THE BALKAN WARS
1912–1913

WARFARE AND HISTORY
General Editor Jeremy Black
Professor of History, University of Exeter

AIR POWER IN THE AGE OF
TOTAL WAR
John Buckley

THE ARMIES OF THE CALIPHS:
MILITARY AND SOCIETY IN THE EARLY
ISLAMIC STATE
Hugh Kennedy

THE BALKAN WARS, 1912–1913:
PRELUDE TO THE FIRST WORLD WAR
Richard C. Hall

ENGLISH WARFARE, 1511–1642
Mark Charles Fissel

EUROPEAN AND NATIVE AMERICAN
WARFARE, 1675–1815
Armstrong Starkey

EUROPEAN WARFARE, 1660–1815
Jeremy Black

THE FIRST PUNIC WAR
J. F. Lazenby

FRONTIERSMEN: WARFARE IN AFRICA
SINCE 1950
Anthony Clayton

GERMAN ARMIES: WAR AND GERMAN
POLITICS, 1648–1806
Peter H. Wilson

THE GREAT WAR 1914–1918
Spencer C. Tucker

ISRAEL'S WARS, 1947–1993
Ahron Bregman

THE KOREAN WAR: NO VICTORS,
NO VANQUISHED
Stanley Sandler

MEDIEVAL CHINESE WARFARE, 300–900
David A. Graff

MEDIEVAL NAVAL WARFARE, 1000–1500
Susan Rose

MODERN CHINESE WARFARE,
1795–1989
Bruce A. Elleman

MODERN INSURGENCIES AND
COUNTER-INSURGENCIES:
GUERRILLAS AND THEIR OPPONENTS
SINCE 1750
Ian F. W. Beckett

NAVAL WARFARE, 1815–1914
Lawrence Sondhaus

OTTOMAN WARFARE, 1500–1700
Rhoads Murphey

SEAPOWER AND NAVAL WARFARE,
1650–1830
Richard Harding

THE SOVIET MILITARY EXPERIENCE
Roger R. Reese

VIETNAM
Spencer C. Tucker

THE WAR FOR INDEPENDENCE AND
THE TRANSFORMATION OF
AMERICAN SOCIETY
Harry M. Ward

WAR AND THE STATE IN EARLY
MODERN EUROPE: SPAIN, THE DUTCH
REPUBLIC AND SWEDEN AS FISCAL–
MILITARY STATES, 1500–1660
Jan Glete

WARFARE AND SOCIETY IN EUROPE,
1792–1914
Geoffrey Wawro

WARFARE AT SEA, 1500–1650
Jan Glete

WARFARE IN ATLANTIC AFRICA, 1500–
1800: MARITIME CONFLICTS AND THE
TRANSFORMATION OF EUROPE
John K. Thornton

WARFARE, STATE AND SOCIETY IN THE
BYZANTINE WORLD, 565–1204
John Haldon

WAR IN THE EARLY MODERN WORLD,
1450–1815
Jeremy Black

WARS OF IMPERIAL CONQUEST IN
AFRICA, 1830–1914
Bruce Vandervort

WESTERN WARFARE IN THE AGE OF
THE CRUSADES, 1000–1300
John France

THE IRISH AND BRITISH WARS,
1637–1654. TRIUMPH, TRAGEDY,
AND FAILURE
James Scott Wheeler

EUROPEAN WARFARE, 1494–1660
Jeremy Black

WAR AND SOCIETY IN IMPERIAL
ROME, 31 BC – AD 284
Brian Campbell

MUGHAL WARFARE: IMPERIAL
FRONTIERS AND HIGHROADS TO
EMPIRE 1500–1700
Jos Gommans

THE BALKAN WARS 1912–1913

Prelude to the First World War

Richard C. Hall

London and New York

To Audrey

First published 2000
by Routledge
11 New Fetter Lane, London EC4P 4EE

Simultaneously published in the USA and Canada
by Routledge
29 West 35th Street, New York, NY 10001

Reprinted 2002 (twice)

Routledge is an imprint of the Taylor & Francis Group

© 2000 Richard C. Hall

Typeset in Bembo by
Prepress Projects, Perth, Scotland
Printed and bound in Great Britain by
Biddles Ltd, Guildford and King's Lynn

All rights reserved. No part of this book may be reprinted or reproduced or utilised in any form or by any electronic, mechanical, or other means, now known or hereafter invented, including photocopying and recording, or in any information storage or retrieval system, without permission in writing from the publishers.

British Library Cataloguing in Publication Data
A catalogue record for this book is available from the British Library

Library of Congress Cataloging in Publication Data
A catalogue record for this book has been requested

ISBN 0–415–22946–4 (hbk)
ISBN 0–415–22947–2 (pbk)

CONTENTS

Preface ix
Maps xi

1 Balkan War origins 1

Congress of Berlin 1
Balkan national aspirations 3
The Bosnian crisis 7
Albanian stirrings 8
Formation of the Balkan league 9
Preparations for war 13
Military forces 15
Conclusion 21

2 The First Balkan War: Thracian theater 22

Preparations 22
Outbreak of war 24
Lozengrad (Kirkkilise) 26
Lyule Burgas–Buni Hisar 28
Chataldzha 32
Adrianople 38
Western Thrace and the Rhodopes 42
Conclusion 43

3 First Balkan War: western theater 45

Serbia 45
Kumanovo 47
Prilep 49

Bitola 50
Other Serbian operations 52
Montenegro 55
Scutari 56
Other Montenegrin operations 58
Greece 59
Thessaly 59
Salonika 61
Epirus 63
The war at sea 64
Conclusion 66

4   The armistice — 69

Chataldzha armistice 69
London peace conference 70
London Ambassadors Conference 72
Bulgarian–Greek dispute 74
Bulgarian–Serbian dispute 76
Bulgarian–Romanian dispute 77
Young Turk coup 78
Conclusion 79

5   Three sieges — 80

Bulair (Gallipoli) 80
Janina 83
Albania 85
Adrianople 86
Chataldzha 90
Scutari 91
Conclusion 95

6   The interbellum — 97

St Petersburg Ambassadors Conference 97
Greek–Serbian alliance 98
Treaty of London 101
Explosion 102
Conclusion 106

7 Interallied war — 107

Military preparations 107
Bregalnitsa 110
The defeat of the Bulgarian 2nd Army 112
Salonika 113
Bulgarian retreats 114
Romanian intervention 117
Ottoman invasion of Bulgaria 118
New Bulgarian government 119
Kalimantsi 120
Kresna Gorge 121
Vidin 122
Treaty of Bucharest 123
Treaty of Constantinople 125
Conclusion 127

8 Consequences and conclusions — 130

Albania 130
The next war 132
Casualties 135
Atrocities 136
Costs 138
Conclusion 139

Notes — 144
Works cited — 158
Index — 168

PREFACE

The complex and obscure Balkan Wars of 1912–13 represent the beginning of an era in European history dominated by nationalism and conflict. These wars were the first concerted effort by the Balkan peoples to emulate the Italian and German examples and establish large nationalist states. The Great Powers of Europe soon intervened. They helped shape the resolution and settlement of the Balkan Wars. The settlement reconfigured the borders of the Balkan Peninsula, expanding the south Slavic states, Greece, and Romania. Bulgaria obtained the Rhodope mountains and western Thrace; Greece took most of Epius; Greece and Serbia divided most of the greatly contested region of Macedonia between them; Montenegro and Serbia divided the former Sandjak of Novi Pazar; and Serbia obtained the largely Albanian region of Kosovo. At the same time, an independent Albania emerged and the multinational Ottoman Empire almost disappeared from the European continent. Because of overlapping rivalries and claims, the nationalist appetites of the post-Balkan War states were not sated. They all persisted in the pursuit of nationalist objectives.

The fighting begun in October 1912 in the Balkan Peninsula had not ended completely by July 1914, when all Europe became enveloped in war. For the peoples of the Balkan Peninsula, the war of 1912 persisted until 1918. Many Balkan War battlefields endured further fighting. Bulgaria occupied most of Macedonia. The Great Powers intervened again. Austro-Hungarian, British, French, German, Italian, and Russian soldiers all fought Balkan battles. At the end of the war, Bulgaria lost Macedonia and western Thrace, and Serbia achieved a maximalist nationalist program with the incorporation of the south Slavic regions of Austria–Hungary, including Bosnia, and Montenegro, into a Serbian-dominated Yugoslavia. Albania barely re-emerged as an independent state.

The Balkan states had little time to recover after the conclusion of fighting in 1918. A mere twenty years separated the First World War from the Second World War. Italy annexed Albania in 1939. The war spread to the Balkans the next year. Yugoslavia collapsed in a week under German and Italian attack in 1941. Italian-dominated Albania annexed Kosovo, and Bulgaria reoccupied

Macedonia and western Thrace. Battles of various sizes and intensities again raged across the Balkan Peninsula for the next five years. Soldiers from Germany, Italy, and the Soviet Union participated in the fighting. When the war was over, Yugoslavia was restored and most of the peninsula was under Soviet domination.

The Communist regimes that emerged in the shadow of Soviet Russia finally brought a period of peace to the Balkan Peninsula. The issues raised by the Balkan Wars lay dormant during the years of Communist rule, only to revive with the collapse of those regimes in 1990. Nationalist wars again erupted there, and continued until the last year of the twentieth century. As with most of the Balkan fighting of the twentieth century, the wars of the disintegration of Yugoslavia drew the diplomatic and military intervention of larger and stronger powers. Albania lurched towards anarchy, Kosovo became a battlefield, and the viability of the post-Yugoslav Macedonian state came into question.

The large nationalist state as exemplified by Italy and Germany proved a poor model for the Balkan peoples. No such states were possible, because the nationalist claims of each Balkan state overlapped with those of its neighbors. Every attempt in the twentieth century to realize this goal has led to war and foreign intervention. Only the adoption of a post-nationalist perspective by the Balkan peoples can break the pattern of war and intervention.

Please note that all dates are given according to the Gregorian or new-style calendar, unless indicated Julian or old style (o.s.). In the twentieth century, the Gregorian calendar was thirteen days ahead of the Julian. All errors of translation are my own.

Richard C. Hall
June 2000

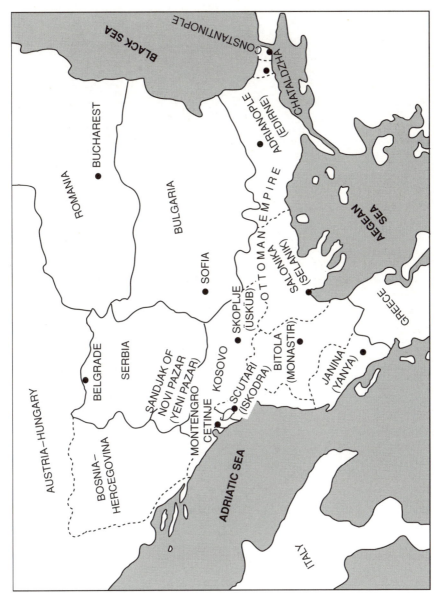

Map 1 The Balkans in 1912

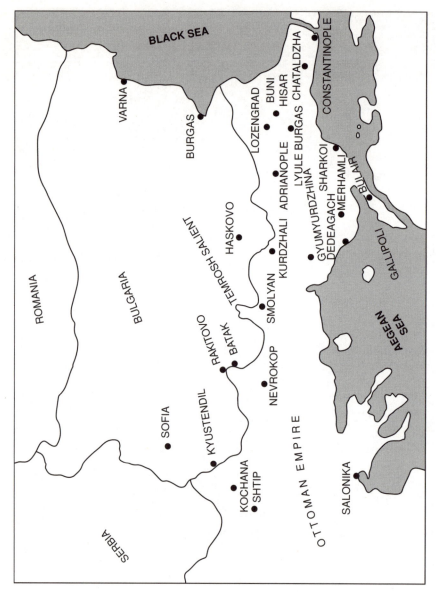

Map 2 Bulgaria in the First Balkan War

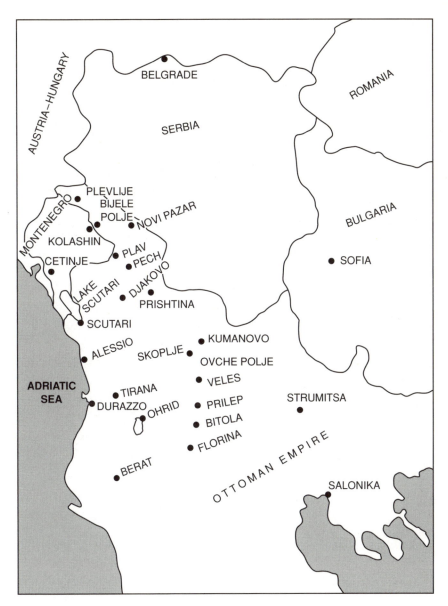

Map 3 Montenegro and Serbia in the First Balkan War

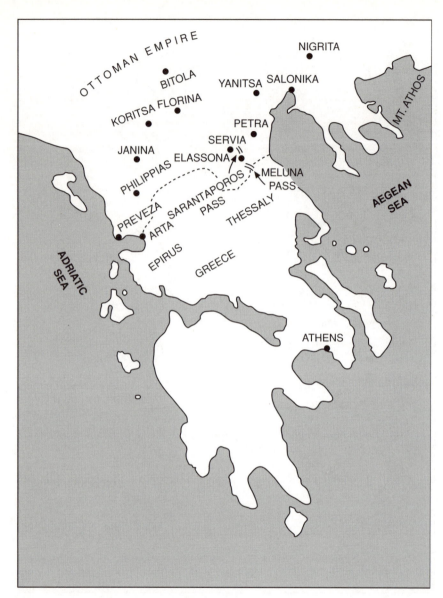

Map 4 Greece in the First Balkan War

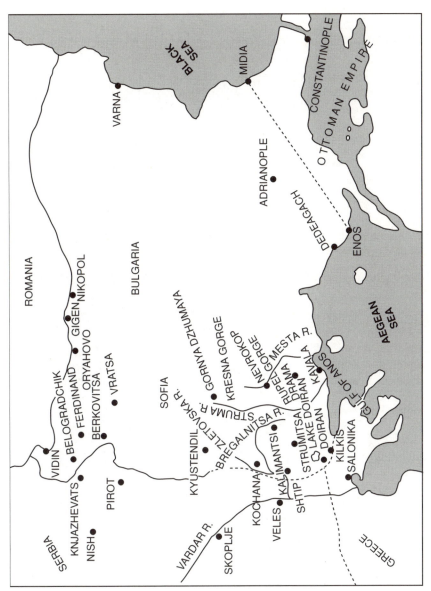

Map 5 The Second Balkan War

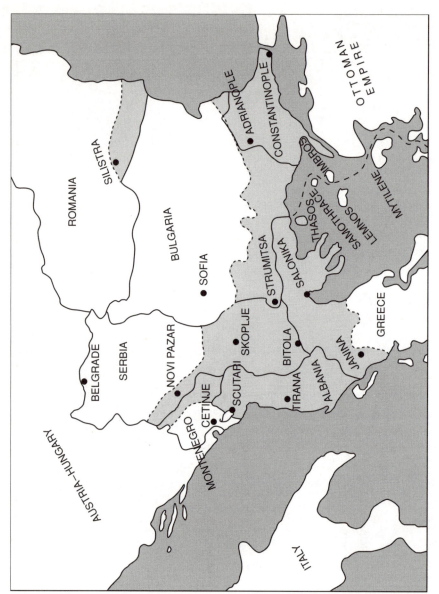

Map 6 The Balkans after the peace settlement in 1913

1

BALKAN WAR ORIGINS

The Balkan Wars were a sharp and bloody series of conflicts fought in southeastern Europe during the autumn of 1912 and the winter, spring, and summer of 1913. In the First Balkan War, the Ottoman Empire fought a loose alliance of Balkan states, which included Bulgaria, Greece, Montenegro, and Serbia. The First Balkan War began in October 1912. An armistice in December 1912 interrupted the fighting until January 1913. Fighting resumed around two besieged cities in Albania, one besieged city in Thrace, and in eastern Thrace until the spring of 1913. The participants in the First Balkan War signed a preliminary peace treaty in London on 30 May 1913.

In the Second Balkan War, Bulgaria fought a looser coalition of Greece, Montenegro, Serbia, Romania, and the Ottoman Empire. Fighting began on 29 June 1913. By the time it ended a little over a month later, the allies had overwhelmed Bulgaria. Peace treaties signed in Bucharest in August 1913 and Constantinople in September 1913 concluded the Second Balkan War. In less than one year the Balkans would again be at war.

Congress of Berlin

The concept of nationalism, appearing from France and the German countries, swept into the Balkan Peninsula early in the nineteenth century. The initial impact was largely cultural. Intellectuals made great efforts to standardize and celebrate the vernacular languages of the Balkans. In doing so, they frequently referred and connected to the medieval states that had existed in the Balkans before the Ottoman conquest.

Soon the emphasis of nationalism became political. A strong desire to achieve national unity motivated the Balkan states to confront their erstwhile Ottoman conquerors. Balkan leaders assumed that only after the attainment of national unity could their states develop and prosper. In this regard the Balkan peoples sought to emulate the political and economic success of western Europe, especially Germany, by adopting the western European concept of nationalism as the model for their own national development. The Balkan peoples perceived nationalism as a justification for the creation of specific geopolitical entities. As Vasil Levski, a nineteenth-century Bulgarian revolutionary activist, explained, "We are a people and want to live in complete freedom in our lands, there where the Bulgarians live, in Bulgaria, Thrace and Macedonia."[1] This concept of western European nationalism displaced the old Ottoman millet system in the Balkans, which had permitted each major religious group a significant amount of self-administration. The millet system allowed Moslems, Orthodox, Catholics, and Jews to all live in proximity to each other without intruding upon each other. It gave the Balkan peoples a limited degree of cultural autonomy.

The Serbs in 1803 and the Greeks in 1821 revolted against their Ottoman overlords, partially in response to the dimly understood western European ethos of nationalism. By 1830 an independent Greek state emerged, and at the same time an autonomous Serbian state came into existence. The Ottomans had conceded Montenegrin autonomy since the eighteenth century. This, however, was more in response to the bellicosity and the remoteness of the Black Mountain than to any overt nationalist stirring.

The successes of the Italians in 1861 and Germans in 1871 in attaining national unity further inspired the Balkan peoples. The military aspects of the Italian and German unifications served as examples to follow. Each Balkan people envisioned the restoration of the medieval empires on which they based their national ideas. The Bulgarians sought the boundaries of the First or Second Bulgarian Empires, the Greeks the revival of the Byzantine Empire, and the Montenegrins and Serbs sought to recover the extent of the empire of Stephan Dushan. In 1876 Serbia and Montenegro went to war against the Ottoman Empire to establish large national states in the western Balkan Peninsula. That same year an anti-Ottoman revolt broke out in Bulgaria. In 1877 Russia intervened in the Balkans on the side of the Bulgarian nationalists. After nine months of unexpectedly hard fighting, the Russians prevailed. The Treaty of San Stefano in March 1878, ending the Russo-Turkish War, created a large independent Bulgarian state and enlarged Serbia and Montenegro. The Treaty of San Stefano fulfilled the maximum territorial aspirations of the Bulgarian nationalists. The new Bulgaria included most of the territory in the eastern Balkan Peninsula between the Danube River and the Aegean Sea. It also included Macedonia. For the first and only time in modern history, a Balkan people had attained all of their national goals.

The Treaty of San Stefano met a negative response from the leading countries of Europe, who had for the past 200 years assumed the prerogative of arbitrating international affairs. These countries as they existed in 1878, Germany, Great Britain, France, Russia, Austria–Hungary, and Italy, were known collectively as the Great Powers. A desire to limit the ambitions of the Russian Empire in the Balkans and to impose order on the chaotic conditions in Ottoman Europe, especially on the part of Austria–Hungary and Great Britain, led the Great Powers to accept the offer of Otto von Bismarck to host a conference to resolve the Balkan issues. Bismarck promised to serve as an "honest broker, who really wants to do business."[2] Bismarck invited representatives of the Great Powers to meet in the German capital. The subsequent Congress of Berlin was attended by the leading diplomats of the time, including Lord Salisbury of Great Britain and Count Andrassy of Austria–Hungary. It greatly diminished the size and independence of the new Bulgarian state. In place of a large independent Bulgaria, the Congress of Berlin established an autonomous Bulgarian principality under Ottoman suzerainty, a semi-autonomous Eastern Rumelia under the authority of the Ottoman sultan, and returned Macedonia to the direct rule of the Sultan. This settlement was a catastrophe for Bulgarian nationalism. Ivan E. Geshov, who would lead Bulgaria into the First Balkan War in 1912, wrote,

> When we in Plovdiv read in the *Times* in the ominous month of July 1878 the first published text of the agreement, in which a short sighted diplomacy in Berlin partitioned our homeland, we were left crushed and thunderstruck. Was such an injustice possible? Could such an injustice be reversed?[3]

The Congress of Berlin also recognized the full independence of a slightly smaller Serbia and deprived Montenegro of San Stefano-sanctioned gains in Hercegovina, the Sandjak of Novi Pazar and northern Albania. Austria–Hungary advanced into the western Balkans by the occupation of Bosnia–Hercegovina and the Sandjak of Novi Pazar. These territories remained *de jure* parts of the Ottoman Empire. They also remained objectives of Montenegrin and Serbian national aspirations. Persistent Greek claims led to something of a corollary to the Berlin settlement. In 1881, the Great Powers sanctioned the Greek annexation of Thessaly and part of southern Epirus.

The Bulgarians soon recovered from the shock of their loses. Geshov wrote to a friend, "Bulgaria is not only truncated but stabbed in the heart. The operation, or better to say this series of operations, inflicted upon Bulgaria, cause us terrible pains and will cripple us for a long time, but will not prove fatal to us."[4] Lord Salisbury, the British advocate of a contained Russia and small Bulgaria, indicated that a big Bulgaria was a matter of time.[5] The Bulgarians were not alone in their frustrations over the Berlin settlement. The Greeks, Montenegrins, and the Serbs likewise perceived in the Treaty of Berlin a barrier to their national aspirations. After 1878 all the Balkan states strove to overcome the Berlin settlement and realize national unity.

Balkan national aspirations

The Bulgarians were the first to act against the Berlin settlement. In 1885, they unilaterally proclaimed the unification of Bulgaria with Eastern Rumelia. The Great Powers did not act directly to preserve the Berlin settlement.

Serbia, however, with some support from its ally Austria–Hungary, attacked Bulgaria later that same year. In the ensuing Serbo-Bulgarian War, the Bulgarians successfully defended their unification and administered a sharp rebuff to the Serbs. Only the intervention of Austria–Hungary prevented a Bulgarian invasion of Serbia. The enmity between these two Balkan Slavic states created an obstacle to the idea of Balkan cooperation against the Berlin settlement and the Ottoman Empire. Nor were relations between Montenegro and Serbia conducive toward the realization of national unity. Dynastic and local rivalries prevented these two Serbian states from mounting a pan-Serb effort against the Ottomans.

The idea of a Balkan alliance extended back to the 1860s, when the Serbian government provided some shelter and assistance for Bulgarian revolutionaries. In 1891, the Greek premier, Kharilaos Trikoupis, had proposed a Bulgar–Greek–Serbian alliance. Neither Serbia nor Bulgaria had responded enthusiastically at that time. The Slavic states remained aloof from their Greek co-religionists because of lack of interest in Greek aspirations in the Aegean and because of rivalries with the Greeks over Macedonia. In 1897 the Bulgarians and Serbs reached an ephemeral agreement for cooperation in Macedonia.

That same year the Greeks made their second assault on the Treaty of Berlin by attempting to annex Crete. The resulting war was over in thirty days. The Ottomans easily deflected the Greek attack. The Great Powers, however, intervened to prevent Constantinople from realizing any meaningful gains from this victory and to maintain the Berlin settlement. They also landed troops in Crete to prevent a Greek occupation and to stop Greek massacres of Moslems. The humiliated Greeks did have to cede several points along their frontier in Thessaly to the Ottomans. Crete, however, received autonomy under the aegis of a Great Power commission but was forbidden a union with Greece. The Greek failure demonstrated the difficulties that any one Balkan state faced in confronting the fading power of the Ottoman Empire. It also greatly undermined the confidence of the other Balkan states in the abilities of the Greek military.

The Bulgarians looked to Thrace, the Greeks to the Aegean Islands, especially Crete, and Epirus, the Serbs to Bosnia–Hercegovina, and the Montenegrins to northern Albania as the locations of their aspirations. Bulgarian, Greek, and Serbian claims all overlapped in Macedonia. The Ottoman vilayets (provinces) of Salonika and Monastir made up most of this fertile region in the center of the Balkan Peninsula. All three Orthodox Christian states considered Macedonia as their own irredenta, based variously on cultural, historical, and linguistic claims. Macedonia first became a problem in 1870, when the Russian government pressured the Ottoman Turks to allow the formation of a Bulgarian Orthodox church independent of the Greek Patriarchate in Constantinople. This so-called Exarchate included churches in Bulgaria and parts of Macedonia. Eight years later a *de facto* independent Bulgarian state emerged from the Russo-Turkish War. The initial Treaty of San Stefano in March 1878 created a big Bulgaria, which included Macedonia. The Treaty of Berlin of July 1878 revised this settlement and returned Macedonia to Ottoman control. Throughout the remainder of the nineteenth century, the Bulgarians, Greeks, and Serbs contested control of Macedonia with the Ottoman Turks and among themselves. The largest revolutionary group, IMRO (Internal Macedonian Revolutionary Organization) was organized in Salonika in 1893. It adopted the slogan, "Macedonia for the Macedonians," and indeed at times even supported the idea of an autonomous Macedonia within the Ottoman Empire rather than annexation of Macedonia to Bulgaria. In part to counter IMRO, the Bulgarian government established the Supreme Committee or External Organization in 1895. Even so, the orientation of IMRO was clearly toward Sofia. The Greeks organized the *Ethniki Etairia* in 1894 to further Greek nationalist aims in Macedonia. The Serbs had already established the Society of Saint Sava back in 1886. All of these groups had educational and propagandistic purposes. They also served as adjuncts for military organizations. Not to be outdone, the Ottoman authorities likewise armed those elements in the population favorable to them and promoted educational and Islamic opportunities. The competition for Macedonia among the Balkan states created an obstacle that prevented a Balkan alliance directed against the Ottomans.

Elsewhere, the Montenegrins and Serbs both aspired to the Austro-Hungarian occupied Sandjak (county) of Novi Pazar. The Sandjak of Novi Pazar was a finger of the Ottoman province of Kosovo, which separated Montenegro from Serbia. The Sandjak of Novi Pazar had a mixed population of Albanians, Serbs, and Slavic-speaking Muslims. Montenegro and Serbia also both claimed Kosovo, which they called Old Serbia because it was the location of the epic battle in 1389 between a Serbian-led Balkan army and the Ottoman invaders of the Balkan Peninsula. This area had a large Albanian population, as well as Serbs and the usual Balkan conglomeration of Turks, Gypsies, Vlachs, and others. These rivalries over Macedonia, Novi Pazar, and Kosovo escalated as the nineteenth century drew to a close.

Increasingly, Macedonia became the focus of Balkan aspirations. The Ottomans preserved their authority in Macedonia by playing the rival Bulgarian, Greek, and Serbian factions against each other. Initially the Bulgarians, favored by the Constantinople government, made educational and cultural gains in Macedonia. The Bulgarians further bolstered their situation by concluding a military alliance with Russian on 14 June 1902, which provided for mutual aid in case of a Romanian attack.[6] The next year a revolt directed against Ottoman authority broke out in Macedonia. Led by IMRO, it resulted in defeat and enabled the Greek and Serbian factions to improve their situations. The failure of this revolt caused tremendous excitement in Bulgaria. As the Bulgarian prime minister at that time, Stoyan

Danev, recalled, "For public opinion at that time Bulgarian foreign policy revolved around only one question, Macedonia."[7] The Bulgarian army was unprepared to intervene at that time, but it began to reorganize the next year.[8] After 1903 the Bulgarians contemplated direct military action against the Ottoman Empire to achieve their national goals. In answer to the Macedonian revolt, the Great Powers, led by Austria–Hungary and Russia, formulated the Mürzteg reform program, which proposed limited reforms for the European part of the Ottoman Empire. It served to support the Berlin settlement, but never really gained the attention of the Ottoman government.

Cognizant of their own weaknesses, the Bulgarians joined an alliance with Serbia in April 1904.[9] The Karageorgeviches had come to power in Belgrade the previous year after a strongly nationalist conspiracy within the army, known as the Black Hand, had murdered the previous king, Alexander Obrenovich, and his wife. Peter Karageorgevich, the new king, was much more overtly nationalistic and coincidentally anti-Habsburg than his unfortunate predecessor. King Peter concurred with the nationalist aspirations of his new prime minister, Nikola Pashich. The Serbo-Bulgarian accord of 1904, actually two separate agreements, addressed economic and political issues. It also provided for mutual military assistance in case of an outside attack and called for united action in Macedonia and Kosovo if these areas were threatened. Ultimately it remained unrealized because of Austro-Hungarian pressures and because of a downturn in Serbo-Bulgarian relations. Because of reservation about the alliance, the Bulgarians sabotaged it by making the agreements public before the Serbs were ready.

The accession of Peter Karageorgevich to the Serbian throne also intensified the rivalry between Serbia and Montenegro for leadership of the Serbian nationalist cause and the establishment of a "Greater Serbia." Montenegro, despite its small size, had enjoyed some advantages in this contest until 1903. Montenegro benefited from the prestige of centuries-long resistance to the Ottomans. Prince Nikola Petrovich Njegosh of Montenegro was a poet of some talent and acclaim. Also, Prince Nikola had succeeded through the marriages of his daughters in becoming father-in-law to some influential European royals. One daughter had married King Victor Emmanuel III of Italy; two others had married Russian grand dukes. A fourth daughter was the wife of Peter Karageorgevich. This made Nikola the father-in-law of the kings of Italy and Serbia and a relation of the Romanovs. These dynastic connections were valuable in securing foreign aid for impoverished Montenegro.

Neither the Karageorgeviches nor the Petrovich Njegoshes had yet produced an heir who seemed capable of continuing the cause. One diplomat described Crown Prince Danilo of Montenegro as, "as good as crazy."[10] Another diplomatic source reported that Crown Prince George Karageorgevich was not fit for any "respectable parlor."[11] Nevertheless, in 1904 the Serbs offered an alliance to Montenegro.[12] Nothing resulted from this Serbian proposal.

The defeat of Russia in the war with Japan and the outbreak of revolution in Russia in 1905 shocked the Slavic Balkan states, who had considered the largest Slavic state to be their protector. The Bulgarian army realized that outside military help, meaning Russian, might not be available for dealing with events in the Balkans.[13] The Russians, who had liberated Bulgaria from the Ottomans and who had sponsored a Great Bulgaria at San Stefano, were too weak to persevere. The Bulgarian army endeavored to strengthen itself further to prepare for the future war against the Ottoman Empire.

The Bosnian crisis

In July 1908 a cabal of junior officers in the Ottoman army, led by Enver Pasha, seized control of the empire and announced a program of reform. They called themselves the Committee for Unity and Progress, but were popularly known as the Young Turks. They immediately announced the restoration of the 1876 constitution, which had never really served as the basis for Ottoman government. They were especially eager to instill among all the various peoples of the Ottoman Empire a sense of Ottoman identity, and thus forestall its further disintegration. The Young Turks were also determined to modernize the Ottoman armed forces. To this end, they invited German army and British naval advisors into the country to initiate the process of the development of a strong and viable military force. After an attempted counter-revolution in April 1909, the Young Turks replaced the aging Sultan, Abdul Hamid II, with the more pliant Mohammad V. The regime then sent Abdul Hamid into exile in Salonika.

This Young Turk revolt reverberated throughout the Balkan Peninsula. The Austrians and Russian, rivals for Great Power domination in the Balkans, attempted to achieve some of their goals before the Young Turk reforms took effect. In September 1908 the Austro-Hungarian foreign minister, Alois Aehrenthal, and the Russian foreign minister, Aleksander Izvolski, agreed to mutually support each other's goals in the Balkans. The Austrians wanted to annex Bosnia–Hercegovina, which they had occupied since 1878. The Russians wanted to control the strategic straits linking the Black Sea to the Aegean Sea. Before the Russians could obtain the sanction of the other Great Powers for their objective, the Austrians acted unilaterally. Amidst the uproar this caused, the Russians lost their opportunity to act. Their demands that the Austrians rescind the annexation of Bosnia–Hercegovina achieved nothing. The only concession the Austrians made was the withdrawal of their garrisons from the Sandjak of Novi Pazar. This crisis over the annexation of Bosnia was a diplomatic defeat for the Russians. They began to seek a means to restore their position in the Balkans.

The Young Turk revolt and the celebration of Ottoman nationhood raised concerns in the Balkan capitals that the Balkan populations in a reformed Turkey would be less susceptible to their nationalistic blandishments. The direct annexation of Bosnia–Hercegovina by Austria–Hungary later that same year caused great agitation throughout the Balkans. Both the Serbs and the Montenegrins perceived in the Austro-Hungarian annexation of Bosnia–Hercegovina a major setback to their national aspirations. Prince Nikola bombastically called for "sacrifices of blood" to prevent the annexation.[14] The Serbs were also aware of their own relative weakness and isolation. To rectify this, they began talks aimed at common action against the Habsburg Monarchy. The result of these talks was an alliance signed on 22 October 1908.[15] A major goal of this alliance was a common border in the Sandjak of Novi Pazar, that finger of Ottoman territory separating Montenegro and Serbia which had been occupied by Austria–Hungary since 1878, in part to isolate Montenegro from Serbia. Although the Austro-Hungarians did evacuate the Sandjak in 1908, the Serbo-Montenegrin alliance did not survive the Bosnian crisis. The old problems of national and dynastic rivalry returned to render it defunct by late 1909. The diplomatic embarrassment of Russia further emphasized the need for the Serbian states to find Balkan allies.

The Bulgarians alone in the Balkans obtained some satisfaction from the Bosnian crisis. They used the annexation as a cover to declare a formal independence from the Ottoman Empire. The Bulgarians gladly perceived in the annexation crisis a further erosion of the Berlin settlement. The Great Powers themselves, and especially Austria–Hungary, appeared to participate in the dismantlement of the Berlin settlement, the most important legal obstacle to the realization of Balkan national aspirations.

The year after the Young Turk revolt, a league of Greek officers likewise rebelled and brought about the collapse of the government. The new Greek government asserted a more overtly nationalistic policy and attempted to take advantage of the ongoing Balkan crisis. It immediately raised the Cretan issue. In 1908, in the aftermath of the annexation of Bosnia–Hercegovina and the proclamation of Bulgarian independence, Crete had announced a union with Greece. The new government, however, was unable to effect this union. Ottoman obstinacy and Great Power indifference again frustrated Greek aspirations. The next year the withdrawal of the Great Power commission, which had controlled Crete since 1898, heightened tensions between Greece and the Ottoman Empire. In 1910 only Prime Minister Eleutharios Venizelos' refusal to seat Cretan representatives in the Greek parliament prevented another war between the Greeks and the Ottomans.

Albanian stirrings

Up until this point the Albanians had staunchly supported Ottoman rule in the Balkans. The majority of Albanians shared the Islamic faith and culture of the Ottomans. Over the centuries they had acquired certain privileges from Constantinople regarding taxation and the possession of weapons. Albanians made up a majority of the population in the Ottoman provinces of Janina, Kosovo, and Scutari and a significant portion of the population of the province of Monastir.

Albanians initially hailed the new regime in Constantinople. They hoped it would initiate reforms leading to a recognition of Albanian autonomy within the empire. These hopes were soon disappointed. The new government's centralization policies aroused fears of loss of privilege and even assimilation in the Albanian areas of the Ottoman Empire. Discontent swept over much of the Albanian-inhabited regions, and open revolt broke out first among the Catholic tribes in the north but soon spread throughout the Albanian regions in the winter and spring of 1910. In May 1911, an Albanian committee in Vlore (Valona) demanded the unification of the Ottoman provinces of Scutari, Janina, Kosovo, and Monastir into an autonomous Albania within the Ottoman Empire. In an effort to restore Ottoman prestige, Sultan Mohammed V visited Kosovo in June 1911. This had little effect on the revolt. The government never completely succeeded in suppressing this uprising before the outbreak of the Balkan Wars.

The growth of an Albanian national self awareness in the Kosovo region challenged Serbian pretensions there.[16] This issue compelled the Serbs to act expeditiously. They feared that Austrian machinations were behind the Albanian unrest. The Greeks were also concerned about the Albanian revolt. The development of Albanian particularism infringed on Greek *desirada* in Epirus and threatened to involve Greece prematurely in a war with the Ottoman Empire.[17] Albanian national stirrings also threatened the aspirations of Montenegro to parts of northern Albania, including the important city of Scutari. Albanian nationalism threatened the national aspirations of Greece, Montenegro, and Serbia. This common problem provided the incentive for these three Balkan countries to act against it and increasingly to act together. By 1911 Nikola, who had granted himself the title of King of Montenegro the previous year, involved his country in the northern Albanian revolt. He supported the rebels against the Ottoman authorities with arms and sanctuary. To retain control of the last important Islamic region of their European holdings, the Ottomans sent troops to suppress the Albanian revolt. Fighting on the Balkan Peninsula then intensified in Albania in 1911.

Formation of the Balkan league

After the crisis of 1908–9, both the Belgrade and the Sofia governments decided to resolve their national unity issues.[18] The Serbs sought support against the escalating anti-Serbian policies of Austria–Hungary. The Bulgarians remained focused on their aspirations in Macedonia and, to a lesser degree, Thrace. Both governments wanted to act before the Young Turks could implement meaningful reforms.

Another reason for the intensification of Bulgarian and Serbian efforts on national issues came from radical activists within their own countries.

After the failure of the 1903 Macedonian uprising, a revolutionary organization, IMRO, had increased its power within Bulgaria and operated effectively beyond the control of the Sofia government. Nor did the Bulgarian government completely control its own Macedonian organization, the Supremeists. Both of these organizations had strong connections within the Bulgarian army. Likewise in Serbia, the shadowy military political action association the Black Hand, or Union or Death, functioned within the army outside of Belgrade governmental circles. Some senior Serbian officers, including the Chief of Staff, General Radomir Putnik, sympathized with the Black Hand. Both the Bulgarian and the Serbian organizations were determined to pursue national unity with or without government sanction.[19] The governments in Belgrade and Sofia recognized that to maintain control of their respective national movements, they had to act forcefully toward the Ottoman Empire.

Contact between Belgrade and Sofia increased in 1909. These centered on the issue of Macedonia. As the then Bulgarian foreign minister, General Stefan Paprikov, noted in 1909, "It will be clear that if not today then tomorrow, the most important issue will again be the Macedonian question. And this question, whatever happens, cannot be decided without more or less direct participation of the Balkan states."[20] After the Bosnian crisis, the Serbs had an additional incentive to make arrangements with the other Balkan states. Serbian Foreign Minister Milan Milovanovich explained to General Paprikov in 1909:

> For us there is another important consideration which speaks for the advantage of an agreement with Bulgaria. As long as we are not allied with you, our influence over the Croats and Slovenes will be insignificant. Outside of the differences of faith, these peoples have to a great degree the same culture we have. They do not see Serbia as a center, however, able to attract them. It will be something else all together, when you and we form a powerful bloc. Then all Orthodox and Catholic Serbs, Croats and Slovenes in the neighboring Monarchy will begin inevitably to gravitate toward us.[21]

The Serbs increasingly saw Yugoslavism as a weapon to use against their Habsburg adversaries, whom they perceived as the major opponent of a Greater Serbia. This issue illustrated that not all Serbian aspirations were in the Balkans. Nor did the Greeks, who dreamed of control of the entire Aegean and Cyprus, and the acquisition of an empire in Anatolia, confine their interests to their north. To transcend the Balkan Peninsula, the Balkan states first had to secure their interests with and against each other.

These attempts among the Balkan states to overcome the issues that divided them coincided with Russian resolve on a more active policy in the Balkans.[22] Since their military defeat by the Japanese in 1905 and their diplomatic defeat by the Austrians in 1909, the Russians had sought a more active role in the Balkans. To this end, St Petersburg began to encourage the formation of an anti-Austrian Balkan union. Beginning in 1911, Anatoli Neklyudov, the Russian ambassador in Sofia, and Nicholas Hartwig, the Russian ambassador in Belgrade, labored to bring Bulgaria and Serbia together again in order to solidify the Russian position in the Balkans.

In the summer of 1911, after the failure of overtures to the Ottomans to resolve the national issues bilaterally, the Bulgarians decided to settle the Macedonian question. In a speech to the Grand National Parliament (*subranie*) in 1911, prime minister Geshov broadly hinted at the direction of Bulgarian foreign policy, "I think it is sufficient that you remember the example of Piedmont."[23] The Geshov government contemplated a *realpolitik* that might not result in a San Stefano Bulgaria, but that could obtain for them much of Macedonia.

The outbreak of the Italo-Turkish war in September that same year provided further incentive for the Balkan Slavs to hasten to reach an agreement. One commentator observed that the Italian attack on the Ottomans, "broke the ice" for the Balkan governments.[24] Obviously the Italo-Turkish war, where one of the Great Powers attacked the Ottoman Empire, further undermined the Berlin settlement. In addition, it diverted the attention of and depleted the resources of the Ottoman Empire to the advantage of the Balkan states.

That same autumn, the Bulgarians and Serbs began to exchange proposals for an alliance treaty. The conservative prime minister Ivan E. Geshov, who also held the portfolio for foreign affairs, oversaw the Bulgarian efforts. His Serbian counterpart was foreign minister Milan Milovanovich, who had also become prime minister in 1911. After three months of negotiations, at times facilitated by Russian diplomatic assistance, the Bulgarians and Serbs arrived at an agreement.[25] This agreement, signed on 7 March 1912, provided for military cooperation against both the Habsburg and Ottoman Empires and an arrangement for Macedonia. The agreement recognized Bulgarian interests in Thrace and Serbian interests in Kosovo and Albania. It stipulated that if autonomy could not be implemented for Macedonia, Serbia and Bulgaria would partition that area. The Bulgarians were to obtain outright southern Macedonia, including the towns of Ochrid, Prilep and Bitola. Northern Macedonia, including the important town of Skoplje, was assigned by the agreement to a "disputed zone," with the Russian tsar acting as arbitrator if the Bulgarians and Serbs could not arrive between themselves at a suitable arrangement for the allocation of the territory. Most Bulgarians understood the establishment of an autonomous Macedonia as being a step toward the Bulgarian annexation of all Macedonia. If this did not prove to be possible, then they could fall back on the provisions in the treaty for division of Macedonia. Although the treaty indicated that Austria was a potential enemy, its main thrust pointed at war between the Balkan Slavic allies and the Ottoman Empire.

The Bulgarians were by and large satisfied with this arrangement. They obtained Serbian recognition for their claims to most of Macedonia. They were confident that their liberator and traditional friend Russia would ensure in the end that the "disputed zone" would also come to Bulgaria. The Serbs, however, were not as enthusiastic about the treaty. Elements in the Serbian army, including the chief of staff, General Radomir Putnik, were dissatisfied with the treaty, and the leader of the Serbian Radical Party, Nikola Pashich, did not like it. He wrote, "in my opinion we conceded too much, or better said, we abandoned some Serbian areas which we should never have dared to abandon even if we were left without an agreement."[26] The source of this dissatisfaction was Macedonia. The agreement with Bulgaria gave Serbia a clear claim only to Kosovo and the Sandjak of Novi Pazar. They would only acquire the "disputed zone," the northwestern corner of Macedonia, as the beneficiaries of Russian arbitration. Many Serbs had aspirations to all Macedonia. Milovanovich's premature death in July 1912 removed a force for moderation in the Serbian government. Six weeks after his death, the ardent nationalist Nikola Pashich became prime minister and minister for foreign affairs. Never a strong partisan of the agreement with Bulgaria, Pashich remained a strong advocate of a maximalist Serbian agenda.

Even before the finalization of arrangements between the Bulgarians and the Serbs, the Sofia government began to pursue talks with Athens toward a Bulgaro-Greek alliance. The Greeks had long been interested in an arrangement with Bulgaria directed against Turkey. In the aftermath of its humiliation in the Cretan crisis of 1909, the government in Athens made numerous overtures to Sofia.[27] These proposals continued until the autumn of 1911, when the Bulgarians, whose negotiations with the Serbs were ongoing, at last responded positively. Negotiations between Greece and Bulgaria continued until the signing of a treaty in Sofia in May 1912.[28] The treaty provided for political and military cooperation against the Ottoman empire without stipulating any specific division of Ottoman territories. This was largely the fault of the Bulgarians. They sought an alliance with the Greeks mainly to secure the assistance of the Greek navy against the Ottomans. The Bulgarians had little faith in the military abilities of the Greeks and were confident that their own larger and stronger army could seize the territories in Macedonia they sought before the Greeks could arrive. This arrogant attitude would have important repercussions.

During the summer of 1912, the Greeks then concluded "gentlemen's agreements" with Serbia and Montenegro.[29] The Serbs and Greeks had negotiated throughout the summer of 1912. Although the Greeks submitted the draft of an alliance proposal on 22 October, the arrangements were incomplete by the time of the outbreak of war, because of issues such as the division of conquered territory and the obligation of Greece to aid Serbia in case of Austro-Hungarian intervention. The Greeks had no firm commitments from any of the Slavic Balkan allies, other than the agreement to fight the Ottomans.

After the signing of the Bulgarian–Greek alliance, the Bulgarians and the Serbs separately approached Montenegro. The Montenegrins were well aware of the Balkan trend toward confrontation with the Ottoman Empire. Since December 1910, King Nikola had begun to arm Catholic tribesmen in northern Albania and to encourage attacks on centers of Ottoman authority. Coincidentally, he began to approach the other Balkan states. In January 1911, Nikola proposed to the Serbian ambassador in Cetinje an agreement for "mutual advance in case of pending events in the Balkans."[30] In June 1911, he approached the Bulgarians.[31] Sofia did not respond until the arrangements with Belgrade and Athens were in place. Then the Bulgarians replied favorably and made an agreement in August 1912.[32] The Serbs finally answered Nikola in September 1912. The two Serbian states signed a political and military alliance "aimed at the liberation of Serbs under the Turkish yoke" in Lucerne, Switzerland, on 27 September.[33]

With the Montenegrin agreements the Balkan League was complete. It was a flawed and flimsy diplomatic instrument, accomplished in haste and based upon self-interest. Bulgaria had formal written alliances with Greece, Montenegro, and Serbia. Serbia had a written agreement with Montenegro. The Greco-Serbian and Greco-Montenegrin agreements were merely oral arrangements, difficult to enforce. The Balkan allies were now ready to fight to complete the process of national unity.

By the summer of 1912, Ottoman control of the Balkans had deteriorated, especially in Albania and Macedonia. Albanian disorders became more widespread. The bombing of a marketplace in Kochana, Macedonia, by IMRO elements as deliberate provocation resulted in the massacre of over one hundred Slavs there and outraged the Bulgarians. Ottoman efforts to disarm the Balkan population came to nothing. The Ottoman military remained engaged in a losing effort against Italy. One casualty of this string of difficulties was the Young Turk government. At the end of August an anti-Young Turk faction in the army brought a new government to power.

Preparations for war

In pursuit of nationalist goals the Balkan states had all built up large military establishments. These armies all received large amounts of the national budgets. They all became strong enough to challenge any constitutional or other political restraint. In addition, they all attempted to pursue strong nationalist agendas of their own. Finally, all of these military establishments viewed the possibility of war with the Ottoman Empire as an exciting opportunity. The Serbian deputy chief of staff, Colonel Zhivojin Mishich, later remembered,

> Among all our people, and especially in the military, an unusually broad mood in favor of this war prevailed. Absolutely no one doubted a

successful outcome. All conscripts and reserve officers, equipped for war, happy and proud, passed through the streets of their collection places. Suddenly all previous quarrels among the officer corps ceased, all were now brothers, and they went off hand in hand to this holy war.[34]

Similar sentiments prevailed in the armed forces of the other three Balkan allies. The announcement of mobilization generally met with enthusiasm throughout the Balkans. Only some socialists and the Bulgarian Agrarian Party expressed reservations about the call to arms.

There was little enthusiasm for the war on the Ottoman side. Some students at the University of Constantinople demonstrated in favor of a war with the Balkan states.[35] Otherwise, the Ottoman capital remained complacent about the prospect of war. The recent wars in Yemen and north Africa had blunted much patriotic enthusiasm.

To coordinate their efforts against the Ottomans, the Bulgarian and Serbian staffs met several times. They signed a military convention in Belgrade on 29 April 1912. This convention provided for mutual assistance against an Ottoman or Romanian attack against Bulgaria and against an Austro-Hungarian attack against Serbia. Subsequent agreements on 2 July and 28 September established the basis for the strategic conduct of the war. The Serbs had wanted a large Bulgarian force of 100,000 men, the equivalent of one Bulgarian army, to go to the Macedonian or Vardar theater to insure an overwhelming victory there. General Fichev, the Bulgarian chief of staff, argued that the eastern or Thracian theater would be decisive and that the Bulgarians needed to use the large majority of their forces there. Fichev's view prevailed. In Belgrade on 28 September the two staffs agreed that the main Bulgarian effort would be in Thrace and that the main Serbian effort would be in Macedonia.[36] Militarily this made sense, for the Bulgarians had the larger army and could expect to encounter larger Ottoman forces because of their proximity to the Ottoman capital. Politically, however, Fichev's demands located Bulgarian forces further away from the major Bulgarian goal of the war, Macedonia. Serbian forces were to take and occupy the parts of Macedonia promised to Bulgaria by the March convention. Fichev himself was not unaware of the complications this military convention would create for Bulgarian aspirations. He made reference to Macedonia when he repeated a Bulgarian saying to Colonel Mishich, "It is difficult for any country an army passes through."[37] Serbian occupation of land promised to Bulgaria would become a source of serious conflict.

The Bulgarians and Greeks also signed a formal military convention in Sofia, but not until 5 October, after the beginning of mobilization. General Fichev and Minister President Geshov signed for Bulgaria, and Captain Ioannes Metaxas, the future Greek dictator, and Demeter Panas, Greek minister in Sofia, signed for Greece. The most important aspect of this convention for the Bulgarians was the assurance that the Greek fleet would dominate the Aegean Sea so that the Ottomans could not transfer troops from Asia Minor to Europe by sea.[38] Bulgaria was obligated to commit the majority of its forces in Macedonia unless the Serbs moved into Macedonia with 120,000 men. In that case, the Bulgarians could utilize the bulk of their forces in Thrace. Both sides also agreed not to accept an armistice without the prior agreement of the other.

The Bulgarians had little respect for the prowess of the Greek army and sought no further agreements. They assumed that they would achieve their goals without the aid or interference of the Greeks. They should have attempted to reach a clearer delineation of activities in southern Macedonia, especially around Salonika. Salonika was an obvious Greek destination but only a fanciful Bulgarian ambition. A definite agreement about areas of action in southern Macedonia might have avoided the race for Salonika and the overt hostility between Greece and Bulgaria that resulted.

Once the alliance arrangements were in place, the Bulgarians began to insist on the implementation of Article 23 of the Treaty of Berlin, which they interpreted to mean the establishment of autonomy for Macedonia. The Bulgarians perceived in an autonomous Macedonia an advantage that might permit the eventual annexation of the entire area. When the Ottomans refused to consider reforms leading to autonomy in their European provinces, the Balkan alliance mobilized. Efforts by the Great Powers to prevent the outbreak of war were feeble and futile. The First Balkan War began on 8 October 1912 with a Montenegrin attack on Ottoman positions. The Greeks signaled their intentions six days later when Venizelos welcomed delegates from Crete into the Greek parliament. This was proof of a union between Greece and Crete and a reason, as in 1897, for war. On 17 October the Balkan League would respond to the Ottoman declaration of war the previous day. The Balkan Peninsula was aflame, a conflagration that would rage for the next six years.

Military forces

In many respects all the Balkan armies were very similar. The all followed European models for training, logistics, communication, and sanitation. Except for Montenegro, they adopted the European General Staff model. Montenegro lacked a General Staff completely. They all fielded a variety of European-manufactured weaponry. They tended to have older Krupp and newer Schneider–Creusot guns. There was little standardization for equipment in any of the Balkan armies. All the Balkan armies perceived that the often illiterate peasant infantryman, indoctrinated to some degree with the appropriate nationalist ideology, was the basis for their military posture.

The Balkan armies were also similar in that they were largely homogenous. None of the four states of the Balkan League contained large national minorities. Many of the existing minorities, such as the Rom (Gypsies), were not expected to serve. A single language of command was a unifying factor in all the armies. Socially they were similar as well, with conscripted peasants forming the bulk of the enlisted personnel. Their officers were a mix of professionals from varied backgrounds, who often had some foreign training. Reserve officers came from the small professional and commercial classes.

Those enlisted personnel who had any education received indoctrination in the nationalist ideology of the particular country, whether it Bulgaria, Greece, or Serbia, replete with references to medieval glories. Bulgarians learned of the empires of Tsar Simeon (893–927), Greeks learned about the Emperor Basil II (known as the Bulgar Slayer, 976–1025), and Montenegrins and Serbs learned about Stefan Dushan (1331–55). These individuals had established medieval states that briefly controlled most of the Balkan Peninsula. The modern national states recognized these earlier ones as lineal antecedents and as models to be emulated. Often the junior officers leading the men off to war had served as the conveyers of this ideology when they had been schoolmasters.

The Bulgarian army was well trained. Both its infantry and its artillery drew praise from foreign observers. In 1910 the American military attaché in Paris, Major T. Bentley Mott, reported after a trip to the Balkans:

> The Army of Bulgaria is recognized in European military circles as having exceptional value. It is small, well instructed, and armed with the most modern weapons, chosen from the best constructors in Europe. It has for years been kept as a sharpened tool, ready for immediate use to defend the country from powerful neighbors which have repeatedly threatened or else to undertake, alone or in conjunction with other powers, the carving out of a larger independence or larger territory from troublesome neighbors.[39]

Its officers had obtained instruction in Russia, Italy, and Germany. Bulgarian staff officers were familiar with the current military theories of the day. They sought to implement the ideas of the French Colonel Louis de Grandmaison to carry out the attack quickly and in force.[40] Greek and Serbian officers had similar backgrounds and similar training experiences.

The Bulgarians had a peacetime army of under 60,000 men, which during war expanded to over 350,000. The army was organized into nine infantry divisions, which were armed with the Mannlicher magazine rifle with a short bayonet, and one cavalry division. In wartime each infantry division included four machine-gun sections, which had four 8-mm Maxim guns each. The Bulgarian infantry prided itself on its use of the bayonet and on its nighttime operations. Each infantry division had attached a field artillery regiment containing nine batteries of four guns each. By the time of the Balkan Wars these were Schneider–Creusot quick-firing 75-mm guns. In addition, the Bulgarians had fifty-four six-gun batteries consisting of older Krupp 8.7-cm guns, and twenty-four six-gun batteries of other older guns. It also had twelve four-gun batteries of Krupp 7.5-mm mountain or light artillery, fourteen howitzer batteries, and a number of other older guns. For the Bulgarians, the artillery had a dual function. It was necessary to attack and reduce the Ottoman fortresses at Adrianople and Lozengrad. Also, since the Russo-Japanese War, the Bulgarians had noted the need for field artillery to utilize against enemy infantry.[41] Finally, the Bulgarians possessed a small navy consisting of six small torpedo boats and the 726-ton torpedo gunboat *Nadezhda* (1898). The main purpose of the Bulgarian navy was the protection of the Black Sea coast and the prevention of any blockade that might hamper the important connection to Russia. When the First Balkan War broke out the Bulgarians had five airplanes of British, French, and Russian manufacture, although they soon acquired seventeen more.

The Greeks had a peacetime army of about 25,000 men, which with mobilization grew to 110,000 men. In war this army consisted of four divisions and six battalions of light infantry (*Evzones*). The infantry weapon was the 6.5-mm Mannlicher–Schonauer rifle. Each division had a regiment of field artillery attached. The Greek artillery regiments consisted of three groups of three four-gun batteries armed with Schneider–Creusot 7.5-cm guns. In addition, the Greeks had two mountain artillery regiments with 7.5-cm Schneider–Canet guns and one heavy artillery battalion. The Greeks also had three cavalry regiments. At the outbreak of the First Balkan War, the Greeks possessed four aircraft. Over the course of the war, they added two sea planes and added floats to one other plane.

Among the members of the Balkan League, only the Greeks possessed a navy of any size and strength. The Greek navy had two main tasks in the war. The first was to guard the mouth of the Dardanelles to interdict Ottoman shipping in the Aegean and Adriatic Seas. This was important as it would prevent the Ottomans from reinforcing and resupplying their European forces. The Greek ambassador to Bulgaria, Demeter Panas, emphasized this point in conversation with Ivan Geshov, the Bulgarian prime minister, on the eve of the war. Panas stated that Greece could provide 600,000 men for the war effort. This assertion met Bulgarian incredulity. Panas explained, "We can place an army of 200,000 men in the field and then our fleet will stop about 400,000 men being landed by Turkey upon the southern coast of Thrace and Macedonia, between Salonica and Gallipoli."[42] The other task was to occupy the Aegean islands still under Ottoman control.

The pride of the Greek navy was the 10,118-ton armored cruiser *Georgios Averov*. Built in Italy in 1910, the *Averov* carried four 23-cm guns and eight 12-cm guns. In addition, the Greek navy had eight destroyers built in 1912, eight built in 1906, nineteen old torpedo boats, and a submarine, the *Dolphin*. It also had some old auxiliary vessels. The Greek navy consisted of over 11,000 men.[43] The commander of the navy was Rear Admiral Paul Kundouriotis.

The Montenegrins lagged behind the other Balkan states in military training, equipment, and education. Essentially the Montenegrin army was a militia composed of most of the males in the country. In wartime it amounted to 35,600 men. These men were armed with a variety of Russian Berdan and other rifles. The Montenegrins had four batteries (twenty-six guns) of light artillery, and eight and a half batteries (thirty-four guns) of mountain artillery. These guns were of Italian and Russian origin. Altogether the Montenegrins had 126 guns, ranging in size from 65 to 240 mm.[44] They also had a small cavalry unit consisting of one officer and thirty men. The Montenegrins depended to a great degree on a martial tradition for the morale of the army. Among the Balkan armies, only the Montenegrins had any recent experience of war. This was largely due to the chronic condition of bellicosity that existed along the Montenegrin-Ottoman frontier. The nature of the fighting tended to season the Montenegrins as individual soldiers, but not as an army.

Serbia had a mobilized strength of 230,000 men organized into ten infantry divisions and one cavalry division. The Serbian infantryman carried the 1889 Mauser model rifle. Every infantry regiment had a machine-gun section consisting of four 7-mm Maxim guns. The Serbs had 228 Scheinder–Creusot 7.5-cm quick-firing guns and some older guns. The Serbian air force expanded from three planes to ten over the course of the First Balkan War.

In population the Balkan states were far inferior to the Ottoman Empire. In 1912 Bulgaria had about 4,300,000 people, Greece 2,666,000, Montenegro 250,000, and Serbia almost 3,000,000. The Ottoman Empire had around 26,000,000 inhabitants.[45] Of these, around 6,000,000 lived in Europe. In the European part of the empire around 3,500,000 inhabitants were mainly Orthodox Christian (Bulgarian, Greek, Serbian) and around 2,300,000 were Islamic. They were of various backgrounds (Turkish, Albanian, Slavic, Circassian, Tartar). This large population was not necessarily an advantage. Even though after 1908 the Ottoman government committed itself to constitutional reform and extended the obligation to serve in the military to all males in the empire, the army could hardly rely on the numerous Bulgarians, Greeks, and Serbs residing within the empire to fight loyally against their co-nationals living in independent states across the frontiers. Many of these Orthodox Christian peoples in the European part of the Ottoman Empire would probably assist any invasion by their co-nationals. Nor did Arab, Armenian, and Kurdish soldiers from Asia offer unconditional loyalty. The diverse population of the Ottoman Empire made conscription and training difficult. The Ottoman army never attempted a sophisticated arrangement like that devised by the Habsburg army, which had a simplified language of command and the officers made intensive efforts to learn the language of their troops.

After their takeover in 1908, the Young Turks attempted to reform the Ottoman armed forces. German army officers and British naval officers oversaw some of the reforms. In 1912 the extent and success of the reforms remained problematical. In particular, the development of an officer corps trained along European (German) lines was open to doubt. The Ottomans had a fairly well-trained and well-equipped regular army (nizam). It also depended upon an infantry reserve (redif), which was ill-trained, ill-equipped, and ill-led. Non-Turkish and non-Islamic people made up a significant portion of the redifs. Many of them had little loyalty to the government in Constantinople and would desert during the campaigns of the Balkan Wars.

Only about half of the Ottoman army was stationed in Europe. The other half was scattered throughout the near-eastern regions of the Ottoman Empire, from Anatolia to Yemen, where a guerrilla war had smoldered since 1904. Some soldiers remained in north Africa in the aftermath of the war against the Italians. While the Ottoman high command could draw upon these Asian forces to obtain decisive numbers in a war against the Balkan states, it still faced the immense difficulties of gathering these soldiers from the remote corners of the empire and transporting them to the European battlefields.

Like the Balkan armies, the Ottoman army had equipment from various European sources. In Europe they had four corps in Thrace based in Constantinople and three corps in the western Balkans based in Salonika. In wartime these corps consisted of three divisions, a sharpshooting regiment, a cavalry brigade of three or four regiments, and an artillery regiment. An artillery regiment had two sections of three batteries with six guns per battery, giving thirty-six guns per regiment. Redif units, all infantry, supplemented the Ottoman division in time of war.

Standardization was a problem. The infantry was armed with either one of three different models of the Mauser rifle, some of 7.65 mm others of 9.5 mm, or an Henri-Martini gun. Its artillery was mostly made up of Krupp 7.5-cm guns. The mixed population and the high levels of illiteracy in the Ottoman army made the effective operation of modern military equipment problematical. This was a problem, especially in the artillery. The Ottoman army also had several cavalry formations. The Ottomans had five airplanes in Thrace at the start of the war. None of them was in condition for flying when war broke out.

The Ottoman fleet consisted of six armored ships, two armored cruisers, eleven torpedo destroyers, thirty torpedo ships, and nineteen other transportation and antiquated vessels. Its two modern vessels were the 3,800-ton light cruiser *Hamidiye* (1903), which had two 6-inch and four 4.7-inch guns, and the 9,250-ton armored cruiser *Mecidiye* (1904), which had two 15-cm guns and eight 12-cm guns apiece. Together they were probably a match for the *Georgios Averov*, but not separately.

The Ottomans could not turn all their attention to the troubles in the Balkan Peninsula until they ended the war with Italy, which had engaged their efforts since 1911. Although Ottoman-supported tribes in the interior of Ottoman North Africa had fought the invading Italians to a stalemate, the Ottoman government in Constantinople decided to resolve this conflict in order to address the more serious one pending in the Balkans. On 15 October 1912, they signed an agreement with Italy at Ouchy, Switzerland, in which they ceded Tripoli and Cyrenaica to Italy. In return, the Italians promised to vacate the Dodecanese Islands and Rhodes, which they had occupied during the war.[46] The Ottomans then turned to Balkan problems.

The Ottomans lacked a clear plan for confronting a threat from the Balkan Peninsula. When asked about plans, the Ottoman Minister of War, Huseyin Nazim Pasha, a graduate of the French military academy at St Cyr, nonchalantly replied, "There is a set of plans prepared during the time of Mahmud Sevket Pasha. I am going to obtain and examine them."[47] This was hardly a sound basis on which to initiate a modern military campaign.

The Ottoman army did have recent knowledge of war, largely through fighting in Yemen, fighting the Italians in Ottoman North Africa, and the fighting in Albania. This was of limited value, however. Yemen was remote. Also, because the war in the Balkans immediately followed the one in North Africa, many of the officers and men who gained military experience there were unable to return before the Ottoman defeats in the autumn of 1912.

The mountainous topography of the Balkan Peninsula made transportation a difficult issue for all the forces involved in the Balkan Wars. Rail lines, where they existed, greatly facilitated movement. A trunk line extended from Belgrade to Sofia to Adrianople and to Constantinople. This, the route of the famous luxury train the *Orient Express*, allowed Bulgarian and Ottoman troops to speed to their respective frontiers. The other important rail line branching off from this line in the Serbian city of Nish was a secondary trunk line that ran down the Vardar valley to Salonika. It connected to another line which ran to the main trunk line south of Adrianople. This line, and two narrow-gauge lines extending from Skoplje to Mitrovitsa in the Sandjak of Novi Pazar and from Salonika to Monastir, helped the Ottomans somewhat offset the presence of the Greek fleet in the Aegean. Unfortunately, confusion in the Ottoman railroad system hindered mobilization. Many of the non-Moslem railroad employees were dismissed.[48] Their replacements lacked the training and experience to facilitate smooth railroad utilization. This undermined the Ottomans' ability to move men and equipment to and from the battlefields. The Greeks also had rail lines extending from Athens to their frontiers at Larissa and Trikala. Montenegro possessed a short but convoluted narrow-gauge line extending from the Adriatic port of Antivari (Serbian: Bar) to Vir Pazar on Lake Scutari. This was useful in bringing supplies from the coast to Montenegrin troops besieging Scutari.

In the absence or destruction of rail lines, the combatants had to utilize the crude roads of the Balkan Peninsula for movement. Often roads barely existed. Motorized transportation was almost entirely lacking. Most Balkan armies depended on horses, donkeys, or oxen to move supplies and the wounded. One source noted that for transportation in Montenegro, "failing other agencies, women are employed."[49] Human power helped move supplies in all the Balkan countries. All this meant that movement of men and material during the Balkan Wars was likely to be very slow.

Conclusion

The Balkan states, which depended on a national ethos for a sense of power and legitimacy at the time of their formation, were painfully aware that they were incomplete. All of these states sought to achieve national unity at the expense of the increasingly decrepit Ottoman Empire, and in the case of the Serbs and Montenegrins also at the expense of the Habsburg Empire. One major obstacle to the attainment of this unity was the desire of the Great Powers of Europe to maintain peace and stability throughout the European continent. The Treaty of Berlin embodied this desire. The other major obstacle was the inability of the Balkan states themselves to overcome their own rivalries and claims. The defeat of Bulgarian interests in Macedonia in 1903 and pressure from Austria–Hungary on Serbia beginning in 1904 led these two states to explore mutual cooperation. This tendency to cooperate became more pronounced after the Bosnian crisis of 1908–9. Fears of Ottoman resurgence following the Young Turk revolt and demonstrations of Ottoman weakness in the Italo-Turkish war further accelerated the preparations of the Balkan states toward war. After 1911, Bulgaria, Greece, Montenegro, and Serbia, with the encouragement of Russia, acted to overcome their intra-Balkan rivalries and create a pan-Balkan alliance directed against the Ottoman Empire. The Russians naively assumed this alliance would serve their interests against the Habsburgs. With the finalization of arrangements in the summer of 1912, however, its anti-Ottoman intent became clear. By then, no amount of posturing by the Great Powers could prevent the outbreak of war. The determination of the Balkan nations upon war was stronger than the resolve of the Great Powers to avert war. The Balkan Peninsula would not know peace for over six years.

The Balkan Wars of 1912–13 occurred because of the determination of the Balkan states to resolve their issues of national unity in the face of the weakness of the Ottoman Empire and the opposition of the Great Powers. By 1912 the Great Powers, who had maintained peace in the Balkan Peninsula since 1878 through the mechanism of the Berlin settlement, lacked the determination to enforce it when confronted by Balkan unity. Because of this failure they would find themselves at war within two years.

2

THE FIRST BALKAN WAR

Thracian Theater

Geography dictated that Thrace would be the major battlefield in a war between the Balkan states and the Ottoman Empire. Thrace is an open, undulating plain with few natural obstacles. This facilitated the movement of large armies. In addition, the proximity of Constantinople to the Balkan Peninsula made imperative the locating of strong armies for its defense. Constantinople was also a natural goal for any Balkan army, a situation that had lured Avars, Bulgarians, and Serbs in Byzantine times. The Bulgarians and the Ottomans would fight the major battles of the First Balkan War in Thrace.

Preparations

Confronted by the hostile Balkan coalition, the Ottomans peremptorily mobilized their European forces on 24 September 1912. These forces consisted of approximately 115,000 men in Thrace and another 175,000 men in Macedonia.[1] Most units were under strength because the Ottoman military authorities had inexplicably reduced the size of the army the previous summer. The Ottoman troops were deployed in the 1st (Thracian or Eastern) Army under the command of Abdullah Pasha and the 2nd (Macedonian or Western) Army under the command of Ali Risa Pasha. The Thracian Army consisted of the 1st Corps of 20,000 men under Djavid Pasha and the 3rd Corps of 38,000 men under Mahmut Muhtar Pasha around Kirkkilise (Bulgarian, Lozengrad); and the 2nd Corps of 14,000 men under Shevket Turgut Pasha and the 4th Corps of 20,000 men under Ahmed Abuk Pasha around Adrianople.[2] In addition, the Ottomans positioned the Kircaali (Bulgarian, Kurdzhali) detachment under Yaver Pasha southwest of Adrianople. Its mission was to maintain a physical link in Thrace between the Macedonian and the Thracian armies. The Ottoman position in Thrace was anchored in the west by the fortress of Adrianople, which had a garrison of over 50,000 men under Sukru Pasha, and in the east by the older and smaller fortress of Kirkkilise. Because of the size of the forces involved and the proximity of the region to the Ottoman capital Constantinople, the

Thracian theater was by far the most important of the First Balkan War. The war would be won and lost in Thrace.

The Bulgarian General Staff recognized the problem imposed by Bulgaria's geography and recognized that Macedonia must be conquered from Thrace. Beginning in 1903, operational plans concentrated the bulk of the Bulgarian forces on the Thracian frontier. The Bulgarians also understood that, with a population of slightly over four million, they were at a distinct numerical disadvantage against the Ottomans, who numbered well over twenty million. Strategic plans developed in 1903, 1904, and 1908 envisioned a defensive posture in the west to prevent a Turkish attack on the Bulgarian capital at Sofia, and a rapid offensive in the east into Thrace.[3] A small detachment would be stationed in the mountainous Rhodope region along Bulgaria's southern frontier to conduct a campaign of harassment against the Turks and to establish Bulgarian claims to Aegean Thrace. Because of the difficult nature of the terrain, the lack of good roads, and the poor food supply, the Bulgarians did not consider an Ottoman offense in this region likely.

The Italian-trained Bulgarian chief of staff, General Ivan Fichev, changed these plans in 1910–11. He insisted that both the western and eastern theaters adopt an offensive posture, based on war preparation and rapid mobilization. Fichev recognized that in a long war Turkey could shift forces from its Asian territories to Europe that could overwhelm the Bulgarians by weight of numbers. Therefore, the Bulgarians had to achieve a decisive result as quickly as possible. In order to accomplish this, Fichev positioned the Bulgarian forces, divided into three armies, near the Thracian frontier. The 2nd Army would face the Turkish fortress at Adrianople but would not initiate an attack. Fichev later observed, "an attack on Adrianople was incompatible with the main object of the war: the destruction of the enemy forces."[4] The Bulgarians wisely did not want to become bogged down by a siege at Adrianople. Time would work against them. The 1st Army would mass between Adrianople and the fortress of Lozengrad and the 3rd Army would form northeast of the 1st Army behind the Bulgarian cavalry division.

The strategic plan envisioned the 2nd Army screening the strong fortress of Adrianople while the 1st Army moved forward and the 3rd Army swept around the Ottoman right flank, overwhelming the less formidable fortifications at Lozengrad and joining with the 1st Army to force a decisive battle around Lyule Burgas. This was a bold idea. The region between Adrianople and Lozengrad is open, undulating downland, inviting an attack. East of Lozengrad, however, where the 3rd Army would make its turn, lie the slopes of the Strandzha mountain, a rugged ridge with heights reaching up to 800 meters above sea level. The Bulgarians thought that the Ottomans would not anticipate a move in this region.[5] The plan depended on the speed and precision with which the 1st and 3rd Armies could coordinate their movements. In the west a detached division would thrust into Macedonia as part of the Serbian 2nd Army, and smaller units would advance into the difficult terrain of the Rhodopes. The plan had to be implemented and executed rapidly, because the Ottomans had large population resources in Anatolia that, in time, could be brought to bear on the much less numerous Bulgarians. The success of the entire Balkan Alliance depended upon the plan, because if the Ottomans were to defeat the Bulgarians, the largest and strongest of the Balkan allies, they could simply continue on westwards to overwhelm the Greeks, Montenegrins, and Serbs.

The Bulgarians responded to the Ottoman mobilization by mobilizing their own forces on 25 September. For the time being they outnumbered the Ottoman forces in Thrace. The Bulgarian forces consisted of the 79,370-man 1st Army under the command of General Vasil Kutinchev, the 122,748-man 2nd Army commanded by General Nikola Ivanov and the 94,884-man 3rd Army led by General Radko Dimitriev. In addition, the Bulgarians had another 48,523 men in the west facing Macedonia and 33,180 men in the Rhodopes. There were also around 16,000 irregulars from the so called Macedonian-Thracian Volunteers in the Rodopes. The total number of men mobilized by the Bulgarians in the First Balkan war was 599,878 men out of a total male population of 1,914,160.[6] The Bulgarian armies were in place by 17 October. Bulgaria declared war the next day.

Outbreak of war

That same day, Bulgarian troops crossed the Ottoman frontier. Initially they encountered little opposition from their Ottoman enemies. The Bulgarians took care to conceal their real intentions. Deputy Commander in Chief Mihail Savov indicated to foreign journalists that the goal of the campaign was the Ottoman fortress of Adrianople. Savov boasted that he was prepared to sacrifice 100,000 men, "like the Japanese," in order to take the fortress.[7] The Bulgarians also, as noted above, masked the 3rd Army behind their cavalry division, and positioned the 1st Army to indicate a descent on Adrianople. One observer identified this hidden position of the 3rd Army as "the great secret of the campaign."[8] The Bulgarian General Staff calculated that the Ottomans could not completely concentrate a 200,000–250,000 army in Thrace until 1 November.[9] They, however, were ready fifteen days earlier.

On 21 October, even before his troops were concentrated fully, Abdullah Pasha launched an ill-conceived offensive along a line from Adrianople to Lozengrad in the direction of the Bulgarian frontier with the intention of enveloping both flanks of an anticipated Bulgarian advance between the two Ottoman forts. He intended this offensive to be a short push against the Bulgarian units advancing across the Tundzha River. This offensive was undertaken on the orders of the Minister of War, Nizam Pasha. A graduate of the French military academy at St Cyr, Nizam Pasha was under the influence of the French idea of *offensive à outrance*.[10] In addition, some Ottoman generals were eager to demonstrate the success of the military reforms begun after the Young Turk Revolution of 1908. The Ottomans realized that once the Bulgarians occupied regions having a Bulgarian majority, they would be unlikely to return these regions to Ottoman control.[11] Finally, the fate of the Ottoman Empire in Europe depended on the Thracian army. The units of the Western army were too scattered, weak, and vulnerable to have a decisive effect on the outcome of the war. The Thracian army sought to seize the initiative to win the war.

In adopting an offensive strategy, Nizam Pasha abandoned the existing Ottoman plan for war against all the Balkan states. This plan envisioned a defensive posture in eastern Thrace until reinforcements from Anatolia could arrive.[12] The German advisor to the Ottomans, General Colmar Von der Golz, had also urged a defensive strategy that envisioned a battle along the upper Ergene River in northern Thrace, where the battle of Lyule Burgas-Buni Hisar would be fought.[13] Instead, Nazim Pasha pressured Abdullah Pasha to begin this offensive. Many other Ottoman officers opposed this ill-conceived attack. Some were reluctant to abandon the prepared positions around Lozengrad. This did not portend a successful offensive.

Many of the Ottoman troops were unprepared for this effort. They marched off toward Bulgaria lacking proper training or equipment, sometimes even lacking weapons. Many units were under strength. These deficiencies were especially evident among the redif, or reserve troops. At the same time, the Ottomans were ignorant of the speed of mobilization and of the disposition of the Bulgarian army. Nevertheless, they were confident of success. In a speech to officers departing for their units, the Ottoman war minister, Nizam Pasha, advised, "Do not forget to take with you your full-dress uniforms, because you will need them for entry into Sofia two months from now."[14] The Ottoman command evinced confidence.

Just as the Bulgarian armies were about to encounter the enemy, the Fichev plan met an unexpected obstacle. The Bulgarian government indicated that it would seek the intervention of the Great Powers to stop the war. The government hoped that the Great Powers would impose a solution to the Macedonian question that would lead ultimately to Bulgarian annexation. This diplomatic move was opposed by the tsar and the military, who wanted to fight. Tsar Ferdinand responded to the government with a telegram on 22 October, "The proposition of the President of the national subranie is very strange, since up to this minute our arms everywhere confirm my hopes and since the spirit of the army is excellent and is directed toward decisive battles with the centuries old enemy."[15] As the success of Bulgarian armies became apparent after the battle of Lozengrad, the government dropped this idea. The General Staff nevertheless had to contend with the problem of the government in Sofia working at cross purposes with it. The government had not intended to fight the war but had wished only to use the threat of war to force the Great Powers to agree to Bulgarian demands in Macedonia. This was not apparent to the army until it had assumed the offensive.

Lozengrad (Kirkkilise)

The Lozengrad battle took place over the course of three days, 22–24 October, along a 36-mile front stretching easterly from Lozengrad to Adrianople. The Ottomans were arrayed with the fortress of Adrianople anchoring the left flank. The Ottoman cavalry division covered a large gap between Adrianople and the 4th Corps, then the 1st Corps, the 2nd Corps, and the 3rd Corps held the right flank and the fortress of Lozengrad.

While the Ottoman offensive met the advancing units of the Bulgarian 1st Army, the Bulgarian 2nd Army moved toward Adrianople from the west on 22 October to block attempts by the troops in the fortress to assist the Ottoman offensive. During the same evening, the Bulgarian 3rd Army, amidst heavy rain, launched an infantry assault, supported by artillery, on the antiquated fortifications of Lozengrad. This northern position was not nearly as formidable as Adrianople. Field Marshall von der Goltz, who was training the Ottoman Army, had optimistically opined several days before the outbreak of war that the fortifications of Lozengrad could hold off the Prussian army for three months.[16] One of the two main forts, however, contained only four guns; the other lacked guns altogether.[17] Von der Goltz's confidence was misplaced.

At the same time, the 1st Army attacked to the southwest of Lozengrad, northeast of Adrianople, encountering the major part of the Ottoman Thracian army as well as units from Adrianople moving to the northeast. Contact between the two forces began on the afternoon of 22 October. The Bulgarian 1st Army, facing the main force of the Ottoman Thracian army as well as the units moving north out of Adrianople, bore the brunt of the fighting. It deflected a weak Ottoman thrust out of Adrianople against its right flank and even managed to move into the gap between Adrianople and the Ottoman cavalry division. If carried out by a stronger force with resolute leadership, this Ottoman sortie out of Adrianople might have turned the Bulgarian right flank and secured an Ottoman victory.

The Bulgarian 3rd Army easily parried a tentative attempt by Nizam Pasha to envelope its left flank. The Bulgarian cavalry division operated in between the two Bulgarian armies. On the evening of 23 October the Ottomans abandoned Lozengrad in panicky flight to the southeast. When Ottoman artillery failed to answer a Bulgarian barrage on the morning of 24 October, a reconnaissance patrol from the 3rd Army advanced toward the forts. It discovered that the Ottomans had fled.

During the battles around Lozengrad, Bulgarian infantry tactics were on display for the first time. Their highly motivated troops were supported by artillery and often attacked in poor light, at dawn, or even at night. Shouting the Bulgarian war cry, "*na nozh*," (by knife) as they charged, the Bulgarians achieved an overwhelming success. The Ottomans responded with their cries of "Allah, Allah." They, however, were unable to withstand the Bulgarian charges.

By 24 October, the Ottoman troops were in an ill-disciplined retreat all along the line between Adrianople and Lozengrad. Heavy rains added to their difficulties and demoralization. In addition, the action of the Bulgarian cavalry in capturing the baggage train of the Ottoman 1st Corps at the beginning of the battles spread trepidation among the Ottomans. In their panic these troops abandoned their weapons, including all kinds of artillery, along the road. The Ottoman 3rd Corps commander, Mahmut Muhtar Pasha, later wrote of this disaster,

> Military history gives no other such example of a similar rout beginning without cause. Without fighting the Bulgarians had achieved a great victory. Without having been pressured by the enemy, beaten only by the bad weather and the conditions of the roads, the Turks fled as if they had suffered an irreparable disaster, and lost one third of their war materials.[18]

Muhtar Pasha was not entirely correct. Serious fighting did occur at Lozengrad, although not much around the fortress itself. The Ottoman troops displayed obvious failings in areas of command, morale, and discipline. Muhtar himself noted that

> The causes of our defeat are to be found in our bad military organization, and in the lack of discipline of our reservists, but the principle cause was the rain, which had continued for a week, completely destroying the moral of our army, and for 3 days, rendering impassable the roads and fields to our trains and artillery.[19]

The effectiveness of the Bulgarian machine guns and shrapnel bursts terrified the Ottoman troops. Clearly the attempts of the Young Turks to modernize the Ottoman army had not yet succeeded.

The Bulgarians losses were 887 killed, 4,034 wounded and 824 missing around Lozengrad.[20] The Bulgarian 1st Army suffered heavier losses than the 3rd Army. The Ottomans losses were around 1,500 killed and wounded and about 2–3,000 were taken as prisoners.[21] In addition, they lost many guns in their disorderly retreat.

The Bulgarians considered that their success was due to the "good form and skillful fulfillment of the strategic plan."[22] Their surprise flanking operation had succeeded admirably. Their success might have been even greater, however, had better coordination existed between their two attacking armies. They were elated by their success. Only six days after the start of the war they had won a major victory. General Dimitriev later wrote, "We Bulgarians, here among the Strandzha hills, after five hundred years of slavery, for the first time aimed by ourselves at the power of the Turkish army, and achieved a decisive ascendancy for the further course of the war."[23] The memory of recent Ottoman domination remained a strong motivating factor for many Bulgarians.

For the Ottomans, however, the loss of Lozengrad was a disaster. One Ottoman general later wrote, "Kirk-Kilisse was the key to the Ottoman Empire. And that key had been surrendered to the enemy."[24] The Ottoman officers and men were completely demoralized. General Abdullah Pasha himself lost his nerve. On 25 October he instructed his subordinate Muhtar Pasha, "With this Army it is not possible to continue the war and defend the country. In order not to fall into a worse situation, I beg you to ask the Council of Ministers, of which you are a member, to settle the question by diplomacy."[25] Northern Thrace now lay open to the Bulgarians.

Lyule Burgas–Buni Hisar

After the Lozengrad victory the friction of war began to affect the Bulgarians. Instead of immediately pursuing the defeated Ottomans, they rested for 2–3 days. The Bulgarian cavalry division under Major General Atanas Nazlumov, which should have at least screened the fleeing enemy, also rested and lost contact with the Ottomans. Had the Bulgarians directly pursued their defeated Ottoman enemies, they might well have achieved a total victory in northern Thrace, especially given the disorganization and demoralization in the Ottoman ranks. One Ottoman commander later wrote that had the Bulgarians attempted a pursuit the Ottoman position would have been "truly critical."[26] At this point the Ottoman army was in a state of near collapse.

Left unmolested, the Ottomans were able to bring up considerable reinforcements from Constantinople and establish a defensive position consisting of a series of shallow trenches along an extended ridge running northeasterly from the Ergene River past the villages of Lyule Burgas and Buni Hisar (Turkish, Lüle Burgaz and Pinarhisar), about 20 miles. These two villages lent their names to the battles for these positions. Ottoman artillery supported the trench positions at irregular intervals. These ridge positions favored the Ottoman defense. In these new circumstances, the Ottoman officers were able to restore a semblance of discipline to their demoralized troops.

General Dimitriev, eager to pursue the enemy, persuaded the Bulgarian high command to order a forward movement. Dimitriev had wanted to initiate the attack even earlier but had been restrained by Generals Savov and Fichev because of concerns that the Ottomans outnumbered him. The Bulgarian command's caution was sensible because of the strength of the Ottoman positions. The Bulgarian armies resumed their advance on 27 October to crush the enemy in the anticipated decisive battle. The 3rd Army, urged forward by its charismatic commander, moved rapidly forward through the open, undulating landscape south of Lozengrad and became separated from the 1st Army. Had these armies moved together and attacked with their combined strength, they might have easily overwhelmed the still disorganized Ottoman forces and achieved a decisive victory.

With their reinforcements, the Ottoman forces now numbered about 130,000 men, outnumbering the Bulgarians by about 20,000 men.[27] The Ottomans now divided their Thracian army into the 1st Army, including the 1st and 4th Corps, around Lyule Burgas under the command of Abdullah Pasha and the 2nd Army, including the 2nd, 3rd, and 17th Reserve Corps, around Buni Hisar under the command of Hamdi Pasha. Abdullah Pasha recovered himself somewhat and retained overall command of the two armies. The fresh Ottoman troops had good morale and training. After a skirmish at the village of Kolibi Karagach on 28 October, a Bulgarian lieutenant noted, "Here the Turks showed themselves to be real soldiers, who know how to die for their country. Now they shoot quickly and accurately and hold tenaciously to their positions."[28] Abdullah Pasha proposed to hold the line on his left and center and to sweep around the flank of the Bulgarian left with his right. The Bulgarian 1st Army would have less room to maneuver because of Adrianople, but had less ground to cover from Lozengrad.

The Bulgarians' general plan was to carry out a frontal attack by the 3rd Army while the 1st Army enveloped the Ottoman left flank. The Bulgarian cavalry screened the Bulgarian right flank and provided some security against a sortie from Adrianople. The Ottomans were arrayed in the same dispositions as at Lozengrad, except that the 17th Reserve (redif) Corps strengthened the position between the 2nd and 3rd Corps.

On 29 October the Bulgarian 3rd Army attacked the Turkish positions along the entire front between Lyule Burgas and Buni Hisar. When the Bulgarian 1st Army, delayed because of the rainy weather and bad roads, finally reached the southern end of the battle zone on 30 October, it came under the command of the general already on the field, Dimitriev. The battle along the Turkish positions lasted four cold, rainy days. The role of artillery on both sides became very important. The Ottomans fought better here than at Lozengrad. On 30 October, they managed to temporarily deflect the Bulgarian attacks in the middle of the line between Lyule Burgas and Buni Hisar and to force the Bulgarians back. At this point, however, the Ottoman logistical system faltered, causing a critical shortage of artillery shells.

The Bulgarians regrouped and renewed their attacks. General Dimitriev, who reminded his contemporaries of Napoleon because of his short stature and his personal involvement in battle, spurned the idea of maintaining a reserve, and threw all his troops into the battle.[29] Dimitriev was probably the most vibrant general of the Balkan Wars. He would lead the Bulgarian army in the Second Balkan War. In 1914, when Bulgarian ambassador in St Petersburg, he would resign his position and accept a commission in the Russian army. He commanded the Russian 3rd and 12th Armies in the First World War and in 1918 was shot by the Bolsheviks.

General Dimitriev attempted to sweep around the Ottoman right flank and block any retreat of Ottoman forces toward Constantinople. The Bulgarians continued to put their night attacks, including the use of search lights, to good effect. After three days of particularly hard fighting, including attacks and counterattacks on both sides, the Bulgarians prevailed. An English correspondent who observed the failure of some fresh troops from the Ottoman 3rd Corps to advance near Buni Hisar later wrote,

> Even the heroic efforts of Mahmoud's previously unbeaten infantry could not drive back the enemy, who fought with unparalleled determination and ferocity, absolutely throwing away their lives in the Japanese manner whenever a point had to be taken or won.[30]

The discipline and morale of the Bulgarians troops was an important aspect of their infantry attacks.

On 31 October the Ottoman left flank began to give way after Bulgarian 1st Army units had managed to move along the Ergene River to envelope the Ottoman positions. At the same time, Bulgarian units in the center advanced and separated the Ottoman right from left. Finally, elements from the Bulgarian 3rd Army worked around the Ottoman right flank. The result was the same as at Lozengrad. The Ottomans again panicked and retreated in disorder on 2 November. Mahmud Muhtar Pasha commented, "One more time we have witnessed the sadness of a new debacle analogous to that of Kirkilisse. It is difficult to explain the reasons."[31]

In fact, the reasons are not difficult to explain. Besides the above-mentioned attitude of self-sacrifice among the attacking Bulgarians, a very effective artillery was also crucial to their success. The Bulgarians were able to rain rapid and sustained fire on the enemy positions. The previously mentioned English observer noted,

> For every battery the Turks seemed to have in action, the Bulgarians were able to produce half a dozen, and whereas the Turkish fire was desultory and ill-directed, the Bulgarian shells burst in a never-ceasing storm on the Turkish positions with a maximum of effect. In fact, the enemy seemed to have so little respect for the Turkish batteries that they seldom directed their fire against them, but concentrated it on the infantry, who suffered enormous losses, and became sadly demoralized.[32]

They also again made effective use of bayonet charges and night attacks. The Ottomans also contributed to their own defeat by their attempt to attack from their defensive positions. They should have just waited for the Bulgarian attack. Finally, the Adrianople garrison, not yet completely surrounded, should have sortied out against the 1st Army on the Bulgarian right flank as it did during the Lozengrad battle. This diversion might have forced the

Bulgarians to shift their forces to the southwest to meet this threat and thus prevent them from achieving a victory over the Ottoman center and right flank.

The battle was costly for both sides. The Bulgarians suffered 20,162 casualties, including 2,534 dead, with the majority of the loses in the more heavily engaged 3rd Army.[33] General Dimitriev's impetuosity and desire to "do the job by himself," contributed to the 3rd Army's loses.[34] The Ottomans lost at least 22,000 men, including 2,000 prisoners of war, forty-five artillery pieces and much other military equipment.[35] This was the largest and bloodiest battle of the entire Balkan cycle of conflict in 1912–13. Lyule Burgas–Buni Hisar was also the largest battle in terms of numbers of soldiers involved and casualties fought in Europe between the Franco-Prussian War 1870–1 and the First World War 1914–18.

The Bulgarians had succeeded in sweeping around the Ottoman right flank and forcing a decisive battle at Lyule Burgas–Buni Hisar. They won in the end by turning both the right and the left flanks of the Ottoman position. General Dimitriev deserved credit for this victory. He was the first to attack, and he maintained his attacks until he forced the Ottomans to retire in disorder. The Ottomans had suffered their second major defeat in a week. Their defeat along the Lyule Burgas–Buni Hisar line was an even greater disaster for them than that at Lozengrad. Not only had they lost control of all Thrace, except for Adrianople, but the way to Constantinople now lay open.

Another major problem for the Ottomans resulted from the Lyule Burgas–Buni Hisar disaster. Their logistical system, never good, completely collapsed. The Ottomans seem to have had difficulty in sustaining the horses necessary for transportation.[36] Organizational skills were often deficient in the Ottoman army. As a result, during their disorderly retreat toward their capital, the tired, cold, and wet Ottoman troops were often unable to find food, water, or shelter. Under these conditions and because of a total absence of sanitary discipline, cholera, and dysentery appeared among these troops, causing a large number of casualties. Refugees fleeing the fighting toward the safety of Constantinople compounded and spread these diseases. The number of cholera causalities remains unclear.[37] Certainly, the dead numbered well into the thousands. Ironically, cholera would become a critical Ottoman weapon in the upcoming fight for Constantinople.

Once again the Bulgarians failed to immediately pursue their defeated enemies. At the very least, the Bulgarian cavalry should have harassed the disorganized Ottomans. Even though the cavalry had not been involved in any of the major fighting at Lyule Burgas–Buni Hisar, General Nazlumov again insisted that his troops were tired and needed to rest. As a result, the Ottomans were able to escape again. This failure to pursue prevented the Bulgarian victory from being decisive. Had the Bulgarian cavalry followed the defeated Ottoman forces and harried them, the breakdown of Ottoman discipline and morale might have become complete. The Bulgarians then might have entered Constantinople without resistance.

After their victory in Thrace, the Bulgarians lacked clear direction. They had assumed that a defeat at Lyule Burgas would destroy the Ottoman army in Thrace. They did not envision further contingencies. Because of the exhaustion of their troops, the bad condition of the Thracian roads and the slow pace of their logistical system, the Bulgarians did not pursue the fleeing Ottomans immediately but rested for five days before resuming their advance. This respite enabled the Ottomans to transfer troops from Anatolia to reinforce their defenses at Chataldzha (Turkish, Çatalca), 20 miles west of Constantinople. By the time the Bulgarian forces arrived in front of these fortifications they were even more exhausted, and cholera had broken out in their ranks.

The Bulgarian offensive plan had used a flanking movement to sweep around the enemy and had achieved initial success. The further the attacking armies advanced into enemy territory, however, the more difficult their logistical situation became and the more tired the troops became. Here was a lesson the Germans would learn two years later as they slogged through Belgium and northern France. The Bulgarian emphasis on psychological factors for troop motivation and their stress on close combat impressed many foreign observers.[38] This tended to reinforce the French emphasis on élan. The Bulgarian military's reluctance to countenance any interference by the civilian government into the pursuit of policy aims once war was declared foreshadowed events in several European capitals in the summer of 1914.

Chataldzha

Meanwhile, propelled by the momentum of their triumphs, the Bulgarian 1st and 3rd Armies slowly pursued their defeated and demoralized enemy. The deplorable condition of the muddy Thracian roads, over which Bulgarian oxcart-drawn transport carried most of the supplies and munitions forward and returned to the rear all the wounded and sick, hampered the Bulgarian pursuit of the Ottomans. The railroad between the Bulgarian frontier and Constantinople was unusable because it ran under the guns of Ottoman-held Adrianople.

Only antiquated fortifications about 20 miles west of Constantinople remained to impede the march of the Bulgarian army to the Bosporus. These fortifications took their name, Chataldzha, from a village and railroad station located slightly west of their center. The Chataldzha fortifications presented political and military problems for the Bulgarians. The government in Sofia had serious reservations over an attack on the Chataldzha positions and entry into Constantinople. Such an action undoubtedly would anger and alienate Bulgaria's Russian patron. The Russians had entertained claims to the ancient imperial city for centuries and certainly did not welcome a Bulgarian infringement on their desideratum. The government understood that the Russians opposed a Bulgarian entrance into Constantinople.[39] Nevertheless, an entry into Constantinople undoubtedly would put the Bulgarians in a position to dictate a definitive peace to the Ottomans. Tsar Ferdinand, who was famous for his theatrical sensibilities, made no secret of his desire to stage a lavish entrance into the Ottoman capital. The Germans and Austro-Hungarians presented no opposition to the Bulgarian occupation of Constantinople. Even the French minister in Sofia, Hector Panafieu, admitted, "It will be almost impossible for the Bulgarian government to avoid having its army enter Constantinople."[40] The feelings of the Russians were scarcely imaginable, with the prize that had eluded them for centuries about to fall to their younger Slavic brothers, whom they had only liberated in 1878.

In response to a request from the Ottoman government on 4 November 1912, and fearing the collapse of Ottoman authority in Constantinople and possible attacks by enraged Moslems on the Christian population residing there, the Great Powers sent warships to the Bosporus. The senior naval officer present, French Rear Admiral Dartige du Fournet, assumed command of an international fleet consisting of warships from France, Germany, Great Britain, Russia, Austria–Hungary, Italy, Spain, the Netherlands, and Romania. On 18 November, this force landed soldiers from a number of European countries to preserve order and protect the Christian population in the threatened city. Not all observers perceived the need for action by the Great Powers. The American military attaché in Constantinople, Major Taylor, reported that despite the approach of the Bulgarian army, the city remained calm. He observed, "I could not but think that the conditions were very different from what they would have been in New York if a beaten United States army was preparing to make its last stand in Yonkers."[41]

The Bulgarian military knew little about the Chataldzha fortifications. They had not anticipated that their forces would come this far. Their best information dated from 1906, when an enterprising staff officer had made an unauthorized inspection of the Chataldzha works.[42] The Chataldzha line stretched about 30 miles from the Black Sea to the Sea of Marmara and was about 4 miles deep. Of this length, about half was disconnected, old-fashioned hill crest redoubts constructed in 1877–8 and renovated several times since then. A German engineer in Ottoman service, von Bluhm Pasha, designed them in 1877. These consisted of trenches, machine guns, and light artillery. Behind these were heavy artillery batteries in several lines, although some of the best guns had been moved to Adrianople at the beginning of the war. The remainder of the lines, especially at each end, was composed of natural obstacles, such as swamps, lakes, and arms of the sea.

Although by no means overwhelming, the Ottoman position at Chataldzha was much stronger than that at Lozengrad and at Lyule Burgas–Buni Hisar. The combination of natural and man-made fortifications was formidable.

In addition, the Ottoman troops, reinforced by fresh soldiers from Anatolia, understood that either they held at Chataldzha or they lost their capital and the war. They were able to man these defenses with around 100,00 men supported by 280 artillery pieces.[43] These were now consolidated into the 3rd Corps on the northern (Black Sea) flank, the 2nd Corps in the middle of the lines, and the 1st Corps on the southern (Sea of Marmara) flank. Nizam Pasha assumed command of the Chataldzha defense. The appearance of the 3rd Corps commander, Muhtar Pasha, on 4 November helped to restore order among the Ottoman troops streaming into the Chataldzha positions from the Thracian battlefields. The American military attaché in Constantinople, Major Taylor, reported that with the presence of Muhtar Pasha, the Ottoman 3rd Corps commander, "A considerable difference began to appear."[44]

Bulgarian patrols appeared before the Chataldzha positions on 9 November, and elements of the 1st and 3rd Armies had occupied the entire front by 14 November. While the Bulgarian troops were making their way gradually over the muddy roads of Thrace toward Chataldzha, Tsar Ferdinand received at the Bulgarian headquarters at Yambol on 12 November a formal Ottoman request through the Russian minister to Sofia, Anatoli Neklyudov, for an armistice.[45] At this point the war might have ended. The imperial prize of Constantinople, however, beckoned to the Bulgarians.

When Ferdinand transmitted the Ottoman armistice request back to Sofia on 14 November, he indicated that he was not disposed to accept it:

> Disagreeably surprised and deeply saddened by the action of the Grand Vizier, I, as a Bulgarian, as the supreme commander of these victorious and fearless armies which are now under the walls of Constantinople, and in the name of the honor of our country, am obligated to forbid you to communicate this request of the Grand Vizier to our allies until I have obtained the opinions of my assistants, of the commanders of the three armies, the five men who are responsible for the outcome of the war.[46]

Ferdinand, like others before him, was mesmerized by the imperial city lying behind the Chataldzha lines. He even possessed a portrait of himself in Byzantine regalia.[47] The tsar wanted to consider the feasibility of an attack on Chataldzha without any governmental or diplomatic interference.

Then on 14 November, Ferdinand issued an order for an attack on the Chataldzha lines and met with the Italian-trained Chief of Staff General Ivan Fichev and Savov. Both officers expressed reservations, since not all of the armies had arrived yet at Chataldzha. Savov, however, agreed to go to Chataldzha himself to discuss the attack with the commanders of the 1st and 3rd Armies before making a final recommendation.[48] For the time being the attack was postponed pending Savov's return.

Anticipating an order for an attack, General Dimitriev assumed command of the combined 1st and 3rd Armies. General Savov journeyed from Bulgarian headquarters in Yambol to Chataldzha on 15 November to meet with him. The Bulgarian forces were tired and undersupplied. In addition, a new complication had emerged: the cholera and dysentery, which had appeared in the Ottoman ranks during the retreat from Lyule Burgas–Buni Hisar, now swept through the Bulgarian army causing significant losses. The epidemic overwhelmed the Bulgarian sanitary services. During the period from 17 November to 3 December the Bulgarian forces at Chataldzha listed 29,719 soldiers suffering from cholera, of whom 4,615 died.[49] This amounted to roughly one-sixth of the total Bulgarian force. At the time of the attack, the Bulgarians had 176,081 men.[50] Of course, the Ottoman forces also suffered greatly from cholera. They, however, were now only 20 miles from the health resources of their capital, which were probably the best available to them at the time. The Bulgarians were at the end of a long and tenuous logistical system that relied in part on oxen for transportation.

Any attack would be under difficult circumstances. After touring the front, Savov overcame his initial reservations. Radko Dimitriev later recounted Savov saying to him at the unified army headquarters:

> What to do! We shall try, God willing. That way the tsar, and the Bulgarian nation, and also you and I will have clean consciences before our posterity that we did everything humanly possible. There is no man in Bulgaria who, under these conditions, would bring down upon himself the terrible responsibility of failing to attack.

Radko Dimitriev responded:

> Yes, history and posterity for the past 1000 years cannot forgive Krum and Simeon for failing to attack and take Constantinople when they came here. Doubtless we would not be forgiven either.[51]

At the beginning of the twentieth century, Bulgarian army commanders justified or at least excused their decisions in part on the basis of events that had occurred a millennium ago. It is remarkable that the figures of medieval Bulgarian rulers appeared in the Bulgarian decision-making process at this critical juncture. Such was the power of Balkan nationalism.

On his return to headquarters, Savov gave a favorable recommendation to the tsar, who then on 16 November for the second time ordered an attack on the Chataldzha positions. Savov claimed that Dimitriev had forecast an 85–90% chance of success if the Bulgarians attacked quickly.[52] He asserted that "The Chataldzha operation was the natural consequence of the development of our strategic consideration, and there was no alternative because peace had not been concluded and the enemy had not ceased operations."[53] The dilemma of the Bulgarian army was summarized by an English commentator, "Who in their wildest dreams a month before expected to see the army of little Bulgaria doing what Russia has so often tried and failed? No wonder, then, the Bulgarian General Staff acted against its better judgement and allowed sentiment to triumph over sound strategy."[54] Having made the decision to attack, Savov affected confidence. He told reporters on 16 November, "Gentlemen, we shall be in Constantinople in eight days."[55]

General Dimitriev drew up the plan of attack at the front. This plan called for a general attack all along the Ottoman positions by both Bulgarian armies, with the 1st in the south and the 3rd in the north. Artillery would support the entire attack. There was no effort at tactical subtlety. Instead, after an artillery barrage, the Bulgarians ordered their infantry to charge and seize the enemy's fortified positions. These were World War I tactics on the eve of World War I.

The attack began in foggy conditions at 05.00 hours on 17 November. This fog made coordination of the Bulgarian forces difficult and hampered their communications. Powder smoke added to these conditions. The intense artillery fire was heard in Constantinople. At first the Bulgarians were able to advance several hundred yards toward the Ottoman positions. After this initial success, however, they found themselves pinned down all along the lines by Ottoman artillery fire. Effective fire from the 8- and 12-inch guns of the old Ottoman battleship *Barbaros Hayrettin* and the cruiser *Mesudiye* in the Sea of Marmara, directed by observers on the shore, supplemented the Ottoman artillery in the south. Bulgarian artillery fire in response was not as impressive as it had been at Lyule Burgas–Buni Hisar. One English observer watching the attacks from the Ottoman side commented that the Bulgarian infantry attacks from their forward positions were "the most futile and wasteful thing, he had ever seen in his life."[56] These attacks continued on through the night into 18 November. During the night of 17–18 November, a battalion from the 3rd Balkan Division of the 3rd Army did succeed in surprising and occupying a fortified position in the northern sector using the night bayonet attack tactics. From this position the Bulgarians might have turned the entire line. They should have immediately reinforced and exploited this success. The foggy night conditions made communication difficult however. Before the Bulgarians could take advantage of their success, several Ottoman officers rode out into the morning mist along their positions. After one was killed and another wounded, they heard Bulgarian being spoken nearby and rode back to sound the alarm. An extensive Ottoman artillery barrage followed by determined counterattack on the morning of 18 November ejected these troops. This position was the closest the Bulgarians came to Constantinople. Despite strenuous effort, the Bulgarians were unable to maintain a sustained presence anywhere in the Ottoman positions. Heavy rain and fog increased Bulgarian difficulties and misery.

At about 14.00 hours on 18 November, General Dimitriev ordered that the attacks be discontinued. The Bulgarians suffered 1,482 dead, 9,120 wounded and 1,401 missing.[57] Ottoman casualties were somewhat lower, around 10,000 in total.[58] The next day the Bulgarians withdrew from their advanced positions and assumed defensive positions in front of the Ottoman lines. The Bulgarians had experienced their first defeat of the Balkan Wars. They also, when assaulting the entrenched Ottoman positions, with both sides supported by artillery, encountered the sort of combat that other European armies would undergo in two years' time.

Many explanations were given for the Bulgarian failure. Both Fichev and Savov attributed the defeat to the lack of modern tactical knowledge in the Bulgarian officer corps.[59] This is difficult to support. No other European army at this time possessed "modern tactical knowledge." Had such knowledge existed, the heavy infantry losses of 1914–18 would not have occurred. Other problems for the Bulgarians were cholera, the effective firepower of the Ottoman naval vessels and the exhaustion of the Bulgarian troops. One major problem for the Bulgarians was their ineffective artillery support. The Bulgarian artillery failed to achieve the superiority that had proved important to the victories at Lozengrad and Lyule Burgas–Buni Hisar. Although they enjoyed a slight superiority in the numbers of artillery pieces, their weapons were lighter than those of the Turks and lacked the range to provide cover for the attack and to counter the Ottoman artillery. Some Bulgarian guns even fired on their own retreating troops. In addition, the Ottoman artillery fire proved to be a formidable obstacle to the Bulgarian attack. A German observer attributed the Ottoman artillery success to the "imperturbability and security" of Krupp guns.[60] Another major problem among the Bulgarians was exhaustion and sickness. Over the last month, they had marched over difficult and often roadless terrain. During that time they had also fought two major battles. Here the rests that they had taken after the battles of Lozengrad and Lyule Burgas–Buni Hisar assumed great importance. The American military attaché in Constantinople, Major J. R. M. Taylor, reported that "If the Bulgarians had attacked on Nov. 5, or even Nov. 10, they would have taken Constantinople."[61] It is unlikely, however, that the Bulgarians could have arrived at Chataldzha any faster than they did, given the muddy roads they had to traverse and the limited transportation means, including ox carts, they used.

The Ottoman recovery was remarkable. They had lost much equipment, many men, and two major battles and were in danger of losing their last toeholds in Europe and of losing their capital. Their victory at Chataldzha rejuvenated the Ottoman forces. For the first time in the war they had prevailed against the Bulgarians. The Ottoman command had preformed the difficult feat of restoring discipline and confidence to their troops under extremely arduous circumstances. The Ottoman victory also heartened the defenders of Adrianople. The failure of the Bulgarian infantry attack against the entrenched Ottoman positions supported by effective artillery foreshadowed the futile allied offensive tactics used on the Western Front in World War I.

The defeat at Chataldzha left the Bulgarian army in a dangerous situation. By 22 November, General Dimitriev reported that the combined strength of the 1st and 3rd Armies was 85,597 soldiers ready for battle.[62] The Bulgarians were numb from exhaustion, starving from lack of adequate supplies, and plagued by cholera. Their offensive potential at least for the time being was finished and no further operations at Chataldzha were contemplated.[63] Fortunately for the Bulgarians, the Ottomans were in a similar situation. The debilitated Bulgarians deflected the feeble Ottoman sorties from the Chataldzha positions on 22 and 23 November without major difficulty. Both sides were exhausted and neither was capable of any meaningful offensive operations. Military stalemate ensued at Chataldzha.

At Chataldzha the Bulgarians were victims of their own success. Their campaign against the Turks had carried them to within 20 miles of Constantinople. Unfortunately, they were not prepared logistically, tactically, politically, or diplomatically to deal with the issues involved in taking and occupying the capital city of their enemy. This battle need not have been fought. The best policy for the Bulgarians at this point would have been to stop in front of the Chataldzha lines while their army was still intact and accept the Ottoman armistice request. Then they could have negotiated a definitive conclusion to the war from a position of strength. This is precisely what the Russians had done in 1878, when they stopped in front of Constantinople and negotiated a favorable peace at San Stefano. The Bulgarians should have learned this from their Russian liberators. Had the Bulgarians taken Constantinople, however, they would have ensured a peace on their terms. They also would have performed a feat replicated only twice in the history of that city. The temptation was too much to overcome.

The Bulgarian army never recovered completely from the defeat at Chataldzha. Many junior officers and soldiers had fallen in front of the Ottoman lines. As long as the weakened army remained in position in front of Chataldzha, it could not counter Serbian and Greek pretensions to the territories in Macedonia claimed by Bulgaria.

Adrianople

The most important position in Thrace was the fortified city of Adrianople (Turkish, Edirne; Bulgarian, Odrin). Adrianople was the capital of the Ottoman province of Adrianople, which corresponded to Thrace. Adrianople and Salonika were the two largest cities of Ottoman Europe, save Constantinople. In 1912, the city had a mixed population of around 76,000, of whom around half were Turkish and the rest were divided among Greeks, Armenians, Jews, and others[64]. There was only a small Bulgarian population in the city, although larger numbers lived in the surrounding countryside.

Because of the small numbers of Bulgarians in Adrianople and in Thrace, Adrianople did not constitute a major policy goal for the Bulgarians.

The Ottomans considered the defenses of Adrianople to be impregnable. They did not think an attacking force could advance beyond it toward Constantinople. At the start of the war the Ottomans shifted some heavy artillery pieces from the Chataldzha positions outside Constantinople to Adrianople. For the defense of Adrianople the Ottomans had almost 52,597 officers and men and 340 artillery pieces of various types.[65] These guns were mainly immobile fortification weapons positioned in the fortification complex. The fortification complex itself consisted of an advanced line of detached positions of trenches and batteries, intended to contain the enemy as far away from the city as possible. These were situated from 4,900 to 13,600 yards in front of the city. The primary line of fortifications consisted of brick, earth, and concrete defensive forts 3–3.5 meters high, with walls 6–7 meters thick. Some of these forts went back to the Russo-Turkish War of 1828–9. Trenches 4 meters deep and 4–5 meters wide surrounded the forts. In front of these positions was a continuous network of 4–6 rows of barbed wire. A secondary line existed from 1–4 kilometers behind the primary line. It consisted of four old forts. These did not play any important role in the siege. The most sophisticated and thorough fortification system of the Balkan Wars defended Adrianople. In the depth of defensive positions, Adrianople resembled positions on the Western Front of the First World War. A secure Adrianople was the first line of defense for Constantinople.

Ferik Mehmed Sukru Pasha, a former student at the French military academy in St Cyr, commanded the fortress in 1912. When war threatened between the Ottoman Empire and Bulgaria in the early autumn of 1912, the commander of the Ottoman Thracian Army, Abdullah Pasha, instructed Sukru, "The task of the Adrianople fortress is to draw as many enemy forces as possible, to impede the enemy advance and to threaten the enemy's rear and flanks."[66] Unfortunately for the Ottomans, the commander at Adrianople, Sukru, was elderly and not well informed about his own forces, let alone the Bulgarians. His ability to accomplish his instructions was problematical.

At the beginning of the twentieth century the Bulgarian General Staff naturally had focused on the major Ottoman stronghold at Adrianople. In 1909 a Bulgarian staff officer had gone to work in the Bulgarian consulate in Adrianople as a cover for investigating the fortifications.[67] A staff study in 1911 concluded that Adrianople should come under immediate attack in the case of war.[68] In the summer of 1912 the Bulgarian army rehearsed an attack on Adrianople.

When war did erupt on 18 October 1912, the Bulgarians initially were reluctant to force Adrianople. Despite their previous efforts, they lacked precise information about the strength of the Adrianople garrison. As a result, they had developed an exaggerated view of the strength of the fortress. The careful plan formulated by the cautious Italian-trained Chief of Staff, General

Ivan Fichev, for attack in the Thracian theater called for the Bulgarian 1st and 3rd Armies to sweep to the north around Adrianople and for the 2nd Army to screen the fortress city. The commander of the 2nd Army, Russian-educated Lieutenant General Nikola Ivanov, opposed this plan. He wanted to rush and seize Adrianople.[69] Fichev's plan was nevertheless consistent with overall Bulgarian strategy. The Bulgarians realized that their enemy enjoyed far greater manpower resources but that these troops required time to consolidate and be transported from Asia Minor to Europe. Therefore, the Bulgarians had to achieve a decisive victory by quickly destroying the main Ottoman force in Thrace. They could not afford to become involved in a prolonged siege at Adrianople.

Political considerations also influenced the Bulgarian decision to avoid a siege at Adrianople. Immediately before the declaration of war the Russian military attaché in Sofia, Colonel Georgii D. Romanovski, warned General Fichev not to attack Adrianople because St Petersburg considered it to be within the hypothetical Russian zone of influence around the straits connecting the Aegean Sea to the Black Sea.[70] Bulgarian policy then was oriented toward the largest Slavic state. Many Bulgarians remembered the Russians gratefully as their liberators from the Ottomans in the Russo-Turkish War of 1877–8. In addition, St Petersburg provided Sofia with material and diplomatic assistance during the war against the Ottoman Empire. For emotional as well as practical reasons, Bulgaria did not want to alienate Russia.

Coincidentally, with the Bulgarian victory at Lyule Burgas–Buni Hisar, the Russian minister in Sofia, Anatoli Neklyudov, informed the Bulgarian government on 4 November 1912 that St Petersburg had withdrawn its objections to a Bulgarian annexation of Adrianople.[71] By this action the Russians acknowledged the success of Bulgarian armies. They could afford to be generous with territory they did not control. In addition, the Russians did not wish to undergo the humiliation of a defiant occupation of Adrianople by their client state.

The prospect of the acquisition of Adrianople elated the Bulgarians. Neklyudov reported, "It is as if we have freed Bulgaria a second time."[72] This action was especially popular because Bulgaria had agreed to accept Russian arbitration on the disposition of northern Macedonia as a condition of the March 1912 alliance with Serbia. The acquisition of Adrianople would compensate to some degree for the loss of northern Macedonia.

Even before the Russian 'gave' Adrianople to Bulgaria, the Bulgarian army had initiated steps to bring the city under siege. As early as 24 October, the Bulgarians widened their screening activity at Adrianople by sending a force south of the Arda River, and on 25 October a cavalry unit was ordered to cross the railroad south of the city. This effectively severed communications between Adrianople and Constantinople. On 29 October, just as the Bulgarian 1st and 3rd Armies were beginning the battles with the Ottomans at Lyule Burgas and Buni Hisar, the Bulgarian high command decided to besiege Adrianople.[73] It ordered the 2nd Army, augmented by the newly formed 2nd Division, to encircle Adrianople. The Bulgarian success at Lozengrad and the excitement of the pending clash at Lyule Burgas–Buni Hisar persuaded the high command that they could take Adrianople. Soon after this an independent cavalry brigade and the 30th Infantry Regiment of the 8th Division occupied Dimotika, southwest of Adrianople, on 31 October, tightening the Bulgarian grip on the city.

At the same time, the Bulgarians called upon their Serbian allies for assistance in conducting the siege. Immediately before the start of the war, the Serbs had agreed to help the Bulgarians at Adrianople if necessary.[74] After their overwhelming victory at Kumanovo on 25 October, the Serbs had overrun much of Macedonia. Transportation of General Stepa Stepanovich's 2nd Army, consisting of the Timok and Danube divisions, to Adrianople began on 30 October and was concluded by 12 November. This added 47,275 men and seventy-two artillery pieces to the besieging forces at Adrianople.[75] The transfer of the Serbs enabled the Bulgarians to dispatch the 3rd Division and two brigades of the 9th Division to the 1st and 3rd Armies, which were slowly pursuing the defeated Ottoman forces toward Constantinople. The 2nd Army continued to screen Adrianople and by 9 November had surrounded the city. The confluence of the three rivers neatly divided the besieging army into four sections: northwest, east, south, and west. Serbian troops took up positions in the western sector and Bulgarians in the other three. The Bulgarians wanted to ensure that the Ottoman garrison could not break out to the southeast and threaten the advance of the 1st and 3rd Armies. The Bulgarians began artillery bombardments of Adrianople on 29 October, but they lacked the heavy artillery to conduct an intensive siege. On 6 November, after an artillery barrage, Bulgarian infantry during a night attack took an advanced Ottoman position, known as Papas Tepe, in the southern quarter. They then used these heights as an observation post for their artillery.

The Ottomans were not inactive as the Bulgarians closed the ring. They recognized the seriousness of their isolated position in the city. They conducted several sorties against the Bulgarians. They attempted one sortie on 22 October to distract the Bulgarians during the battles around Lozengrad. This had little effect. On 29 October, the Ottomans attempted a sortie in strength to the west, in an attempt to recapture some positions. Bulgarian artillery, directed by airplane and balloon, drove the Ottoman troops back to the shelter of their fortifications.[76] This was a wasted effort. Sukru probably should have directed his efforts a day or two sooner and in a more northerly direction, toward the rear of the Bulgarian 1st Army, then engaged in battle around Lyule Burgas. Such a sortie might have greatly disrupted the Bulgarian communication and logistical lines. The raid to the west gained little for the Ottomans except heavy casualties. Around 1,200 of their men were killed.[77]

The Chataldzha defeat increased the importance of Adrianople for Bulgaria. On 14 November, even before the Chataldzha attack, the Bulgarians initiated an intensive bombardment of Adrianople. The Bulgarian command did not anticipate that the bombardment would result in a capitulation of Adrianople, but merely hoped that it would increase strain and tension within the besieged city.[78] The bombardment continued until the end of November. An infantry sortie on 15 November brought minimal gains to the besiegers. Tsar Ferdinand even ordered an infantry attack on Adrianople during the armistice negotiations, "in order to force more favorable conditions for the conclusion of peace for us."[79] The General Staff dissuaded him from implementing this order by the staff because of an agreement to suspend military activity during the armistice negotiations. The defeat at Chataldzha demoralized the high command and the General Staff of the army. They were unwilling to risk another battle at that time.

Western Thrace and the Rhodopes

Small Bulgarian forces, fewer than 25,000 men, from the 2nd Thracian Division under the command of General Stiliyan Kovachev and several other units advanced into western Thrace from southern Bulgaria. These Bulgarian forces were divided into the Haskovo detachment and the Rhodope detachment.

The Ottomans had some strength in this region. Their Kircaali (Bulgarian, Kurdzhali) detachment, including one division of about 10,000 men near the Temrosh salient and two divisions totaling 20,000 near Kurdzhali, was under the command of Yaver Pasha.[80] These forces singularly failed to offer the invading Bulgarian significant resistance. They retreated to the southeast in the face of the Bulgarian invasion.

The Haskovo detachment moved south into Kurdzhali. Having taking that city part of the detachment moved to Adrianople to participate in the siege. The other part assumed the name Kurdzhali. As the Kurdzhali detachment, it then proceeded to Gyumyurdzhina on 22 November and entered the Aegean port of Dedeagach on 26 November. There it found that Bulgarian irregulars from the Macedonian–Thracian Legion had been in control since 19 November.

Anxious to bolster their position in Thrace after the Chataldzha defeat, the Bulgarians augmented their forces in eastern Thrace with troops from Salonika. On 21 November the 13th Infantry Regiment of the 7th Rila Division embarked on six Greek steamers at Salonika and arrived near Dedeagach five days later. The 7th Rila Division entered the Aegean port of Dedeagach on 27 November. There it combined with troops from the Kurdzhali detachment and moved to the east.

The appearance of Bulgarian troops on the Aegean cut the railway link to the west and effectively isolated the Ottoman Macedonian army from the

Thracian army. These Bulgarian units continued to move into eastern Thrace and occupied the north shore of the Sea of Marmara at Sharkoi and the northern part of the Gallipoli Peninsula. Their pursuit of the Ottomans ended at the village of Merhamli in southern Thrace on 26 November. There, after a brief fight, Yaver Pasha surrendered his force of 10,131 officers and men.[81] Yaver Pasha's surrender effectively isolated the Ottoman Macedonian Army in the Western Balkans.

Meanwhile, the Rhodope detachment crossed the Ottoman frontier in three locations. One section took the Temrosh salient and then the town of Smolyan on 26 October. From there it moved south to Dedeagach. A second section moved southwest from Batak in Bulgaria to Nevrokop (now Gotse Delchev), taking that city on 30 October. From there it advanced to Drama, which it took on 5 November. The third section moved west from Rakitovo in Bulgaria to Bansko, joining the second section in Nevrokop. These Bulgarian forces moved fairly quickly over difficult terrain. They encountered little resistance from Ottoman units or from the indigenous Pomaks (Bulgarian-speaking Muslims). By 30 October, the Bulgarians had occupied the entire Rhodope region.

After the battle at Merhamli, the Bulgarians had occupied almost all of Thrace. The Ottomans clung to Thrace, and thus to Europe, behind the fortifications of Adrianople, Chataldzha, and Gallipoli. The small Bulgarian forces had chased a larger Ottoman force out of the Rhodopes and away from the Aegean seaboard. A more resolutely led Ottoman force might have reversed the situation. It might have itself crossed the Rhodopes and emerged on the plain of the Maritsa River, threatening the major Bulgarian town of Plovdiv. Such a threat could have forced the Bulgarians to withdraw forces from Adrianople or from eastern Thrace. A weaker Bulgarian position in Thrace could have afforded the Ottomans the opportunity to defeat the invaders. The Bulgarian success in the Rhodopes then was an important aspect of their victories in Thrace.

Conclusion

The campaign in Thrace in the autumn of 1912 began with stunning Bulgarian victories at Lozengrad and Lyule Burgas–Buni Hisar. Their strategic plan had succeeded in inflicting demoralizing defeats on their Ottoman adversaries and brought them to the Chataldzha lines only 20 miles from the fabled imperial capital at Constantinople. There they spurned an Ottoman offer of peace and attacked. The Bulgarians, however, were unable to summon sufficient reserves of energy to push past the Ottoman positions and enter their capital. The Bulgarians were exhausted, at the end of a tenuous logistical system and were plagued by cholera. Had they managed to take Constantinople, they would have achieved a feat that few armies in history had managed. They also would have thrown the Great Powers, especially Russia, into a state of envy and confusion.

The Ottoman Eastern Army began the campaign with terrible defeats. Because of these, the Ottomans lost not only Thrace but also Macedonia and Albania. At the Chataldzha lines, however, the Ottoman defense obtained an important victory. They rallied from complete defeat to stop the Bulgarian onslaught. The Ottoman troops protected their capital and gained a sense of confidence and purpose lacking in the previous battles of the war. This was the most important Ottoman victory against a European army for 200 years. It set a precedent for the victory at Gallipoli three years later.

After the Chataldzha battle, stalemate ensued. Because of heavy losses of men and material, both sides were exhausted and for the time being were incapable of further military activity. The Ottomans clung to three small pieces of eastern Thrace, at Chataldzha, Gallipoli, and Adrianople. Their continued presence in these locations remained questionable.

More outsiders, military observers, and journalists witnessed the campaign in eastern Thrace in the autumn of 1912 than any other theater during the Balkan war cycle. Their efforts to comment on these battles, however, did not serve to preserve the names Lyule Burgas–Buni Hisar and Chataldzha in popular European or American memory. The shadows of the First World War rapidly obscured these battles and their lessons.

3

FIRST BALKAN WAR

Western Theater

The western region of the Balkans, including Albania, Kosovo, and Macedonia, was less important to the resolution of the war and the survival of the Ottoman Empire than Thrace was. Nevertheless, this region was the object of the national aspirations of Montenegro and Serbia and most of the aspirations of Greece. To a considerable degree, the goals of the Montenegrins and the Serbs overlapped in the Sandjak of Novi Pazar and in Kosovo.

Serbia

In preparation for war against the Ottoman Empire, the Serbs arrayed their forces in four groups. Crown Prince Alexander commanded the Serbian 1st Army, the largest Serbian force. It numbered around 132,000 men.[1] It was concentrated in the lower Morava valley. The Serbian 2nd Army, under General Stepa Stepanovich, had around 74,000 men. It consisted of the Serbian Timok Division and the Bulgarian 7th Rila Division. It was concentrated in southwestern Bulgaria between Kyustendil and Dupnitsa. The Serbian 3rd Army, led by General Bozhidar Jankovich, had around 76,000 men. It was concentrated in two groups in western Serbia: one at Toplica and the other at Medvedje. The remaining two Serbian concentrations were in northwestern Serbia. The Ibar Army, with only 25,000 men, was led by General Mihail Zhivkovich. In addition, the Javor brigade, commanded by Lieutenant Colonel Milovoje Andjelkovich, had 12,000 men.

 The Serbian General Staff, under the direction of Chief of Staff General Radomir Putnik, planned an all-out attack on the Ottomans. The General Staff reasoned that the Ottomans would concentrate their forces in the direction of the Morava and Vardar Rivers, that is central Macedonia, and hold out until forces from Anatolia could relieve them.[2] The main Serbian force, the Serbian 1st Army, would confront the Ottomans directly. It was to advance down the Morava valley, across the gap to the Vardar valley into Macedonia and occupy that region. This would destroy Ottoman control of central Macedonia. It would also establish a Serbian presence in the "contested regions" that had been established in the March treaty with Bulgaria. The

2nd Army was to advance into eastern Macedonia from Bulgaria. It would cut off Ottoman forces escaping down the Vardar and prevent reinforcements from reaching Macedonia. The Serbian 3rd Army was to move south into Kosovo. From there it would attack the Ottoman left flank in central Macedonia. The Serbian General Staff expected the three armies to meet at Ovche Polje, a fairly level region east of Skoplje, where it anticipated the main Ottoman force would be[3]. The united Serbian armies could then overwhelm the Ottoman force there.

Further north, the Ibar Army and Javor detachment would move into the Sandjak of Novi Pazar from the south and the north respectively. The Ibar Army would make a move on the town of Novi Pazar and protect the flank of the 3rd Army. The Javor detachment at first would monitor Austro-Hungarian activity. The Serbs were concerned that in the event of a Balkan war, the Austro-Hungarians might reoccupy the Sandjak of Novi Pazar to keep Serbia and Montenegro physically separate. The Austro-Hungarians, after all, had only evacuated the Sandjak in 1908. If they did not move against Serbia after the opening of hostilities, the Javor detachment would cross over into the northern Sandjak. The Serbs developed an aggressive plan that depended on rapid movement. If successful, it would ensure a quick defeat of the Ottomans.

In the west the Ottomans had the impossible task of defending the large salient of Macedonia and Albania, which was vulnerable to Greek, Montenegrin, and Serbian attacks. The Greek navy's control of the Aegean increased the difficulties of the Ottoman situation. Under these circumstances, if the Bulgarians moved across the narrow neck of western Thrace to reach the Aegean Sea and cut the Constantinople–Salonika railroad, the Ottoman forces in all Albania and Macedonia would become completely isolated. The Ottomans concentrated their largest force, the Vardar Army, in northern Macedonia. Its task was the defense of the Macedonian core. Smaller units were stationed in the Sandjak of Novi Pazar, Albania, and around Salonika. The Ottomans depended on Albanian irregulars to defend that region against the Greeks and Montenegrins. The Ottomans planned a vigorous defense of the west. A successful rebuff of Greek, Montenegrin, and Serbian attacks might open the way for the Vardar army to launch an offensive against Sofia, and thus the major power in the Balkan Alliance would be crushed between the Vardar army advancing from the east and the Thracian army advancing from the east.[4]

At the beginning of the war, the Ottomans had 175,000 men in Macedonia and Albania.[5] This actually amounted to more soldiers than they had at the time in Thrace. The Ottoman forces in Thrace, however, could be easily strengthened from Anatolia. Because of the presence of the Greek fleet in the Aegean, those forces in Albania and Macedonia could not be strengthened. A number of Albanian volunteers and irregulars augmented the Ottoman forces. Ottoman authorities supplied the Kosovo Albanian leader Isa Boljetini with 63,000 rifles.⁶ The Albanians reasoned that Ottoman rule was preferable to that of the other Balkan nationalities. The Ottoman forces, although scattered throughout the region, were concentrated in the Vardar and the Struma valleys. The largest concentrated Ottoman force in the west was the Vardar Army, around 65,000 men commanded by Zeki Pasha.⁷ It consisted of the 5th, 6th and 7th Corps, which included both nizam and redif divisions. Smaller forces were scattered throughout Ottoman territories in the western Balkans. The overall commander of the Ottoman forces in Macedonia was Ali Riza Pasha. He maintained his headquarters in Salonika.

Above all, the Ottomans in the west had to play for time. If they could hold out long enough, they anticipated that their superior numbers brought from Asia could preserve their rule in the Balkans. For this strategy to succeed, of course, they had to defeat the Bulgarians in Thrace. This would protect the vital Constantinople–Salonika railroad connection. Otherwise, their forces in the western Balkans would become isolated from their source of strength in Anatolia. In the west their only strong position was Albania. For the Ottomans, as one officer wrote, "the only protection, the only refuge, was in Albania."⁸ The Ottomans should have based their western defenses there.

Kumanovo

On 19 October the Serbian 1st Army crossed the frontier advancing south into Ottoman territory. The Serbian cavalry division screened the Serbian left flank. Three days later the 1st Army encountered Zeki Pasha's Vardar Army consisting of the 5th Corps (Salonika) under Kara Said Pasha, the 6th Corps (Bitola) under Djavid Pasha, and the 7th Corps (Skoplje) under Feti Pasha arrayed respectively east, north, and northwest of the Macedonian town of Kumanovo. The Ottoman forces numbered around 58,000 men, about half the size of the oncoming Serbs.⁹ The size of the Ottoman army came as a surprise to General Putnik.¹⁰ He had not expected to encounter so large a force so early in the war, and he had not anticipated a major battle this far north.

Following the instructions of Nizam Pasha, the Ottoman commander in chief, to take the offensive, Zeki Pasha initiated the battle at Kumanovo.¹¹ He attacked the Serbian right flank on the morning of 23 October. Major fighting developed along a 10-mile front that afternoon in the cold and rain. Initially the Serbs sustained heavy casualties, especially on their right flank. At first the Ottomans enjoyed a numerical advantage. Many Serbian units were still moving toward the battlefield and were not yet available to fight. In addition, the Serbs had some trouble bringing their artillery into position.

As the Serbian soldiers arrived on the battlefield, they immediately began to attack the enemy. A colonel of the Morava Division explained, "I think that we must go over into attack immediately, because in the Bulgarian War of 1885, we had a bitter lesson in a similar situation, while one division fought, the other rested and played music."[12] The Serbian soldiers threw themselves into the battle. One journalist later wrote, "This Serbian fight was a real Japanese assault of the kind I had witnessed at Port Arthur, where no one tried to save his life."[13] Nevertheless, after the first day of fighting, Zeki Pasha thought that the situation, "concluded to our advantage."[14]

Serbian counterattacks against all Ottoman positions intensified on 24 October as additional Serbian units arrived on the battlefield. By that morning, many Serbian batteries began appear. Their fire overwhelmed the Ottoman artillery to such a degree that the Serbs could press their attacks in the open. Here, as in Thrace, the Ottomans did not handle their artillery well. Ottoman artillery acted separately from the infantry and lacked forward observers to help determine the effectiveness of its fire. Furthermore, Zeki Pasha failed to position eighteen heavy artillery pieces that had arrived at Kumanovo from Skoplje.[15] This additional fire power undoubtedly would have given the Ottomans a great advantage in their initial attacks and in their defense against the Serbs.

In the afternoon, the Ottomans began to retreat all along the line. Their redif units in particular proved unreliable and liable to panic. At Kumanovo the Serbian 1st Army suffered 687 dead, 3,208 wounded, and 597 missing.[16] The Ottomans suffered 12,000 dead and wounded and about 300 were taken prisoner.[17]

Even though initially caught by surprise, the Serbs adjusted quickly to inflict what became the decisive defeat of the campaign in Macedonia on the Ottomans. In celebration of the victory King Peter awarded General Putnik the title Vojvoda (Marshall). As Vojvoda, Putnik would lead the Serbian army in two successful defensive campaigns against Austro-Hungarian invasions in 1914. After supervising the Serbian retreat across Albania in 1915, Putnik was relieved of command by Crown Prince Alexander, ostensibly because of illness but also because the Serbian army needed a scapegoat after its defeat.

With the victory at Kumanovo the Serbian army controlled northern Macedonia. Much of the "disputed zone" was now under Serbian occupation. This gave Serbia a tremendous advantage in this "dispute" with Bulgaria. Having expended lives and much treasure to conquer this territory, the Serbs were unlikely to relinquish it willingly.

The Ottomans had begun the Kumanovo battle aggressively, hoping to break through the oncoming Serbs. They lacked the number of soldiers to sustain their attacks however. If they had overrun the Serbs before the Serbian artillery arrived on the battlefield, they might have achieved a victory and with it bought the time to maintain their position in northern Macedonia. This was a forlorn hope. After the Serbs positioned their artillery and began sustained fire, the battle turned decisively against the Ottomans. Within half a day, the Vardar Army began to retreat south in some disorder.

The Ottoman offensive ordered by Nizam Pasha was no more successful in Macedonia against the Serbs than it had been in Thrace against the Bulgarians. This strategy was seriously flawed. The Ottoman forces were not sufficiently well trained and ably led to carry out a successful offensive. Kumanovo was not the place to meet the Serbs. This extreme northern position was vulnerable to attack on its flanks, just as the Serbian plan envisioned. By fighting at Kumanovo in northern Macedonia, the entire Vardar Army risked being cut off and surrounded by the actions of the Serbian 2nd and 3rd Armies. The Ottomans should have established a strong defensive position further south in Macedonia around Bitola. There, with access to Albanian resources, they might have been able to hold out for a time. This at the very least would have bought them the time that they needed to draw on their reserves from Anatolia. As a result of their offensives at the very beginning of the war, the Ottomans forfeited their potential numerical advantage.

The Kumanovo defeat panicked and demoralized the Ottomans. They retreated in a southerly direction toward Bitola. The Ottomans made no attempt to defend the important town of Skoplje (Turkish, Uskub; Bulgarian, Skopie), southwest of Kumanovo, abandoning there many guns and much supplies, including the eighteen heavy guns unused at Kumanovo. The attempted assassination of the defeated Ottoman commander, Zeki Pasha, in Skoplje by a disgruntled Ottoman soldier contributed to the panic.

The Ottomans should have established some defensive positions north of Skoplje. This would have forced the Serbs to fight for the main city of central Macedonia and would have slowed them down considerably. The Serbian 1st Army entered Skoplje without opposition on 26 October. Three days later the Morava Brigade, which had been attached to the 3rd Army, arrived from Prishtina.

Vojvoda Putnik and his staff failed to appreciate the extent of their victory. They continued to adhere to their plan to concentrate their forces at Ovche Polje. The main part of the 1st Army, strengthened with a division from the 3rd Army, pursued the Ottomans toward Bitola. Another part followed disorganized Ottoman units toward Veles. Because they did not realize the extent of their victory at Kumanovo, the Serbs did not closely follow the fleeing Ottomans. Had they pressed their victory, they might have destroyed the main force of the Vardar Army in central Macedonia and ended their campaign two weeks after it had begun. The failure to pursue the defeated enemy was the same mistake that the Bulgarians had made after their big victories at Lozengrad and Lyule Burgas–Buni Hisar.

Prilep

Bad weather and difficult roads hampered the 1st Army's pursuit of the Ottomans after Kumanovo. Road conditions forced the Morava Division to move ahead of the Drina Division. On 3 November, in the autumn rain, forward elements of the Morava Division encountered fire from Kara Said Pasha's 5th Corps from positions north of Prilep. This started the three-day battle for Prilep. The fighting was broken off that night and was renewed the next day. When the Drina Division arrived on the battlefield, the Serbs gained an overwhelming advantage. The Ottomans withdrew south of the city.

On 5 November, as the Serbs moved south of the city they again came under Ottoman fire from prepared positions. The Ottomans controlled the heights on the road to Bitola. The Serbs required the better part of the next day to force the Ottomans to retreat. Bayonets and hand grenades gave the Serbs the advantage in hand-to-hand fighting. The overt and guileless nature of the Serbian infantry attacks impressed one Ottoman observer, who noted,

> The development of the Serbian infantry attack was as open and clear as the execution of a barracks exercise. Large and strong units covered the entire plain. All the Serbian officers were seen clearly. They attacked as if on parade. The picture was very impressive. One part of the Turkish officers were struck dumb by the wonder of this mathematical disposition and order, the other sighed at this moment because of the absence of heavy artillery. They remarked on the arrogance of the open approach and clear frontal attack.[18]

The artillery abandoned in Skoplje would have helped the Ottoman defenders south of Prilep. The Serbs demonstrated the same lack of subtlety in their infantry attacks that caused heavy casualties among all the combatants during the Balkan Wars and would cause many during the First World War. During this battle, the Serbian 1st Army was without the presence of its commanding general, Crown Prince Alexander. Ill from the rigors of the cold and wet campaign, he maintained telephone contact with his army from his sickbed in Skoplje.

The short, sharp battles around Prilep demonstrated that the Ottomans were still capable of opposing the Serbian march through Macedonia. Even after abandoning the city of Prilep, the Ottoman 5th Corps fought stubbornly south of town. The size and enthusiasm of the Serbs overcame the Ottomans, but at a cost. The Ottomans suffered around 300 dead and 900 wounded, and 152 were taken prisoner; the Serbs had losses of around 2,000 dead and wounded.[19] The road southwest to Bitola now lay open to the Serbs.

Bitola

Lacking a territorial agreement with the Greeks, the Bulgarians feared that their ally might attempt to occupy large parts of southern Macedonia that had fallen to Bulgaria under the terms of the treaty of March 1912. To forestall this possibility, Minister President Geshov asked the Serbs to occupy Bitola

(Serb, Bilolj; Turk, Monastir) in southwestern Macedonia before the Greeks could get there.[20] The Bulgarians had faith in the Serbs because of the ties of Slavic solidarity, but more so because of the March 1912 treaty guaranteed by Russia. The Bulgarians were confident that the Russians, who had liberated them in 1878, would not fail them now. As events unfolded, the Bulgarians need not have worried about a Greek move into Bitola. Such an advance made sense militarily, because it would cut off the Ottoman line of retreat. The Greeks, however, like the Bulgarians, were distracted by the prize of Salonika.

The Bulgarian request notwithstanding, the Serbs were eager to complete their conquest of Macedonia. The Serbs were happy to comply with this request, because this would bring almost all of western Macedonia under Serbian occupation. On 8 November the Serbian high command ordered the 1st Army to advance on Bitola. The Serbs approached Bitola in two groups: one from the northwest and the other from the northeast. The cavalry scouted ahead of the main forces, generally on the Serbian left flank. The destruction of the railroad line between Veles and Bitola by the Ottomans, as well as the usual cold and rainy weather and miserable roads, hindered the movement of Serbian artillery and slowed logistical efforts.

Much of the Vardar Army had retreated directly to Bitola after the Kumanovo defeat. There the Ottomans consolidated their units and established defensive positions for what would be their last stand in Macedonia. The Vardar Army was arrayed around Bitola; the Ottoman 7th Corps commanded by Feti Pasha held the left flank; the 6th Army Corps commanded by Djavid Pasha held the center; and the Ottoman 5th Corps commanded by Kara Said Pasha held the right flank. Zeki Pasha retained overall command of the Vardar Army. The Kochana and Janina independent divisions supplemented the Ottoman defenses. Since the Kumanovo battle, the strength of the Vardar Army had dwindled to only 38,350 soldiers and 100 artillery pieces at Bitola, and the advancing Serbian 1st Army heavily outnumbered them with 108,544 men.[21] After their previous defeats, the Ottoman command faced a formidable task in organizing this force and instilling a sense of discipline and purpose. They did manage to establish a strong position on the Oblakov heights northwest of the town.

The fighting began on the morning of 16 November with an artillery duel. The Serbian infantry then advanced against the Ottoman positions. At first some Serbian units attacked without artillery support because the mud and bad weather hampered the movement of the Serbian guns down the road from Prilep. The difficult terrain north of the town and Ottoman artillery fire held off the Serbian attacks for two days. On 17 November, the Serbs succeeded in storming the Oblakov heights. This was the key to breaking Ottoman resistance in front of Bitola. The next day, the Serbs succeeded in bringing up all their artillery. Serbian heavy artillery then identified and destroyed the Ottoman batteries that had held up the Serbian infantry. The Serbian right flank pushed past the Ottoman defenders. This caused the entire Vardar Army to break up and retreat. As usual with Ottoman retrograde movements in the First Balkan War, the retreat became disorganized and panicky.

For the second time in three weeks the Vardar Army had suffered a major defeat. The demoralized Ottoman forces sustained heavy casualties in the Bitola battle. They lost 1,000 men and 2,000 were wounded; the Serbian casualties amounted to 539 dead, 2,121 wounded and 329 missing.[22] In addition, the Serbs took 5,600 Ottomans as prisoners, and around 5,000 redifs deserted and probably returned home after the defeat. Among the Ottoman dead was the 7th Corps commander, and former Ottoman ambassador in Belgrade, Feti Pasha. He was the highest ranking officer on any side to fall in battle in the Balkan Wars. After this defeat, the Ottoman 5th Corps fell back toward Florina, and the Ottoman 6th and 7th Corps retreated toward Berat in Albania.

The Serbs then entered Bitola on 19 November. With the conquest of Bitola the Serbs controlled southwestern Macedonia, including the symbolically important town of Ohrid. Until 1767, Ohrid had served as the seat of an autonomous Bulgarian church authority. Serbian cavalry took Ohrid on 22 November. After the battle of Bitola, the five-century-long Ottoman rule of Macedonia was over. So, for the Serbian 1st Army, was most of the fighting in the First Balkan War.

At this point some Serbs wanted the 1st Army to continue its advance down the valley of the Vardar to Salonika. Vojovoda Putnik refused.[23] The threat of war with Austria–Hungary loomed over the issue of a Serbian presence on the Adriatic. In addition, with the Bulgarians and Greeks already in Salonika, the appearance of Serbian forces there would only muddle an already complicated situation.

The remnants of the Vardar Army withdrew south toward Kostura, Korchi, and Lerin, seeking safety and shelter in southeastern Albania. The Albanians offered the only possible shelter and source of supplies for the defeated army. The commander of the Ottoman Western Army, Ali Riza, and his staff fled north from Salonika to meet them around Korchi. Some of these forces reinforced Janina, which was under attack from the Greek Epirus Army. There they would hold out until 6 March. Djavid Pasha's 6th Corps, still largely intact, moved to the southern Albanian towns of Berat and Koritsa, where it continued to fight on until the spring of 1913. Over the course of the campaign, the Vardar Army had retreated from northern Macedonia to southern Albania. That Ottoman soldiers could continue to fight at all after three major demoralizing defeats and a long and difficult retreat is remarkable.

Other Serbian operations

Because of the early battle at Kumanovo and the rapid Ottoman retreat afterwards, neither the Serbian 2nd Army nor 3rd Army was able to carry out the planned attacks on the Ottoman flanks. The Serbian 2nd Army crossed the frontier from its positions in Bulgaria and brushed aside the Ottoman resistance offered by two divisions of the 5th Corps at Katovo and Kochana in eastern Macedonia. On 24 October, the 7th Rila Division occupied Kochana, in the Vardar valley. General Stepanovich attempted to move forward sufficiently to cut off the Ottoman Army's retreat from Kumanovo. Before he could accomplish this, two events occurred that changed the 2nd Army's mission.

On 26 October General Georgi Todorov, the commander of the Rila Division, informed General Stepanovich that, on orders from Bulgarian high command, he would now move south toward Seres and ultimately to Salonika, instead of advancing west into Macedonia.[24] The Serbian high command was "unpleasantly surprised" by the Bulgarian troops' movement to the south.[25] This does not seem to have caused much hardship for the Serbs however. The major Ottoman force was in retreat. In addition, this move removed the only significant Bulgarian force from central Macedonia. This left the Serbs in sole possession of not only the "disputed zone" but much of the remainder of the region. Had the Bulgarians left a division in central Macedonia instead of chasing after Salonika, they might have retained control of more of this region, bolstered their claim to Macedonia, and saved the lives of more of their soldiers.

That same day, the Serbian high command ordered General Stepanovich to send his other division to Adrianople to support the Bulgarian siege. On 27 October the united army entered Shtip. The Serbs then prepared for moving into Thrace, where they would fight for the next five months.

The Serbian 3rd Army was the first Serbian force to fight in the First Balkan War. On the night of 15–16 October it repulsed an attack by Albanian irregulars. The 3rd Army crossed the frontier four days later. It pushed away the Ottoman forces on the frontier. Meeting significant resistance only at Teneshdol Pass, the 3rd Army took Prishtina in Kosovo on 22 October. The entry of the Serbs into Prishtina evoked memories among them of medieval glories. A Serbian journalist accompanying the soldiers wrote, "Prishtina! There for some time was the capital of the Nemanjich Dynasty, especially King Milutin. There was also the capital of Vuk Brankovich, who during the time of Tsar Lazar held the lands between Lava and Sitnitse." At the same time he admitted that "Prishtina is a nest of the Albanians. It is their capital of Kosovo."[26] With this easy victory, the icon of Serbian nationalism, Kosovo Polje, the location of the epic battle between a Serbian-led Balkan coalition and the invading Ottomans in 1389, fell into Serbian hands. Not all Serbs gave themselves over to nationalist ecstasies with the conquest of Kosovo however. When the 3rd Army commander General Bozhidar Jankovich, organized a celebration, the austere Vojvoda Putnik remarked with some exasperation to his aide Colonel Mishich, "What the hell is *Uncle Bozha* (General Jankovich) doing with a religious procession for Kosovo. Please tell him, to quit it and see to that later."[27] The war still had to be fought.

On 23 October the 3rd Army moved south along the railway line to Skoplje. Some soldiers remained behind as a garrison force in Kosovo. They imposed a harsh rule on the Albanians, and the Albanians immediately began to oppose the Serbs with such arms as they could muster.

Beginning on 9 November, the remaining divisions of the 3rd Army, around 16,000 men, advanced in a westerly direction into northern and central Albania. As the 3rd Army advanced toward the Adriatic Sea, it divided into two columns. All the Serbian columns encountered resistance from irregular Albanian bands in Kosovo and Albania. The Serbs often responded to Albanian resistance with great brutality directed toward the civilian population.

On 28 November the left column reached the port of Durazzo (Albanian, Durrës; Serbian, Drach), having passed through Tirana several days earlier. The right column crossed the White Drin River and proceeded into northern Albania. It entered Alessio (Albanian, Lezhe; Serbian, Ljesh) on 17 November. On the right, the Serbs made contact with the Montenegrin forces besieging Scutari. On the left, the Serbs moved south toward Elbasan to confront elements of Djavid Pasha's 6th Corps, which had retreated into Albania after its defeat at Bitola.

As they moved through Albania, both Serbian columns met strong resistance from Ottoman regulars and Albanian irregulars. Three years later the Serbian army would take some of these same routes, not in victory but in defeat, seeking the shelter of Adriatic ports after an Austro-Hungarian and Bulgarian invasion of Serbia. Again the Albanians would fight them all the way to the Adriatic.

The arrival of a Serbian army on the Adriatic aroused strong diplomatic opposition from Austria–Hungary and Italy. They perceived the Serbs as a threat to their domination of the Adriatic Sea. In addition, they feared that a Serbian Adriatic port could become a Russian base.

The Ibar Army crossed the frontier on 19 October and entered Novi Pazar on 23 October.

When it become clear that the Austro-Hungarians would not oppose a Serbian move into the Sandjak militarily, the Javorska Brigade moved into the northern Sandjak on 20 October. On 25 October it took the town of Sjenica. Several days later the whole of the Sandjak was in Serbian and Montenegrin hands. Neither force encountered serious opposition. The small number of Ottoman troops in the Sandjak of Novi Pazar either retreated toward Kosovo or, if redifs, simply went home. For the first time since the Treaty of San Stefano, the two Serbian states had a direct physical connection, an important precondition for unification. This connection was cause for Austro-Hungarian discomfort, because it strengthened the Orthodox Slavs on the southern frontier and could possibly attract southern Slavs living within the empire. It also gave Serbia uninterrupted access to the Adriatic Sea, a circumstance that raised the possibility Serbian and Russian cooperation to bring about Austro-Hungarian maritime isolation, a nightmare for Vienna.

Montenegro

Tiny but warlike Montenegro had two major objectives in the war against the Ottomans. One was the Sandjak of Novi Pazar and Kosovo proper, where their aspirations rivaled those of the Serbs. King Nikola hoped to advance as far as the medieval Serbian capital of Prizren, in southwestern Kosovo. The other goal was the northern Albanian town of Scutari (Albanian, Shkoder; Serbian, Skadra; Turkish, Iskodra). Scutari, the largest town in northern Albania, was the administrative capital of Scutari Vilayet. It was especially important for Montenegro for commercial as well as political reasons. Control of Scutari might enable Montenegro to end its dependence on foreign subsidies, and allow it to establish a viable economy. By taking Scutari, Montenegro could dominate Albania as far south as the Drin River.

In pursuit of these objectives, the Montenegrins divided their forces into three groups. The Eastern Division, commanded by Brigadier Janko Vukotich, had 12,000 men and thirty-two guns. Its objective was the Sandjak of Novi Pazar. After occupying Novi Pazar, it was to advance rapidly to the south to Prizren in Kosovo. Most Montenegrin forces, however, were positioned to attack Scutari. The location of Lake Scutari, which separated the city of the same name from Montenegro, forced the Montenegrins to again divide their forces. The Zeta Division, consisting of 15,000 men and forty guns and led by Crown Prince Danilo, was to move around the eastern shore of Lake Scutari toward the city. The Coastal Division, commanded by Brigadier Mitar Martinovich, had 8,000 soldiers and thirty-four guns.[28] A volunteer force of around 500 supplemented the Montenegrin forces.[29] After the start of the war, immigrants returning home, mainly from the United States, and additional volunteers from among the South Slav population in the Habsburg Empire eventually added around 4,500 men to the Montenegrin forces. Some Catholic Albanian tribesmen (Maltsors) supplemented the Montenegrins, but these irregulars were of dubious military value and doubtless of questionable loyalty to the Montenegrin cause. As with the other members of the Balkan League, the monarch, King Nicola, was the commander in chief of his forces.

At the outbreak of the war, a significant Ottoman force confronted the Montenegrins. This was the Scutari Corps of 13,600 men and ninety-six guns commanded by Hasan Riza Bey[30]. Immediately after the war began, Esad Pasha Toptani, an ambitious Albanian reserve commander, brought his redif unit into the city. He became second in command. Other Albanian irregulars soon supplemented the garrison. The Ottomans had only defensive intentions in this area. The hills, rivers, and the lake around Scutari made it a natural strong point. The defenses of Scutari were based on the three hills of Tarabosh in the west, Brda in the south and Bardanjolt in the east. To the north was an open, relatively flat area known as Stoj. All these positions were fortified with barbed wire, trenches, machine-gun emplacements, and artillery. The Ottomans had improved the fortifications around the city as recently as the summer of 1912. There were also 13,350 Ottoman troops from Djavid Pasha's 6th Corps stationed in the Sandjak of Novi Pazar and Kosovo. Most of these troops subsequently became involved in the major battles in Macedonia against the Serbs.

Montenegro was the first member of the Balkan League to act against the Ottomans. In accordance with the terms of the agreement with Bulgaria, the Montenegrins declared war on 8 October. They liked the idea of beginning to fight before their Serbian rivals in order to emphasize their Serbian patriotism and their aggressive spirit. At the outbreak of war, they belittled the military prowess of their Serbian allies. One Montenegrin told M. E. Durham, an English observer of the Balkans, that the Serbian army was "a lot of swineherds."[31] The next day their soldiers began shooting, with King Nikola's youngest son, Prince Peter, ceremoniously firing the first shot across the Ottoman frontier.

The Montenegrin declaration of war gave the Ottomans advance notice that they would have to fight a war in the Balkans. They rushed to conclude peace with Italy. The Treaty of Ouchy ending the war was signed near Lausanne, Switzerland, on 15 October. It had lasted a year and two weeks.

Scutari

The day after Montenegro's declaration of war, the Zeta Division left its positions around Podgoritsa and moved south along the eastern shore of Lake Scutari. It advanced against moderate Ottoman resistance for five days. Then the army rested. This gave the Ottomans the opportunity to reinforce Scutari with 8,000 additional troops. The Zeta Division then resumed its attacks north of Scutari on 18 October, the same day Montenegro's Balkan allies entered the war. At the same time, the Coastal Division moved the short distance along the west shore of Lake Scutari from the Montenegrin frontier to the Ottoman fortifications west of Scutari. It too, encountered relatively light Ottoman resistance until it came up against the outer fortifications of Scutari, especially the positions on the round hill called Tarabosh, so named because its truncated conical shape resembled a piece of traditional Turkish headgear.

Having reached their goal, the Montenegrins began an active siege. The efforts of the Zeta Division to rush Scutari from the north across the open area of Stoj on 24 October failed in the face of determined resistance. In another attempt to take the city on 28 October, the Zeta Division tried to outflank the open area by attacking the fortified hill Big Bardanjolt east of Scutari. Initially, the Montenegrins had some success. They, however, could not maintain their troops on the hill. The Ottomans launched counterattacks from additional positions on Little Bardanjolt, behind the main hill, and forced the Montenegrins to retreat to the northeast and to reorganize.

The shortcomings of the Montenegrin army now became apparent. Their infantry tactics were simplistic. They often merely massed in front of and charged an objective, spurning cover. Not surprisingly these 'rush tactics' resulted in high casualties. Although they bombarded the city intermittently, they lacked sufficient artillery to support their attacks. More importantly, they failed to develop a coordinated command at Scutari. The Coastal Division remained relatively inactive while the Zeta Division attacked. This enabled Hasan Riza Bey to transfer troops from the Tarabosh positions to meet the threat from the east. Obviously, the two Montenegrin forces should have attacked simultaneously. Finally, the Montenegrins lacked enough forces to completely surround Scutari. Their siege was incomplete. As a result the defenders could still obtain provisions and reinforcements from the south. By mid-November, the defenders of Scutari had grown to 24,000 Ottoman troops and around 5,000 Albanian irregulars, and the Montenegrins had surrounding Scutari 15,000 in the Zeta Division, 8,000 in the Coastal Division, 5,500 transfers from the Eastern Division, and around 4,500 volunteers from Bosnia and other parts of Austria–Hungary.[32] This meant that the Montenegrins enjoyed only a very slight advantage in numbers over the Ottomans.

The advance of the Serbian 3rd Army into Albania eliminated that problem for the Montenegrins. Elements of the Serbian 3rd Army made contact with the Montenegrin Coastal Division on 18 November near Alessio. With the seizure of Alessio by the Montenegrins and Serbs, the gap was sealed. Scutari was finally completely surrounded. Even then, the seal was not tight. The Ottoman defenders sortied several times in December after the armistice to gather food from the Albanian countryside.

After the defeat of Ottoman forces in Thrace, Kosovo, and Macedonia, the Montenegrins considered another attempt to capture their main goal. Concerns of Austro-Hungarian support for a new Albanian state that could include Scutari also helped King Nikola decide to take action. He transferred 5,500 soldiers of the Eastern Division from the Sandjak of Novi Pazar; Nikola, however, decided against another assault, hoping that he might obtain the city through diplomatic means. The conduct of their military only added to Montenegrin frustrations.

Under the terms of the armistice signed on 3 December 1912, Scutari remained in Ottoman hands, but it could not receive provisions. The situation reached a stalemate. The Montenegrins lacked the power to take the city, and the Ottomans did not have the forces to break the siege. Time, however, was on the side of the besieging army. The now underutilized Serbian army could reinforce its allies to give the besiegers an overwhelming advantage in men and artillery.

Other Montenegrin operations

The day after the declaration of war, detachments of the Eastern Army entered the Sandjak of Novi Pazar, advancing in three directions. One detachment moved north from Kolshin, taking Bijele Polje on 11 October. After some hesitation because of fears of Austro-Hungarian intervention, it turned to the southeast to take Berane on the 16th. A second detachment moved out of Andrijevitsa in Montenegro toward Plav and Gushinje. They entered these towns on 20 October. On 23 October, the Ottomans, led by the energetic Djavid Pasha, mounted a serious counterattack near Chukor. The Montenegrins managed to deflect this attack and drove back the Ottomans.

Then, both detachments moved in three columns to the southeast into Kosovo. Two of these columns converged on Pech on 2 November. They then joined the other column to take Dechani on 15 October, near the site of a monastery of the same name important to the Serbian Orthodox Church. This combined force then advanced into Kosovo in a southerly direction to Djakova, an important market town. On 4 November, the Montenegrins together with a detachment of the Serbian 3rd Army that had advanced into Kosovo, took Djakova.

The third of the three detachments of the Montenegrin Eastern Division left Zhabljak in northern Montenegro and crossed into the northern part of the Sandjak of Novi Pazar. It remained stationary for several weeks because of King Nikola's concerns of an Austro-Hungarian thrust into the Sandjak of Novi Pazar. It finally moved on at the end of October, when King Nikola realized that the Austro-Hungarians would not oppose any occupation. On 28 October, elements of the Montenegrin Eastern Army together with the Serbian Javor Brigade, which had advanced into the Sandjak from the east, took Plevlja.

Of the four Balkan allies, Montenegro enjoyed the least success in the first phase of the fighting. Most of the army was mired in a frustrating siege around Scutari. King Nikola had expended Montenegro's limited resources fruitlessly. The only success had been the conquest of the western portion of the Sandjak of Novi Pazar.

Montenegro, however, had to share the Sandjak with its Serbian ally. This was the cause of jealousy between the two Serbian rivals, especially when Montenegrin troops entered Prizren in Kosovo after the Serb conquest of the city. King Nikola dreamed of making Prizren, the capital of a medieval Serbian state, the center of his united Serbian state. Indeed, Nikola, something of a poet, had written a song with the words, "onward, onward, let me see Prizren."[33] The Montenegrins never did reach their goal of Prizren. Had King Nikola seen that town, he would have observed Serbian troops already in occupation.

The relative lack of success of Montenegrin arms only intensified the rivalry with the Serbs. The Montenegrin population began to compare the failure of its troops before Scutari with Serbian successes in Kosovo and

Macedonia, to the detriment of the Petroviches. This was compounded by the situation that Crown Prince Alexander had commanded a successful Serbian army, whereas Crown Prince Danilo displayed a singular lack of military talent. This situation boded ill for the unification of the Serbian people under the Petrovich–Njegosh dynasty, and indeed for the survival of the ruling dynasty in Cetinje.

Greece

The Greeks fielded two armies. The Army of Thessaly, commanded by Crown Prince Constantine, was the main force of the Greek army. Its objective was in general to occupy Thessaly and specifically to take Salonika (Bulgarian, Solun; Greek, Thessaloniki; Turkish, Sélanik) before the Bulgarians arrived there. The Greek General Staff and Crown Prince Constantine wanted the Thessaly Army, concentrated at Larissa, to advance as far as Bitola to insure the defeat of Ottoman troops in southern Macedonia. This would also have placed much of southern Macedonia under Greek control. The Greek prime minister, Eleutherios Venizelos, however, insisted that the primary objective of the army should be Salonika, the largest city in the region.[34] The secondary Greek force was the Army of Epirus, which was under the command of General Constantine Zapundzakis. Its objective was the southern Albanian town of Janina.

The Ottomans had a relatively strong force to oppose the Greeks. In Thessaly they had the 8th Corps, consisting of three divisions, one brigade, and a cavalry regiment of around 40,000 men. Hassan Tahsin Pasha commanded the 8th Corps. In Epirus they had initially two infantry divisions of around 18,000 men, led by Esad Pasha (not to be confused with the Albanian opportunist Esad Pasha Toptani).[35] There the Ottomans could count on the assistance of the local Albanian population. Unlike his colleagues in Macedonia and Thrace, Hassan Tahsin Pasha did not contemplate an offensive against his more numerous enemies. The size of his forces gave him a sound basis for a defensive strategy.

Thessaly

On 18 October, the day of the declaration of war, the Army of Thessaly crossed the frontier in two main columns. One column advanced through the Meluna Pass toward Elassona and on to Servia (Serfidze). To its east the other column moved in the direction of Petra. Since the war of 1897, the Ottomans had possessed the key passes along the frontier, but they did not contest the Greek army marching there. They evidently anticipated a Greek attack on Elassona and arrayed their troops to the northwest. They did not envision the Greeks driving directly toward Salonika. The first major engagement occurred at the Sarantaporos Pass on 22 October. This was the major Ottoman defensive position in Thessaly. It controlled the route into Macedonia. In a day-long battle in the usual October rain, the Greeks, using frontal attacks against Ottoman positions and shouting *zeto* (hurrah), pushed through the Ottoman defenses. The Greeks sustained losses of 187 dead and 1,027 wounded, and at least 700 Ottomans were killed and 701 were taken prisoner.[36] The demoralized Ottomans retreated northward, abandoning stores and equipment. The Greeks pursued them leisurely. The exhaustion of their troops and the difficulties of transportation prevented them from chasing the enemy and delivering a decisive blow. They also lacked an effective appreciation of reconnaissance. One observer noted, "There is no such thing as a scout in the whole Greek army."[37] The same inability and disinclination to pursue the defeated enemy beset the Serbs after Kumanovo and the Bulgarians after Lozengrad.

Only after this victory was the conflict between the army and the government over Salonika resolved. King George overruled his son's insistence that the army pursue a military rather than a political agenda.[38] This meant that Salonika became the chief objective of the Greek army. It also reinforced the divide between the Crown Prince and the prime minister, which would result in the former being ousted by the latter in 1917.

On 1 November, Ottoman positions at Yanitsa (Turkish, Yenije Vardar) held up the Greek advance. The two sides fought a bloody battle. The Ottomans, reinforced by troops from Bitola, resisted stoutly at first. On 2 November, the Greeks overran the Ottoman positions at a cost of 1,200 dead and wounded, with around 1,960 dead and wounded Ottomans.[39] They then turned to the east toward their goal. The Ottomans had destroyed the road bridge, but not the railway bridge over the Vardar River. Using the railway bridge, the Greeks continued their advance. The way to Salonika was now open.

For the move into Salonika, after the fighting around Servia the Greeks attempted to protect their left flank by detaching their 5th Division under Colonel Mathiopulos and sending it north toward Florina. This would also give the Greeks a foothold in southwestern Macedonia and possibly the important southern Macedonian town of Bitola.

The Ottomans still had some forces from their Vardar Army in southwestern Macedonia. The Greek advance met the Ottomans, who had been sent reinforcments by rail from Bitola and were also strengthened by irregulars. The Ottomans attacked on the night of 5–6 November and defeated the Greek division at Klidion. It retreated to the southeast in disarray. It had to rest and regroup before returning to combat.

After entering Salonika, Crown Prince Constantine ordered a push toward Bitola and southwestern Macedonia. Three additional divisions moved north and northwest, encountering significant Ottoman resistance. After resting and reorganizing, the 5th Division entered Florina on 20 November. The Ottomans had hoped to retain Florina to keep their line of retreat from

Macedonia to Albania open. This time, they could not withstand the Greek advance. After resting at Florina, the Greek column resumed its march into Albania, reaching Koritsa (Albanian, Korce) on 20 December. The entry of troops into this Albanian town alarmed Austria–Hungary and Italy. They perceived this region as vital to the new Albanian state.

Salonika

After their victory at Yanitsa, the Greeks neared their goal of Salonika. The largest city in Macedonia and the port for the entire region, Salonika was an important prize sought by both the Bulgarians and the Greeks. The population of the city was cosmopolitan. It was a center of the early Christian church as well as the birthplace of the Young Turk leader and founder of the Turkish Republic, Mustapha Kemal Ataturk. In 1912, Shephardic Jews formed the largest community in the city, about 80,000 out of a total population of 120,000, which also included Greeks, Turks, Bulgarians, and others.

The Greeks began to surround the city. On 7 November, in response to an Ottoman initiative, they entered into negotiations for the surrender of Salonika. With the Greeks on hand, and the Bulgarian 7th Rila Division moving rapidly from the north, Hassan Tahsin Pasha considered his position to be hopeless. The allied victories in Macedonia and Thrace and the sinking of the old warship *Fetik Bouled* in Salonika harbor by the Greek navy on 31 October thoroughly demoralized the Ottoman garrison. Hassan Tahsin Pasha, seeking favorable capitulation terms, negotiated with both armies. The Greeks offered more attractive terms than the Bulgarians did.[40] On 8 November Tahsin Pasha agreed to terms, and 26,000 Ottoman troops passed over into Greek captivity.[41] Before the Greeks entered the city, a German warship whisked the former sultan Abdul Hamid out of Salonika to continue his exile across the Bosporus from Constantinople. With their army in Salonika, the Greeks took positions to the east and northeast, including Nigrita. With their navy, they occupied the Chalcidice Peninsula, including the ancient Orthodox monastery complex at Mt Athos.

Competing with the Army of Thessaly for the prize of Salonika was the Bulgarian 7th Rila Division of about 24,000 men, late of the Serbian 2nd Army. Under the command of General Georgi Todorov, and accompanied by Crown Prince Boris and Prince Kyril, the 7th Rila Division reached Salonika the day after its surrender to the Greeks. After parting from its Serbian allies, the 7th Rila Division, in three columns, had advanced south down the valleys of the Struma and Mesta Rivers. They linked up north of Seres, which they took on 5 November. None of the Bulgarian columns encountered serious Ottoman resistance as they hastened toward Salonika.

Although the 7th Rila Division did little fighting, it did have an important political task. It represented Bulgarian claims to Macedonia and also to the important port of Salonika. Salonika was the largest town in Macedonia and the major outlet for its agricultural produce. With the bulk of the Bulgarian army fighting for Macedonia in Thrace, the 7th Rila Division embodied the aspirations of the nation. When pressed by the Bulgarians to come to terms with them, Tahsin Pasha replied, "I have only one Thessaloniki, which I have surrendered."[42]

Nevertheless, when the 7th Rila Division reached Salonika on 9 November, the commander of this force, General Petur Todorov, telegraphed Tsar Ferdinand, "From today Salonika is under the scepter of Your Majesty."[43]

Although the Bulgarians had narrowly lost the race to Salonika, they still intended to enforce their claims to the city. About 25,000 Greek soldiers and 15,000 Bulgarian soldiers occupied the city. An uneasy co-dominium ensued. Initially, the Greeks denied the Bulgarians entry into the city. They finally agreed to a formula in which Crown Prince Boris, his brother, and most of the 7th Rila Division were admitted as guests of the Greek army. Overjoyed by this success, Ferdinand telegraphed Crown Prince Boris, "How I envy you, my dear son, for your historic entry into the City of St Paul."[44] The Bulgarian tsar possessed a romantic sensibility, which made the annexation of Salonika attractive. Economic realities, however, were the main reason for Bulgarian interest in Salonika. It was the only important port of central Macedonia. The Serbs also were interested in establishing a presence in Salonika. Prime Minster Pashich wanted the Serbian army to push down the Vardar to Salonika, but Vojvoda Putnik wisely refused.[45] This move would have created unnecessary military as well as political complications for Serbia. It probably would have strengthened the Bulgarian position in Salonika. The dispute over Salonika could then be cast in terms of Slavs versus Hellenes.

The occupation of Salonika was of great political value to Bulgaria and Greece. It bestowed little military benefit, however, on either side. By turning toward Salonika, the Greek army allowed the retreating Ottomans to concentrate at Bitola. Likewise, the south turn of the Bulgarian 7th Rila Division allowed some Ottoman forces fleeing from Kumanovo to escape to Prilep. The Serbs had to fight further battles because of Salonika. The Greeks also had to pay for their focus on political rather than military goals. Many of the Ottoman troops defeated at Bitola retreated into Albania, where they reinforced the garrison at Janina. The Greek failure to advance on Bitola cost them time and lives in Epirus.

The Ottomans sold Salonika cheaply. Although the Greek fleet cut off the city and any hopes of reinforcement by sea, the Ottomans still had significant forces in Macedonia at the time of surrender. They might have resisted for a while on the east bank of the Vardar River, which formed a significant natural obstacle. Unfortunately, they did not even destroy the railway bridge across the river. They also might have bought valuable time by extending the negotiations and exploiting the rivalry between the

Bulgarians and the Greeks. These failures were the fault of the Ottoman command. Clearly Hassan Tahsin Pasha was not up to his responsibilities.

Epirus

In preparation for the invasion of Epirus, the night before the Greek declaration of war on 18 October, two Greek torpedo boats slipped into the harbor of Preveza and rendered the two Ottoman warships lying there unusable. The next day, the army in Epirus crossed into Ottoman territory at Arta. It moved slowly in a northwesterly direction and occupied the town of Philippias on 26 October. There, General Zapundsakis divided his forces. One column continued to advance north. The other column moved along the north side of the Gulf of Arta, and crossed difficult terrain and encountered Ottoman resistance. By 2 November the old fortifications at Preveza were under siege. This lasted until 4 November, when the Ottoman defenders of Preveza surrendered. With the conquest of Preveza, the Greeks could support their advance into Epirus from the sea.

From the beginning of this campaign, Esad Pasha had demonstrated much more determined resistance to the Greeks than his counterpart in Thessaly. He forced the Greeks to fight for every step into Epirus. This resolve, and some of the most difficult terrain of the First Balkan War, slowed the Greek advance considerably. After the surrender of Preveza, the main Greek force, supplemented by a corps of foreign volunteers under the Italian General Ricciotti Garibaldi, the son of Giuseppe, advanced toward the Ottoman stronghold of Janina (Greek, Ioannina; Turkish, Yanya). General Garibaldi had led a similar corps on behalf of the Greeks in the war of 1897.

Janina was the southern counterpart of Scutari. It was the economic capital of southern Albania and the seat of the administration of the Vilayet of Janina. It was located on a lake in a valley whose mouth opened to the northwest. Although the city itself had a majority of Greek inhabitants, the majority of the inhabitants in the countryside was Albanian. At the outbreak of the war, two Ottoman divisions held well-fortified machine-gun and artillery positions containing about ninety big guns. The Ottomans had recently modernized the fortifications at Janina under the direction of General von der Goltz. The main positions at Janina were Fort Bezane (Bizanion), south of the town, and Fort Kastirsa, southeast of the town. These had permanent concrete gun emplacements with bunkers, searchlights, and trenches. A ring of barbed wire surrounded the forts. Five smaller forts with similar construction guarded the western and northwestern parts of the city. In addition, there was a small fort northeast of the city and one on a small island in the lake. Most of the guns were 5.25 cm or 6 cm caliber. Some Ottoman troops retreating toward the southwest after the battle at Bitola reinforced the Janina garrison. The Greek besiegers were unable to surround Janina and thus could not cut it off from its Albanian hinterland. Here, as at

Scutari, the local Albanian population in the countryside by and large supported the Ottoman defenders. By mid-December, the Ottomans had 35,000 soldiers confronting only 25,000 Greeks.[46] Ottoman soldiers retreating from Macedonia and Albanian irregulars reinforced the defenders of Janina. The 2nd Division from the army of Thessaly and an assortment of volunteers and irregulars from Crete and elsewhere arrived by sea at Santi Quaranta and marched overland to supplement the Greek forces. By 25 November, the Greeks had besieged Janina on the west, south, and east. Only the north remained open.

The Greeks located their artillery on the hills south of the town. From there they could fire on the Ottoman positions to great effect. This artillery fire, however, was unable to damage the forts sufficiently for a successful infantry assault. By the middle of December, the Greeks, like the Bulgarians at Adrianople and the Montenegrins at Scutari, had stalled outside a well-fortified Ottoman city. Because the Greeks did not sign the December armistice, their operations continued at Janina without interruption.

The war at sea

The Greek navy had an important task in the First Balkan War. It had to blockade the mouth of the Dardanelles and the coast of Asia Minor. This would prevent the Ottomans from sending troops from Smyrna to the Aegean ports of Dedeagach or Kavala, where the Ottoman war plan intended them to reinforce either their Thracian or Macedonian armies. The Greeks blockaded the Dardanelles with the occupation of the strategic islands of the northern Aegean. On 20 October they seized Tenedos. The next day they landed on Lemnos, where fighting lasted until 27 October. The conquest of Lemnos effectively closed the Dardanelles. By 1 November, Imbros, Samothrace, and Thassos were also under Greek control. They met little resistance on these islands. At the same time, the Greeks patrolled the waters off Smyrna to prevent Ottoman troopships from leaving that port.

After these relatively easy victories, the Greeks turned to the Aegean islands further to the south, including Chios, Mytiline, Tenedos, and Psara. They landed at Mytiline on 21 November and on Chios on 27 November. Here the Ottomans strongly resisted the invaders. On both islands the Ottoman garrisons withdrew inland and continued to fight: on Mytiline until 22 December and on Chios until 3 January 1913. Because of a desire to avoid diplomatic complications with Italy concerning the Italian-occupied Dodecanese, the Greeks did not land on Samos until 13 March 1913.

The largest sea battle of the Balkan Wars occurred near the mouth of the Dardanelles on 16 December, when a part of the Ottoman fleet, including the old armored ships *Barbaros Hayrettin* and the *Mesudiye,* which had recently participated in the successful defense of Chataldzha, sortied out of the Dardanelles in an attempt to break the Greek blockade. Fire from Ottoman land forts on the European and Asian sides of the Dardanelles supported their ships. Both sides sustained some damage, but the Ottomans were unable to get past the Greek blockade and retired after about an hour back into the Dardanelles. This was a Greek victory because the Ottoman fleet remained blockaded. Two days later the Ottoman fleet made another sortie out of the mouth of the Dardanelles, but once again failed to break the Greek blockade and retired back into the Dardanelles. On 6 February a Greek airplane flew over the Ottoman fleet in the Dardanelles and dropped several small bombs, which missed. This was the first airplane attack on naval vessels.[47]

This was not the first time in the twentieth century that the Dardanelles had been the scene of naval action. In April 1912 during the Italo-Turkish War the Italians had bombarded the Ottoman forts at the mouth of the Dardanelles. Less that three years later the same location would be the sight of further naval action, when British and French warships attempted and failed to force the Dardanelles against determined Ottoman resistance.

The victories off the Dardanelles in January 1913 confirmed Greek control of the Aegean Sea. The Greek fleet proved its worth to the Balkan cause by closing the Aegean to Ottoman shipping. In addition to its combat duties, the Greek fleet carried out the movement of Bulgarian troops to Dedeagach and Serbian troops to San Medua, Albania. On a visit to the harbor of Salonika on 7 June 1913, on the eve of the Second Balkan War, General Ivanov, commander of the Bulgarian 2nd Army, acknowledged the role of the Greek fleet in the defeat of the Ottomans. On board the *Averov*, he stated, "The activity of the entire Greek fleet and above all the *Averov* was the chief factor in the general success of the allies."[48] Three weeks later with the outbreak of the Second Balkan War, General Ivanov's army would come under fire from the Greek fleet.

The Greek navy was also active in the Ionian and Adriatic Seas. In addition to its role in transporting and supplying the army's effort in Epirus, the Greek Navy attacked and blockaded the Albanian port of Vlore on 3 December. It imposed a blockade on the Albanian coast extending from the Greek frontier to Vlore by 3 December and Durres by 27 February. This had the effect of isolating the Albanian provisional government in Vlore.

One important Ottoman naval success was the role the fleet played in the successful defense of the Chataldzha lines. The fleet served as a floating heavy artillery position. Another was the voyage of the light cruiser *Hamidiye*. The *Hamidiye*, under the command of Rauf Bey, eluded the Greek fleet. It slipped out of the Dardanelles on 22 December 1912. On 15 January it sank the auxiliary cruiser *Makedonia* in the harbor of Syra in the Cyclades. The *Hamidiye* proceeded to Beirut and Port Said. Its apparent ability to cruise the eastern Mediterranean at will greatly concerned the Greeks, who tried without success to find and destroy it. The voyage of the *Hamidiye* was also a source of great satisfaction to the Ottomans, who had had little else to boost their morale over the course of the war.

The Ottomans should have used their fleet to better effect. Although it played an important role in the defense of the Chataldzha lines, it did little to contest Greek control of the Aegean Sea. A more aggressive attitude in the Aegean might have had important results for the Ottomans. They could have seriously disrupted the Greeks' movement of men and material in the northern Aegean, and even maintained contacts with the Western Ottoman army.

The minuscule Bulgarian Navy did enjoy one success against the Ottomans in the Black Sea. When the Ottoman light cruiser *Hamidiye* appeared off the port of Varna on 21 November 1912, a squadron of four Bulgarian torpedo boats under the orders of Commander Dimitur Dobrev confronted it and scored at least one hit. The *Hamidiye* suffered damage to its bow and some casualties. It limped back to Constantinople for repairs before resuming its activities against the Greeks.

The *Hamidiye* represented a substantial threat to Bulgaria. It could cut the important Black Sea connection to Russia. The Bulgarians had to do whatever they could to keep this connection open to receive Russian aid. The attack on the *Hamidiye* remains the greatest victory in the history of the Bulgarian navy.

Conclusion

The Serbian army had preformed well in the First Balkan War. It had adjusted quickly and successfully to the unexpected Ottoman challenge at Kumanovo. The victory there enabled the Serbs to advance more quickly than if they had adhered to their original plan, which envisioned that the decisive battle for Macedonia would be south of Skoplje. The Serbs were the big victors in the west in the initial phase of the First Balkan War. Not only did they defeat and expel all Ottoman forces from the areas of northern Macedonia and Kosovo to which they aspired, but they occupied central Macedonia and the northern half of Albania all the way to the Adriatic. These successes had come at a relatively small cost in human and material terms. At the time of the armistice, the Serbs faced a problem, not from their Ottoman enemy but from the Great Powers. Would the Great Powers, especially Austria–Hungary and Italy, allow them to retain their Albanian conquests? Closely related to this issue was the problem of Macedonia. The Serbs had taken all of northern and central Macedonia, including large areas promised to Bulgaria in the March 1912 alliance. Could the Serbs surrender this territory to Bulgaria after they had spilt Serbian blood to take it? The withdrawal of the Bulgarian 7th Rila Division to southern Macedonia and the transfer of the Serbian 2nd Army to Adrianople further complicated the issue.

For Montenegro, the initial phase of the First Balkan War was extremely frustrating. Initial Montenegrin expectations of military glory were sorely disappointed. Although Montenegrin troops had occupied a significant part of the Sandjak of Novi Pazar, they did not reach their goal of Prizren in Kosovo. Even worse, the Montenegrins were stuck in front of the important northern Albanian town of Scutari, with no clear expectation of victory. Montenegrin military frustrations emphasized the weakness and backwardness of the Petrovich regime. After the first two months of the First Balkan War, Serbia and the Karageorgevich dynasty were the clear winners in the contest for the unity of the Serbian people. Because of military incompetence demonstrated during the First Balkan War, Montenegro and the Petrovich dynasty could no longer contend for leadership of the Serbian national movement.

The results of the first round of the fighting for the Greeks were mixed. They had achieved their main goal, the occupation of Salonika. In political and military terms, however, their victory remained circumscribed. A Bulgarian force contested Greek claims to the city. The Greeks still lacked a territorial settlement with Bulgaria. Conflicting claims to Salonika and elsewhere between Greece and their larger and stronger ally undermined the Balkan League. Nor had the Greek army preformed particularly well. Unlike their Bulgarian and Serbian allies, the Greeks had not achieved any overwhelming military victories over the Ottomans. Most battles they had fought were on a comparatively small scale. They had suffered a real setback at Klidion. At the time of the armistice, an armistice they ignored, Greek troops remained bogged down outside Janina. The war brought the Greek army little glory, and the armistice gave it no respite.

The Greek navy, as anticipated, proved to be a critical advantage for the success of the Balkan League. It successfully prevented the Ottomans from bringing troops from Asia to the western Balkans, and enabled Greece to seize the Ottoman-held Aegean islands. The success of the Greek fleet in Aegean operations demonstrated the weakness of the Ottoman navy and emphasized the Ottomans' need to acquire a modern navy. This led to an attempt to obtain British warships and ultimately to the *Goeben* and *Breslau* steaming into the Dardanelles in August 1914.

The Ottoman situation at the start of the war in the west was not promising. They applied their offensive strategy at Kumanovo, with no better success than they had in Thrace. The Ottomans were unable to halt the advance of the Serbian army all the way to Bitola. Nor could they stop the Greek march on Salonika. The successful defenses of Scutari and Janina indicate one strategy that might have gained the Ottomans the time to muster their Asian forces for ultimate victory. They could have withdrawn their Western Army into Albania immediately after the outbreak of war instead of after their defeats in Macedonia. By the time the remnants of the Western Army arrived in Albania, they were defeated and demoralized. Had the Ottomans established a "fortress Albania" at the beginning of the war they would have enjoyed some advantages. Only there in the west did the Ottomans enjoy the support of the local population against the allies. From there, with fresh, motivated troops they could have harassed their Balkan enemies as they moved into Macedonia. In Albania they might have held off their Balkan enemies indefinitely. This could have gained them the time they needed to bring their troops from Asia to Europe and use their superior numbers to crush the Balkan League.

4

THE ARMISTICE

By the end of November 1912, the armies of the Balkan League were victorious almost everywhere. The exertion of war, however, had exhausted them. Likewise, the Ottomans were debilitated by their defeats. Their victory at Chataldzha, however, had given them some hope. Neither side was in a position to continue the fighting at the previous levels. Nor did either side have any serious expectation of outside help.

Chataldzha armistice

After the Bulgarian defeat at Chataldzha, Tsar Ferdinand changed his position and urged the government to begin the peace process. On 20 November he wrote to President Geshov, "the main thing is that the peace negotiations begin no matter how."[1] Negotiations for the armistice began on 25 November at Chataldzha and were concluded on 3 December after only five sessions. The opposing armies would remain at Chataldzha until the conclusion of a definitive peace. Negotiations for an armistice began at Chataldzha on 25 November. At this point the Ottoman Empire in Europe had shrunk to the small portion of eastern Thrace east of the Chataldzha lines, the Gallipoli Peninsula (Bulair), and the three besieged fortress cites of Adrianople, Scutari, and Janina, which was just now coming under siege by the Greeks. That the Ottomans could negotiate at all, however, was due to their victory at Chataldzha and their continued retention of the three fortresses. The main purpose of the armistice was to establish conditions for a cease-fire. After this, negotiations for a peace treaty would begin in London. The Bulgarian delegation, composed of Generals Savov and Fichev and Stoyan Danev, the president of the Bulgarian parliament, also represented Serbia and Montenegro. The Greeks sent their minister in Sofia, Demetur Panas. Nazim Pasha, the failed Ottoman commander, was the chief representative for his side.

The talks concluded after only five meetings with the signing of the armistice on 3 December. The Balkan allies had demanded that the Ottomans concede all of their European territories west of the Chataldzha lines. They did not quite get all of this. According to the armistice terms, the three fortresses would receive no new provisions, the armies were to stay in their respective positions, and the Ottomans were to lift their blockade of Bulgarian Black Sea ports and allow the Bulgarians to use the railroad running past Adrianople to provision their troops at Chataldzha.[2] The Greeks did not sign the armistice because it did not give them possession of Janina. Consequently, they continued their siege there.

The terms of armistice favored the Balkan allies. The Serbs alone had attained all of their military objectives. The Bulgarians did receive an advantage by securing the right to supply their exhausted troops in front of Chataldzha by using the railroad running through the Ottoman positions at Adrianople. The allies did not receive total satisfaction however. Bulgaria, Greece and Montenegro still endeavored to acquire the besieged fortresses. Ottoman resistance was due largely in the case of Adrianople to its proximity to Constantinople, and in the cases of Janina and Scutari to the determination of the Albanian inhabitants to avoid foreign rule.

The Bulgarians had hoped that they could secure the surrender of Adrianople during the armistice negotiations.[3] This expectation, however, was inconsistent with their military situation. Both sides were exhausted and incapable of further military action for the time being. Both sides insisted on ruling the city. Had the Bulgarians relinquished their claim to Adrianople, they probably could have obtained a final peace at Chataldzha rather then merely an armistice.[4] Because they had agreed to arbitration over the question of northern Macedonia, which raised the possibility that they would not obtain all Macedonia, the Bulgarians were anxious to obtain compensation in Thrace. Their insistence on obtaining Adrianople insured that this question would be on the agenda of the London Peace Conference.

London peace conference

After the signing of the Chataldzha armistice, the diplomatic arena shifted to London. Two simultaneous conferences met there in December 1912 to determine the fate of the Balkan Peninsula. On 16 December 1912 representatives of the Balkan League and the Ottoman Empire met at St James's Palace to negotiate a peace settlement. The energetic Dr Danev was the main Bulgarian representative. His somewhat abrasive personality was an asset neither for dealing with his allies nor for dealing with the ambassadors of the Great Powers. The Greek Prime Minister Eleutherios Venizelos represented his country. He skillfully and sympathetically delineated Greek interests. Former Prime Minister Lazar Mijushkivich represented the Montenegrins and former Serbian prime minister Stojan Novakovich represented the Serbs. Mustafa Reshid Pasha, the Ottoman ambassador to Paris, was the chief Ottoman delegate.

From the beginning, the Ottomans adopted delaying tactics. They hoped that by gaining time they could rest, reinvigorate, and, where possible, reinforce their armies. In addition, they perceived that they might benefit from the signs of discord appearing among the allies. Reshid Pasha immediately protested the Greek presence at the peace table since they had not signed the armistice. This delayed the talks until 24 December, when the Ottomans conceded the Greek presence. Then the negotiations stalled over the issue of Adrianople, demanded by Bulgaria, and the four Aegean islands near the mouth of the Dardanelles, Samothrace, Imbros, Lemnos, and Tenedos, claimed by Greece. The Ottomans regarded Adrianople and the four islands as vital to the defense of their capital.

At London, Danev demanded that Adrianople become Bulgarian. The Bulgarians wanted Adrianople to make up for the possible loss to the Serbs of the disputed zone of Macedonia and to justify their own heavy losses in the Thracian fighting. The American military attaché in the Balkans, Lieutenant Sherman Miles, reported, "It is doubtful if the present Bulgarian Government could survive the popular indignation which would surely be aroused by a peace in which the vilayet and the city of Adrianople were given to the Turks."[5] Adrianople was a valuable prize that would help make up for the great sacrifices the Bulgarians had made in conquering Thrace.

At the same time the Ottomans resolutely rejected the cession of the city. They refused to surrender Adrianople because it commanded the European approaches to Constantinople. An Ottoman diplomat later explained to Dr Danev, "For you Adrianople is a window into our harem."[6] In addition, the Ottomans had a sentimental attachment to Adrianople as the location of their first European capital and as the site of the sixteenth-century mosque of Sultan Selim II.

In their peace proposal of 1 January 1913, the Ottomans accepted the loss of all territory west of the province (vilayet) of Adrianople (Thrace), but refused to concede the cession of Thrace or the Aegean Islands.[7] This was completely unacceptable to the Bulgarians and the Greeks. As a result, negotiations stalled. After 6 January talks were suspended.

The Ottoman New Year's Day offer was not a bad deal for the Balkan allies. It meant that the Ottomans conceded Janina and Scutari. In the absence of the settlement, the fighting continued for three months in Janina and for four months in Scutari. A settlement at this point might have enabled the Montenegrins to acquire Scutari without arousing the opposition of the Great Powers. Acceptance of the New Year's Day offer also meant that the Balkan allies could turn to the resolution of their differences before these became manifest. Bulgarian insistence on Adrianople was the main obstacle to the peace. Danev later asserted that had Bulgaria not insisted on Adrianople she could have signed a final peace at London in the winter of 1912–13.[8] This is almost certainly the case. Had the Bulgarians abandoned their dreams of obtaining the city and region, which had only a small Bulgarian population, the Greeks would have been hard pressed to maintain a lone defiant posture against the Ottomans and ultimately against the Great Powers. The First Balkan War could have ended in January 1913, and the Second Balkan War might never have taken place.

London Ambassadors Conference

The second conference held in London was the more important of the two London meetings. It met as the "Reunion of the Ambassadors of the Six Great Powers, signatories of the Treaty of Berlin." Although it lacked participants of the stature of the luminaries who had attended the Congress of Berlin, it represented the same idea of congressional oversight of European affairs. It was clear from the start that the Great Powers, through their ministers in London, and not the representatives of the belligerent states meeting there, would have the ultimate prerogative in the determination of the settlement of the Balkan war.

The London Ambassadors Conference had developed from concerns among the Great Powers that the Balkan war might escalate into a wider conflict involving other states. The military measures taken by Austria–Hungary in November 1912 in Galicia and Bosnia–Hercegovina because of the Serbian move into Albania and directed not only against Serbia but also against Russia exacerbated the situation.[9] Clearly, a Balkan issue could quickly escalate into a European war. The Great Powers sought to prevent this. Sir Edward Grey, the British foreign secretary, suggested that a conference should be held in London for this purpose. The other Powers were eager to agree. As Leopold Berchtold, the Austro-Hungarian foreign minister explained to a subordinate, "I could easily provoke a war in twenty four hours, but I do not want to do that."[10] The prospect of a European war growing out of the Balkan War was a real danger. This of course was what happened in July 1914.

Beginning on 17 December, the ambassadors of the Great Powers accredited to Great Britain met under the leadership of Sir Edward Grey to oversee the Balkan peace process and to protect the interests of the Great Powers there. The Ambassadors Conference also intended to resolve differences among the Great Powers themselves, particularly those three with direct interests in the Balkans: Austria–Hungary, Italy, and Russia. The Great Powers endeavored to replace the Berlin Settlement with a London Settlement. This was the last gasp of the congress system, which had contained the ambitions of the Great Powers since the Congress of Vienna ended in 1815.

The ambassadors had to contend with such issues as the disposition of the Aegean islands and the determination of a new Thracian border between Bulgaria and the Ottoman Empire, but the major area of contention for them was the problem of Albania. On 28 November 1912, a national assembly in Vlorë had proclaimed the independence of Albania under a provisional government headed by Ismail Kemal Bey.[11] The advance of the Balkan armies and the Ottoman collapse forced the Albanians into action. By mid-December, the Greeks were besieging the southern gate of Albania at Janina, and the Montenegrins had besieged the northern gate at Scutari. Early in the war the Serbs had overrun Kosovo. Furthermore, by the end of November 1912, the Serbian 3rd Army had occupied the Adriatic port of Durrës (Italian, Durazzo; Serbian, Drach), giving the Serbs a long-sought outlet on the sea and establishing a Serbian presence in central Albania.

This Serbian presence on the Adriatic aroused opposition from the Albanians, who perceived Durrës as a vital commercial port in the middle of their newly declared independent state. They naturally wanted to include as many of their fellow nationals as possible in the new state. Without Durres there could be no Albania. It also received strong objections from the Italians, who saw in the Serbian presence on the Straits of Otranto a challenge to their control over the mouth of the Adriatic. The Serbian appearance on the Adriatic especially antagonized the Austrians, who discerned the hand of Russia behind the Serbian pretensions as a check to Austrian ambitions in the western Balkans.

The Dual Monarchy strongly resisted any Serbian expansion into the Adriatic. This narrow arm of the Mediterranean was Austria–Hungary's only maritime outlet to the wider world. Its relations with its Triple Alliance partner across the Adriatic, Italy, were at best problematical. Austria–Hungary could not permit another problem to emerge on the eastern shore of the Adriatic. In the view of the Viennese government, a Serbian Adriatic port was a Russian naval base and a challenge to the Monarchy's only access to maritime connections. To prevent this Austro-Hungarian policy was determined to create a viable Albanian state. The Austrians decided that, "The territorial boundaries of this new state will be whatever is proper to insure the interests of its vitality and stability and should include if possible all the Albanians living on Turkish soil within natural borders."[12] In particular, they wanted the new Albania to include such towns as Scutari, Prizren, and Djakova. All of these places were objects of Serbian and Montenegrin aspirations. For the Austro-Hungarians, no strong advocates of nationalism in general, a large and strong national Albania was a good way to guarantee control of the Adriatic. The alleged detention or even murder of the Austro-Hungarian consul in Prizren, Kosovo, by Serbian troops exacerbated the situation. Even though the consul, Oskar Prochaska, turned up safe in Skoplje at the end of November, this incident only increased Austro-Hungarian determination to prevent a Serbian presence on the Adriatic.

The Austrian-Hungarians, however, were not overly concerned about the southern frontiers of Albania. Since they had no conflict with Greece, they were not so vigilant about the future Greco-Albanian frontier. The only time the Austrians and Italians bestirred themselves about the southern frontier of Albania was to forbid a Greek occupation of Vlorë after the Greek navy had shelled the town on 3 December.[13] The Greeks had no Great Power opponent and no Great Power patron to press their interests in southern Albania. The Greek navy imposed a blockade on the Albanian coast, isolating the Albanian Provisional Government in Vlore. As a result, no Great Power made any serious effort in London to deny Janina to the Greeks so long as they could take it. The remainder of the southern Albanian frontier, however, remained unresolved for some time because of the lack of direct interest by the Great Powers and because of its remoteness.

The Serbs naturally resented Austrian opposition to their presence in Albania and their acquisition of an Adriatic port. Pashich insisted that Serbia had to obtain the part of the Adriatic coast from Durrës to Alessio and a wide corridor to link this to Kosovo.[14] He insisted that, "Serbia absolutely cannot renounce a port on the Adriatic Sea."[15] Mindful of their alliance obligations, the Bulgarians offered support for their Serbian ally's claims.[16] With the Serbs occupying most of Macedonia, the Bulgarians did not want to give the Serbs any excuse to claim that the March 1912 alliance was invalid because of Bulgarian failure to uphold their responsibilities. The Serbs did not activate the anti-Austrian portion of the March 1912 alliance. They hoped for a diplomatic resolution of the Albanian issue in their favor. Specifically, Pasich expected Russian intervention for the Serbian position.[17] Although the Russians did support the Serbs, their help proved insufficient. On 20 December the ambassadors recognized an independent Albania and soon agreed that the new Albanian state would include Durres.

Through the winter of 1912–13 and the spring of 1913, the ambassadors wrangled over the frontiers of the new Albanian state. The Austrians and Italians supported a large Albania in order to contain Serbia and Montenegro, and thus control of the Adriatic Sea. Russia advocated a smaller Albania in order to insure Serbian and Montenegrin gains. The Albanians themselves had little or no influence over the proceedings.

The focus of Austro-Hungarian efforts on behalf of Albania became the northern city of Scutari, still besieged by Montenegrin forces. As an Austro-Hungarian report specified, "In the opinion of experts, a viable Albania is inconceivable without Scutari and its environs."[18] On 26 January, the Russians demanded that if Scutari was to go to Albania, the ethnically Albanian market town of Djakova in the western part of the Kosovo vilayet should go to Serbia, rather than the new Albanian state. This caused a deadlock lasting until the end of March, when the Austro-Hungarians agreed to allow Serbia to retain Djakova. By this time, the Ambassadors had already recognized that Albania would obtain Scutari, whatever the outcome of the siege.

Bulgarian–Greek dispute

The separate Greek delegation at the armistice talks was indicative of a growing fissure in the Balkan League. Even before the signing of the

December armistice, disputes had developed among the victorious allies. The first problem, not surprisingly, arose between the Bulgarians and the Greeks. This centered on the important port of Salonika. The Greeks entered the city on 8 November, the Bulgarians arrived the next day. An uneasy condominium ensued with units of both armies stationed in the city. While the war was still ongoing, the Bulgarians unwisely rebuffed a proposal by the Greek Prime Minister, Venizelos, for a division of southern Macedonia. The Greeks wanted Salonika, Kavala, Seres, and a common frontier with Serbia.[19] In response, the Sofia government insisted on the principle of proportionality. The Bulgarian Prime Minister, Ivan E. Geshov, asserted, "Let Venizelos compare the size of our army and the amount of our sacrifices with those of the Greeks, and he will understand the outlandishness of the project and our categorical refusal to accept it even as the basis for discussion."[20] The principle of proportionality obviously favored the Bulgarians because of the major Bulgarian military effort in Thrace and the high casualties they had suffered there. The Greeks, not surprisingly, showed little enthusiasm for this idea as the basis for negotiation.[21]

The lack of a clear line of demarcation between Bulgarian and Greek interests had also begun to cause trouble. As early as December 1912, the Bulgarian government protested against the efforts of the Greeks to establish administrations in regions occupied by Bulgarian troops.[22] In addition, in November the Greeks began to release Ottoman prisoners of war captured at Salonika. The Bulgarians feared that these troops would return to Ottoman authority and rejoin the army to be used against them.

The armistice in the Balkan War brought no end to the dispute between the Balkan allies, Bulgaria, and Greece. After their quick victories over the Ottomans, neither Balkan ally demonstrated any inclination toward resolving their intra-alliance problem. In London the Greeks were determined to secure recognition of their claims to Salonika. Skouloudis, a member of the Greek delegation, remarked, "If we do not bring back Salonika, we cannot return to Athens!"[23] While in London, Venizelos and Danev met on three separate occasions. The Greek prime minister again proposed a frontier that gave much of southern Macedonia to Bulgaria but allotted Salonika to Greece. Danev claimed to have no authority to negotiate. Afterwards he advised Sofia that the Bulgarians might have to fight Greece for Salonika.[24] This impudence was based on confidence in the power of the Bulgarian army.

The Bulgarians should have made a greater effort to reach an agreement with the Greeks. An acknowledgment that Salonika was Greek might have gone a long way to resolving this problem. In London they missed an excellent opportunity to settle this issue. Had they done so, they would have been in a much better position to confront the growing problem with Serbia over the disposition of Macedonia.

Bulgarian–Serbian dispute

By the turn of the year, the diplomacy of the Great Powers had thwarted Serbian aspirations to the Adriatic. In response the Serbs sought compensation in Macedonia. They had always regarded Macedonia as a part of the Serbian historical legacy. Many in the Serbian army and government had never been completely reconciled to the March 1912 treaty, which had conceded most of Macedonia to Bulgaria. Indeed, important elements in the Serbian military, including members of the organization Unity or Death (Black Hand), opposed any idea of arbitration with Bulgaria based on the March 1912 treaty.[25] The apparent loss of northern Albania made the Serbs determined to retain their conquests in Macedonia. This brought them into conflict with their Bulgarian allies.

Even before the decisions of the London ambassadors on Albania, the Sofia government began to receive alarming reports that Serbian forces were consolidating their hold over the portions of Macedonia that they had occupied but which were Bulgarian according to the terms of the March 1912 treaty. Serbian authorities were arresting Bulgarian administrators, closing Bulgarian schools and harassing Bulgarian priests.[26] These reports caused considerable distress in Sofia. Concerns about Macedonia caused the Bulgarians to rely further on the good faith of Russia in maintaining the March 1912 treaty. The Bulgarians could not imagine that Russia would fail to support them.

The Serbs were also concerned that their reception by the Slavic inhabitants of Macedonia did not meet their expectations. When the Serbs entered Macedonia, they were surprised and disappointed to discover that many of the inhabitants identified themselves as "Bulgarians." The Serbs attributed this situation to the successful Bulgarian educational efforts that had begun at the end of the nineteenth century. As the Serbian armies advanced into Macedonia, one Serbian journalist wrote, "What falls under Serbia, remains Serbian, what falls under Bulgaria, is assimilated."[27] This perception allowed for little tolerance of pro-Bulgarian sentiment in the regions under Serbian occupation.

A Serbian diplomatic note of 13 January 1913 increased Bulgarian concerns for Macedonia. In the note, the Serbs formally requested a revision of the March 1912 treaty.[28] The main basis for this request was the Serbs' failure to obtain territory in Albania and an Adriatic port and the Bulgarians' apparent conquest of more territory in Thrace than anticipated in the March 1912 treaty. The Serbs noted that the Bulgarians had not sent the agreed upon troops to the Vardar theater, but they had sent soldiers to support Bulgaria at Adrianople.

The Bulgarians had no desire to provide the compensation for their allies frustrated advance to the sea. Macedonia, after all, was the major Bulgarian objective of the war. For the time being, however, the Bulgarians did not respond to what they regarded as Serbian provocation. Serbian troops were entrenched alongside Bulgarians at Adrianople. The Bulgarians had confidence that Russia, which had guaranteed the March 1912 alliance, would resolve the dispute according to the treaty.

Serbia's rapid and overwhelming victory at Kumanovo rendered their arguments directed to the Bulgarians as somewhat fatuous. The Serbs had really not needed additional troops in the Vardar theater. In fact, they had more easily consolidated their control over Macedonia in the absence of Bulgarian troops. The Bulgarians victories in Thrace, however, had insured that the Ottomans could not launch a counteroffensive to regain Macedonia. Nevertheless, the presence of Serbian soldiers in most of Macedonia, and the absence of Bulgarian troops there, rendered the legality of the dispute to be irrelevant. A real danger of war between Bulgaria and Serbia lay behind this conflict.

Bulgarian–Romanian dispute

After the turn of the year, another problem emerged to confront the Bulgarian government. This was a Romanian demand for compensation after the Bulgarian successes against the Ottomans changed the power dynamic in the Balkan Peninsula. The Romanians regarded themselves as the 'gendarmes of the Balkans' and wanted to insure that they would remain the single strongest power in the region.

This problem had not gone undetected by the Bulgarians. On the eve of the war in the summer of 1912, the Sofia government had attempted to reach some kind of accommodation with Bucharest because of concerns over Romania's alliance with Austria–Hungary and friendship with the Ottoman Empire. The Bulgarians sought to secure their rear before the fighting broke out. At that time, the Romanian prime minister, Titu Maiorescu, replied evasively to the Bulgarian approach. He equivocated, "Events have not yet occurred which necessitate a discussion."[29] The Romanians wanted to wait until the outcome of the war was clear before presenting a bill.

When the extent of the Bulgarian victories over the Ottomans became apparent in the autumn of 1912, the Romanians proffered in Sofia a demand for territorial compensation in northeastern Bulgaria.[30] Initially, they indicated they wanted the important Danubian port of Silistra. By January 1913, however, their demand had expanded to include generally the fertile corner of northwestern Bulgaria called Dobrudzha (Romanian, Dobrogea), and specifically on the territory north of a line drawn from the Danube city of Tutrakan to the Black Sea port of Balchik northeast of Varna. Dobrudzha is the flat and fertile land between the Black Sea and the bend in the Danube River. The Berlin settlement had divided it between Bulgaria and Romania, but both countries had vague aspirations to each other's portion. Annexation of Dobrudzha would bring a rich agricultural region to Bucharest and also further secure Romanian control of the south bank of the mouth of the Danube River. The Romanians initially considered the immediate occupation of Bulgarian, or southern, Dobrudzha, but their German and Austro-Hungarian allies' assurances of eventual gain dissuaded them from this action.

The Bulgarians naturally resisted what they regarded as blackmail. They were particularly disinclined to cede territory when their victorious armies were adding to the size of Bulgaria. They replied with diplomatic evasions of the issue and offers of minimal border adjustments. These tactics bought them some time. Finally on 24 February 1913, when their armies were again active at Adrianople and Chataldzha, while they were under pressure from Russia and other Great Powers to make concessions, and with their relations with their allies becoming problematic, the Bulgarians agreed to submit the dispute with Romania to the ambassador of the Great Powers at a conference in St Petersburg. Two days earlier, the Romanians had also agreed to the conference. The location of the conference inspired Bulgarian hopes that in the end Russia would protect its traditional Balkan ally from the minion of the Triple Alliance. Bulgarian faith in Russia during the Balkan Wars was somewhat naively misplaced.

Despite their disinclination to surrender ethnically Bulgarian territory to what amounted to Romanian extortion, the Bulgarians should have accommodated their northern neighbor. Some Bulgarians recognized the need to reach an agreement with Romania. Even Tsar Ferdinand urged a cession of territory, which he hoped Bulgaria could regain at some future date.[31] Instead, the Bulgarian government resisted the Romanian demands and relied on Russia to ward off any attempt by Bucharest to use force. This was a fatal mistake for Bulgarian policy. Because of the growing disputes with Greece and Serbia over the disposition of Macedonia, the Bulgarians needed to have their northern frontier secure. Bulgaria's failure to relinquish southern Dobrudzha resulted in the much greater loss of Macedonia when Romania joined Greece and Serbia to overwhelm Bulgaria during the Second Balkan War.

Young Turk coup

On 23 January the Young Turks, led by Enver Bey, again seized power in Constantinople. Enver Bey was at the time the chief of staff of the Strategic Reserve in Constantinople. The assumption that the Ottoman grand vizir, Kamil Pasha, was preparing to concede Adrianople to the Bulgarians, was a major motivating factor for this action.[32] The Young Turks were determined to continue the war and to save Adrianople by whatever means possible. They forced Kamil Pasha to resign at gun point. Nazim Pasha, the minister of war and originator of the Ottoman Empire's failed military efforts in the war, was shot and killed. This was the brutal penalty for his poor leadership.

A non-political soldier, Mahmut Shevket Pasha, a former minister of war, became grand vizir. His task was to do everything possible to retain Adrianople. The new government then made new proposals in London, offering to partition Adrianople by ceding that portion of the city on the right bank of the Maritsa River to Bulgaria and leaving the disposition of the Aegean Islands to the Great Powers.[33] The Bulgarians, with problems mounting on every side, would have been wise to accept this offer. Instead, the Balkan allies immediately rejected the proposal and denounced the armistice. The war, now limited to the besieged towns of Adrianople, Janina, and Scutari and the eastern extremities of Thrace, resumed on 3 February 1913.

Conclusion

The period from the beginning of December 1912 to the end of January 1913 was one of disappointment for the members of the Balkan League. None of them obtained their objectives. The Bulgarians remained bogged down outside of Adrianople, likewise the Montenegrins at Scutari and the Greeks south of Janina. Pressure from the Great Powers had forced the Serbs to withdraw from some of their conquests in northern Albania.

This period also saw the isolation of Bulgaria. Bulgaria had sustained a major military effort during the war, with the big victories in Thrace. These victories, however, had not brought corresponding territorial and political gains. Bulgarian disputes with their Greek and Serbian allies over Macedonia had arisen to threaten the security of the March 1912 Treaty. In addition, the Romanians, jealous of Bulgaria's new power, and backed by the Triple Alliance and also apparently Russia, proposed to amputate the northeastern corner of the country. The Ottomans had derived little advantage from the duration of the armistice and from the fraying of the Balkan League. Their garrisons in the three besieged cities remained beyond the help of the government in Constantinople. The two months of the armistice, in fact, had not even seen the cessation of fighting at Scutari and Janina. Meanwhile, in all three cities, the soldiers and civilians there had consumed valuable food and other irreplaceable resources. The return to power of the Young Turks might have afforded these beleaguered locations and the troops at Chataldzha and Gallipoli some psychological lift, but did little else to alleviate their situations. The Ottoman army, only slightly rested, now had to fight again in an effort at which it had conspicuously failed previously.

5

THREE SIEGES

After the denunciation of the armistice on 30 January 1913, five locations became combat zones. Fighting had continued at Janina, Scutari, and elsewhere in Albania throughout the armistice. Adrianople, the Bulgarian–Ottoman fronts at Chataldzha and at Gallipoli also became active. Their victory at Chataldzha in November 1912 and the Young Turk coup in January 1913 to some extent reinvigorated the Ottoman forces. The Bulgarians had exhausted themselves with their efforts in the autumn of 1912 and had yet to recover their offensive spirit. Likewise the Montenegrins had debilitated their meager resources in their futile efforts at Scutari. The Greeks, still besieging Janina, had yet to experience any major fighting. The Serbs, after the fighting at Kumanovo, had virtually cleared Macedonia and Kosovo of Ottoman troops. Their soldiers now were prepared to assist their allies at Adrianople and Scutari.

Bulair (Gallipoli)

The Young Turks had seized power in order to continue the war and to save Adrianople. The new Ottoman Foreign Minister Noradounghian Effendi boasted, "If Adrianople continues to resist, we shall fight to relieve her. If Adrianople falls, we shall fight to retake her."[1] Enver Bey, who held a subordinate military position as the chief of staff with the rank of colonel in the 10th Corps but exercised primary power in the new regime, immediately decided upon bold action. On 7 February, the Ottomans began an audacious effort at Gallipoli and at Sharkoi on the Sea of Marmara to relieve pressure on Adrianople. This operation was intended as the first step toward the relief of that beleaguered garrison. Fourteen months later Enver, now a pasha, would lead the Ottoman Empire into the First World War on the side of the Central Powers.

Confronting the Ottomans was the newly organized 4th Bulgarian Army, commanded by General Stiliyan Kovachev. This army included the 7th Rilski Division, two divisions recruited in the recently occupied areas of the Rodopes and Thrace, and the Macedonian–Thracian Volunteers. It had

92,289 officers and men.² The 4th Army's main purpose was to defend the Gallipoli front, which the Ottomans had considerably reinforced during the armistice. The Gallipoli front guarded the rear of the Bulgarian operations at Adrianople and Chataldzha.

The Ottomans launched an attack against the Bulgarians at Bulair, about midway down the Gallipoli Peninsula. At the time of the armistice, the situation at Bulair resembled that at Chataldzha, with the Ottomans occupying positions first prepared during the Crimean War by the British and French, and the Bulgarians arrayed in newly dug trenches in front of them.³ The Bulgarian positions, however, did enjoy the advantage of occupying several low hills. The Bulgarian 7th Rila Infantry Division, commanded by General Georgi Todorov, occupied a line stretching across the width of the peninsula, about 4.5 miles. The Ottomans intended this attack to clear the Gallipoli Peninsula and to link up with Ottoman forces landing at Sharkoi on the Sea of Marmara.

The Bulgarian right flank at Gallipoli abutted the Gulf of Saros, an arm of the Aegean Sea, and the left flank bordered the Sea of Marmara. The Ottoman Bulair Army, consisting of the 27th Division and the Myureteb Division, about 50,000 men, under Fahri Pasha outnumbered the Bulgarians, who had only about 10,000 men.⁴ The Bulgarians did have an advantage in artillery, however, with seventy-eight guns to only thirty-six Ottoman guns.⁵

The fighting at Gallipoli began on the morning of 8 February. The cruiser *Mesudiye*, the bane of the Bulgarians at Chataldzha, supported the advance by firing into the left and center of the Bulgarian positions. The main blow came on the Bulgarian left flank, on the Marmara side of the peninsula. At first, the Ottomans succeeded in driving the Bulgarians back, capturing positions on the Bulgarian extreme left flank. They also advanced on the Bulgarian right flank after the Bulgarian defenders ran out of ammunition. Among the officers leading the Ottoman attack was Major Mustafa Kemal, recently returned from North Africa. He would distinguish himself in the same location two years later fighting in the opposite direction.

In the center of the Gallipoli Peninsula, the Bulgarians held their positions in the face of intense Ottoman artillery fire. Reflecting the desperate situation, one Bulgarian officer instructed his men, "If you retreat you will be shot, if I retreat, shoot me."⁶ As the Ottoman troops advanced into a thick mist, however, they became disoriented. At the same time, they encountered intense Bulgarian artillery and machine-gun fire. One Bulgarian soldier noted in his diary that, as a result of the fire, "There was nothing alive to even stir."⁷ With the Ottomans in disarray, the Bulgarians counterattacked in the early afternoon. The Ottoman troops retreated, pursued by the Bulgarians. By evening both sides had returned to their original positions, with the Bulgarians even gaining an Ottoman fort. The Ottomans suffered catastrophic loses, about 6,000 men dead and up to 18,000 wounded.⁸ Bulgarian loses were much lower, 114 killed and 416 wounded.⁹

Meanwhile, the Ottomans launched the other part of their operation, a landing near the Marmara port of Sharkoi. This began on the evening of 7 February with a bombardment by the Ottoman warships *Barbaros Hayrettin*, *Turgut Ries*, and *Mecidiye*. The Bulgarian troops, elements of the Macedonian–Thracian brigade, retreated about 2 miles inland and began to shell the Ottomans. The next day, Ottoman troops of the 10th Corps, 30,000–40,000 men under the command of Hurshid Pasha and the direction of Enver Bey, went ashore slightly west of Sharkoi. Supported by naval guns, they attacked slowly toward Sharkoi. This attack posed a great danger for the Bulgarian forces in eastern Thrace. Had the Ottomans succeeded in establishing themselves on the north shore of the Sea of Marmara, they could have threatened the rear of the Bulgarians at Chataldzha and even broken through the Bulgarian lines to relieve Adrianople. Fighting continued for three days. General Kovachev rushed reinforcements to contain the Ottoman landings. On 10 February, the Bulgarians aided by air reconnaissance successfully counterattacked and halted the Ottoman advance.

Casualties on both sides were comparatively light. The Bulgarians suffered five dead and thirty-two wounded, while the Ottomans suffered 100 dead and seventy wounded. News of the failure of the Gallipoli operation persuaded the Ottomans to withdraw.[10] On 11 February, they re-embarked their ships without much difficulty. Tsar Ferdinand later fumed that his forces missed an opportunity to capture Enver at Sharkoi.[11] The Ottoman troops then went to Gallipoli, where they augmented the forces already there. The low casualty figures indicate a lack of determination on the part of the Ottomans and a failure of leadership. A more sustained effort at Sharkoi might have given the Ottomans a better result. Initially they faced small numbers of Bulgarian soldiers. Had they used the firepower of their fleet more effectively and attempted to move off the shore more quickly they might have succeeded in establishing a strong position from which they could have cut off the Bulgarian forces at Gallipoli and threatened the rear of the Bulgarians besieging Adrianople. This was a real lost opportunity for the Ottomans.

To divert attention from their Gallipoli–Marmara operation, the Ottomans undertook a supplementary attack against the Bulgarian 1st Army positions on the southern part of the Chataldzha lines. This attack began on 7 February. After sustaining heavy casualties and fearing an Ottoman landing to their rear the 10th and 4th infantry divisions fell back about 20 kilometers to secondary defensive positions. There they deflected the Ottoman offensive.

The Ottomans undertook an aggressive offensive in eastern Thrace with which they hoped to alleviate pressure on Adrianople and possibly lead to the relief of the beleaguered city. The audacity of their offense was indicative of their success in November at Chataldzha and of the fighting spirit of the Young Turks. Unfortunately, they still lacked the abilities of command and the training for success. In particular, they failed entirely to coordinate the

Gallipoli attack with the Sharkoi landing. The cruiser *Mesudiye* might have proved decisive if it had supported the Sharkoi operation.[12] The Ottoman experiences at and familiarity with Bulair, however, undoubtedly proved advantageous two years later when, facing the opposite direction slightly to the south, they again fought at the Gallipoli Peninsula. Although their offensive at Gallipoli in 1913 failed, their defense in 1915 succeeded.

The fighting on the Gallipoli Peninsula and on the north shore of the Sea of Marmara gave the Bulgarians a scare. They did not panic however. Their command responded well to the Ottoman attacks. The Bulgarians held on in the face of superior numbers and decisively repulsed the bold Ottoman offensive. These actions were the most successful Bulgarian defensive battles of the Balkan Wars. The defeat exhausted Ottoman offensive capabilities for the present. The initiative passed to the Bulgarians. This helped insure the fall of Adrianople in March.

Janina

Because the Greeks had not signed the armistice at Chataldzha in December 1912, they hostilities continued in Epirus. They were in a difficult position there. The region was remote and could only be reached by bad roads over rugged terrain. Winter conditions in the mountains were arduous and many soldiers suffered from the cold and exposure. In addition, the Greeks lacked the numerical strength to completely surround Janina. Nevertheless, they were eager to take Janina before the conclusion of any formal peace. To accomplish this, they transferred three divisions from the Army of Thessaly to reinforce the besieging forces. By January 1913, the Greeks had five divisions, with about 28,000 men, at Janina, supported by eighty artillery pieces and six airplanes. Because of their growing dispute with Bulgaria over Macedonia and especially Salonika, they dared not transfer any more troops or supplies to Epirus.

The situation within the city was also difficult for the Ottoman defenders. Unlike in Adrianople and Scutari, they could not depend on the loyalty of the civilian inhabitants, most of whom were Greeks. In addition, the inability of the Greeks to completely surround Janina afforded deserters the opportunity to leave. Some defenders bolstered their spirits with the hope that if Janina held out, it might become the capital of an autonomous Albania.[13]

The Greeks improved their position in Epirus somewhat by taking Koritsa (Albanian, Korce). After their eviction from Macedonia, the Ottoman 6th Corps of around 24,000 men under Djavid Pasha had established a strong position there which protected Janina on the northeast.[14] On 20 December, three Greek divisions pushed Djavid Pasha out of Koritsa. The Ottoman force retired deeper into Albania to Lushe. The seizure of Koritsa enabled the Greeks to control access to Janina from the northeast. The flow of men and supplies into the besieged city abated.

Fighting intensified around Janina toward the end of the year. Daily artillery duels ensued. The Ottomans, as elsewhere, demonstrated poor utilization of their big guns. An American volunteer in the Greek army noted, "The Turkish batteries have fired shells by the thousands and none did any damage."[15] His comment also indicates that the defenders of Janina had plenty of ammunition. The Ottomans maintained an active defense, retaking on one occasion a lost outer fort. A small Greek air detachment flew over the city observing and dropping hand grenades. All the time, the main Ottoman fortification of Bezane resisted every Greek effort to take it. The attacks by Albanian irregulars harassed Greek positions throughout Epirus. Especially important in this regard was the destruction on 12 January of the port facilities at Santi Quaranta, the main supply port for the besiegers, by an attack of Albanian irregulars.

On 20 January the Greeks undertook a large-scale general attack in heavy rain. They achieved some success on their flanks, but the attacks in the center against Fort Bezane failed and resulted in heavy casualties. The Greeks lost around 1,200 men.[16] Because of their losses, the Greeks discontinued their attacks that same evening. Nevertheless, the attack came close to success. The Ottomans were convinced that had the Greeks pressed their attacks, they would have entered Janina.[17]

Time now became an important consideration for the Greeks. Attempts by Venizelos at London to resolve the dispute with Bulgaria by talking to Danev had come to nothing. Furthermore, the London Ambassadors Conference was making progress in determining the boundaries of the new Albanian state. If Janina continued to hold out, the ambassadors might well assign it to Albania. Then the Greeks would have to contend with the Great Powers.

After the defeat of 20 January, General Zapundzakis was relieved of command. Crown Prince Constantine assumed command of the Greek forces in Epirus three days later. He carefully prepared for a final assault, marshaling men and resources. On 5 March, the Greeks began their attack. In his report to the War Office, Crown Prince Constantine explained his strategy, "While the right wing kept the enemy in play, my left pushed home their attack."[18] Essentially, the Greeks feinted an attack on the forts southeast of the town and made their major attack southwest of the town. All the while, they poured artillery fire from the hills south of the town onto Berane. These efforts overwhelmed the Ottoman defenders of Janina. On 6 March, Esad Pasha surrendered unconditionally. The Greeks took 33,000 prisoners and acquired 108 artillery pieces and a great deal of war material.[19] Unlike those in Adrianople and Scutari, the defenders of Janina did not suffer from great material want. This was because the siege was the briefest of the three, and because the Greeks never succeeded in completely surrounding Janina. In the final assault, the Greeks incurred losses of only 500 men dead and wounded.[20]

Janina was the first of the besieged Ottoman cities to fall. The Greek army had confronted strong opposition at Janina and had overcome it. This was their greatest military effort of the First Balkan War. The success instilled confidence in the Greek army. Furthermore, their victory, while the Bulgarians were still bogged down outside Adrianople, enabled the Greeks to transfer their army back to Macedonia in preparation for a confrontation over Salonika.

Albania

Fighting between Serbian troops from the 1st Army and Ottoman regulars supported by Albanian irregulars continued in central and southern Albania even after the signing of the armistice in December 1912. By mid-December the Serbs had taken Elbasan and established control over the north bank of the Shkumba River. This left the Serbs in effective control of northern Albania, roughly the portion they had hoped to obtain in the war. Albanian bands continued to oppose their presence in northeastern Albania.

The renewal of the war in February did little to change the situation. Albanian guerillas, supported by Djavid Pasha's forces south of the Shkumba River, resisted the Serbs. Serbian units crossed the Shkumba into southern Albania in pursuit of these guerillas.

The fall of Janina did not end the fighting in southern Albania. Not all of the Janina garrison accepted Greek captivity. Several thousand soldiers fled northwards during the night of 5–6 March. They joined the remnants of the Vardar Army that had withdrawn into southern Albania after the Battle of Bitola on November 1912. This force, led by Djavid Pasha, had remained north of Janina.

Djavid Pasha's 6th Corps of around 24,000 men continued to fight on after the fall of Janina. On 26 March 1913, it clashed with Serbian units near the village of Balagat, north of Lushe. Here the Serbs suffered losses of twenty-two dead and fifty-one wounded and took 188 Ottoman prisoners.[21] This was the final battle of the First Balkan War for Serbia. The Ottomans sustained a clear defeat. Afterwards they withdrew south of Lushe. The Serbs entered Lushe on 6 April 1913 and Berat on 12 April. Pressure from the Great Powers, escalating because of the siege of Scutari, forced the Serbs to surrender its holdings in central Albania that same month. By the first week of May, most of the Serbian forces had withdrawn from northern Albania. The remaining Ottoman troops returned home beginning in the middle of May. Although Djavid Pasha and his 6th Corps had suffered defeat several times during the course of the war, they never stopped fighting. Djavid Pasha and Esad Pasha, the defender of Janina, were the two most intrepid Ottoman commanders of the First Balkan War.

The Serbian efforts in central Albania represented more than a counterinsurgency operation. Despite the Austro-Hungarian warnings of the previous autumn and amidst the threats of April 1913 directed at Scutari, the Serbs stubbornly endeavored to maintain a strong presence in Albania. Their retreat in May did not represent the end of their aspirations there.

Adrianople

The armistice conditions had depressed the defenders of Adrianople.[22] The inability of the Ottomans to resupply Adrianople insured that the city would fall during the winter for lack of food and fuel unless they could launch a major attack for its relief from their positions at Chataldzha or Gallipoli. Nevertheless, the Ottomans utilized the armistice to improve their fortifications as much as possible.[23] They laid mines, reinforced the structures of their forward positions, installed floodlights, and improved radio connections with Constantinople and within the fortifications.

The Young Turk coup in Constantinople and their determination to relieve Adrianople meant that the Bulgarians now had to fight. Severe winter conditions made any immediate activity impossible. General Savov recognized that of the three fronts where the Bulgarians faced the Ottomans, only Adrianople offered a reasonable chance for success. Yet he and his army were not eager for the fray. General Fichev succinctly summarized the Bulgarian dilemma, "If we attack Adrianople, we can fail and sustain great losses, if we do not attack, the war will continue."[24]

After the Chataldzha defeat, Savov hesitated to risk a major frontal assault. He wanted to attack Adrianople, but did not want the responsibility for the resulting losses. Furthermore, the Bulgarians at Adrianople lacked the material basis for an assault, especially heavy artillery. Savov hoped that the winter weather and lack of food would cause the expeditious surrender of Adrianople without the loss of another Bulgarian soldier. Additional heavy artillery might insure a Bulgarian victory without the risk of an infantry assault. This consideration led the Bulgarians to again approach Serbia for help with the siege of Adrianople. The Serbs agreed to a Bulgarian appeal on 9 February for artillery to attack the besieged fortress-city of Adrianople, but reserved the right to specify compensation at a later date.[25] The Bulgarians responded, however, that they would provide only financial remuneration for use of the guns.[26]

The growing disputes with their Greek and Serbian allies over the disposition of the spoils in Macedonia forced the Bulgarians to attempt to resolve their campaign in Thrace and prepare to assert their claims in the west. Having occupied the greater part of Macedonia in the autumn campaign, both Greece and Serbia balked at surrendering any of their gains to their erstwhile Bulgarian ally.

Tensions between Bulgaria and Serbia increased after the expiration of the armistice and renewal of the war on 30 January 1913. Then on 22 February, Serbian Prime Minister Nikola Pashich formally requested a revision of the Serbo-Bulgarian treaty.[27] He noted that Serbia had provided assistance to the Bulgarians beyond the stipulations of the March 1912 Treaty. The Serbs wanted additional territory in Macedonia to make up for the loss of an outlet to the Adriatic. They insisted that the territory the Bulgarians had conquered in Thrace, unforeseen by the 1912 treaty, would recompense for the loss of more of Macedonia. The Bulgarians officially ignored this Serbian request. They did not want to cause friction while Serbian troops were fighting alongside Bulgarians at Adrianople. Above all, however, they relied on Russian support for the legality of the treaty.

After the denouncement of the armistice, the Bulgarians renewed their bombardment of Adrianople. Their purpose was to raise the moral of the besiegers and depress the spirits of the defenders. They apparently succeeded in demoralizing some of the civilian population. One inhabitant of the city described the shelling as "furious, implacable, inhuman."[28] The bombardment of the previous autumn had demonstrated that the Bulgarian artillery lacked the strength and precision to do any great damage to the prepared defensive positions. The Bulgarians directed some intense shelling at the European quarter of Adrianople in the hope that foreign consuls posted in the city would pressurize Sukru Pasha to surrender.[29] This questionable tactic emphasized Savov's impatience and desperation. At the same time, the Bulgarians attempted to jam the Ottoman radio link between Adrianople and Constantinople.[30] This was perhaps the earliest attempt at electronic warfare.

The bombardments stirred the defenders into action. During February, Ottoman troops attempted several sorties directed at the guns that were making existence in Adrianople precarious. These attacks met with no success. The Bulgarian ring of artillery continued to pour fire on Adrianople.

On 13 February, the Serbian heavy siege guns arrived at Adrianople. There were seventeen batteries including fifty-eight Schneider guns. Twenty-four of these were 120- and 150-mm howitzers, some of which had been sent direct from the factory.[31] With the addition of the Serbian siege guns, pressure mounted on the Bulgarians to mount a final assault on Adrianople. General Ivanov unceasingly sought the order to begin the attack. The Russian military attaché in Sofia, Colonel Georgi Romanovski, urged the storming of Adrianople, as did the Russian General Staff.[32] In addition, the titular commander in chief of the Bulgarian army, Tsar Ferdinand, "burned with desire" to attack the city.[33] Pressure on Savov increased even further after Janina surrendered to the Greeks.

Conditions during the winter were difficult for the besieging forces. A Serbian soldier reported,

> The troops suffered greatly. The region around Adrianople was for a distance of 15 kilometers treeless and for the most part without water. In February a terrible snowstorm raged, and we had to fight against typhus

and for a while also against cholera. Bread, meat and later on also wood had to come from Serbia.[34]

An alarming decline in the moral of the Bulgarian troops ringing Adrianople due to the intense cold and inactivity greatly disconcerted the high command.[35] Nevertheless, several Bulgarian leaders, notably, Chief of Staff Fichev and Dr Danev, still opposed an assault because of the risks involved.[36] Prime Minister Geshov told Savov that the government did not want him to attack Adrianople.[37] The risk of heavy casualties was too great. All of the political and military leaders, however, were anxious to conclude the siege in order to address the pressing issue of Macedonia.

Savov could not withstand this combination of factors. On 20 March he decided to attack and three days later gave the order to begin the assault.[38] General Ivanov's staff had developed the plan of attack. This plan called for a preliminary bombardment on the northwestern, southern, and western sectors, with the final assault beginning from the eastern sector. The other three sectors would attack in support of the main attack. The staff selected the eastern sector as the sight of the main attack because the northwest was the strongest and because the Bulgarians had learned through espionage that the Turks felt vulnerable in the southern sector and felt relaxed about the eastern sector.[39] Since November, the Bulgarians had occupied the Papas Tepe heights in the south, from which they commanded the entire area. Furthermore, an attack from the eastern sector would encounter no rivers blocking access to the main part of the city. Coincidentally with the assault on Adrianople, the Bulgarian forces at Chataldzha would launch a diversionary attack to prevent any desperate attempt at relief from these positions.

The Bulgarians maintained a tenuous watch on their opponents with observation balloons and airplanes. In an effort to further pressure the defenders of Adrianople, the Bulgarians took photographs of, dropped leaflets on, and later bombed the city using their airplanes.[40] The Bulgarians thus introduced Europe to the outrage of psychological bombardment and the horror of aerial bombardment. There is no evidence from Adrianople that the aerial bombardment had any effect.

By March food supplies in Adrianople, strained by the large number of refugees in the city, were running low.[41] The energies of the garrison and the population suffered. The Ottoman forces had reached the limits of their continued capacity to resist when the attack began.

The initial bombardment on 24 March surprised the defenders. In the dark early the next morning, the infantry moved forward. Attacks continued until noon, when they were suspended and the artillery bombardment renewed. At moonrise on the evening of 25 March, the Bulgarian attacks began again. At this point fearing a breakthrough, the Ottomans rushed reinforcements to the southern sector.[42] This was a major mistake because only one bridge from the city crossed the Maritsa River to the southern sector. Thus Sukru Pasha, the Ottoman commander, could not transfer his troops quickly to the eastern sector when he perceived the main thrust of the attack. The supplementary attacks began at 03.00 hours and the main assault on the eastern sector began at 04.00 hours on 26 March. They achieved immediate success, crossing the wire and making their way into the first line of defense. The exhausted, hungry, and demoralized defenders offered serious resistance only in the morning. Some Ottoman soldiers fought stubbornly. After the Bulgarians had crossed the primary defensive positions, however, the Ottoman soldiers in forts in the eastern sector ceased resistance. Some even met the Bulgarians with, "welcome."[43] Undoubtedly, the exhausted Ottomans were relieved that the siege ordeal was finally over. By 09.00 hours the Bulgarian cavalry had entered the city and captured the Ottoman commander. Sukru Pasha formally surrendered at 13.00 hours to General Ivanov.

After the conquest of Adrianople, relations between the Bulgarian and Serbian troops began to deteriorate further. Until this point, despite growing difficulties between the Bulgarian and Serbian governments over the division of Macedonia, relations between General Ivanov and the Serbian commander at Adrianople, General Stepa Stepanovich, had remained good.[44] After receiving the congratulations of General Stepanovich on the victory, General Ivanov graciously responded, "This action serves notice to the enemies of Slavs what can be attained by a sincere alliance among Slavic nations."[45] Nevertheless, a dispute, mainly in the Bulgarian and Serbian press, arose over the capture of Sukru Pasha. The Serbs claimed him as their prisoner, since he had surrendered in the western sector, where their troops had fought.[46] Bulgarian cavalry units had first found the Ottoman commander, and the Bulgarian general in overall command of the Adrianople operation had received the formal surrender. This incident emphasized the growing unease between the allies, even in the aftermath of their joint triumph.

Although infantry and cavalry units were the first to enter the city, the Bulgarian and Serbian artillery were the most important factors in maintaining the siege and in suppressing the Ottomans for the final assault. The French military attaché in Sofia, Major Martharel, reported, "The taking of Adrianople is all to the glory of the artillery, as a weapon."[47] This role of the artillery prefigured its importance in the First World War. Artillery would be the most important weapon used against established positions in that conflict.

News of the fall of Adrianople brought great joy and relief throughout Bulgaria. Ferdinand staged a triumphant entry into the city the next day. Pan-Slavic demonstrations occurred in St Petersburg in support of the Bulgarian victory. Somewhat patronizingly, the Russian War Minister General Vladimir A. Sukhomlinov told the Bulgarian minister in St Petersburg, Stefan S. Bobchev, "I congratulate you on the Adrianople victory not because you would not have obtained it, but because you took it by yourselves, and by storm. The Russian army is justifiably proud of the fraternal Bulgarian army."[48] With the capture of Adrianople, the Bulgarians appeared to have seized the prize and won the war.

The Bulgarian victory had a high price. In the final assault, they suffered 9,558 casualties, including 1,591 killed, out of a total force at Adrianople of 149,224.[49] The total Bulgarian casualties for the entire campaign amounted to 18,282.[50] Ottoman losses were over 15,000 casualties during siege plus 60,000 taken prisoner.[51] These were heavy losses incurred during an unnecessary endeavor.

The lack of provisions and the inability of the Ottoman army to relieve Adrianople insured that the city would fall to the besieging army. As the Bulgarian Chief of Staff, General Fichev, later wrote, "I think that if we had waited several more days, either the fortress would have surrendered, or the Turkish government would have been forced to conclude peace, because the situation was hopeless."[52] The Bulgarian troops had died to satisfy the élan of Bulgarian and Russian officers and inflate the national pride of Tsar Ferdinand and some Bulgarian politicians. Adrianople was the first fortified city in Europe in the twentieth century to fall to an assault. The final attack was conceived intelligently and executed skillfully but was ultimately unnecessary. After their defeat at Chataldzha, Adrianople assumed an exaggerated importance for the Bulgarians. It did not contain a significant Bulgarian population. Its strategic significance lay in its position astride the main route to Constantinople, a city the Bulgarians had small hope of capturing much less retain after the Chataldzha defeat. They should have accepted the peace terms offered by the Ottomans and then concentrated their political and military efforts to obtain their real national goal, Macedonia.

The Bulgarian capture of a large city with modern fortifications was a testament to the courage and initiative of the soldiers from a small country that lacked material and human resources. This effort, however, also signified a serious distortion of national priorities. The Bulgarians were dazzled by the prospect of the acquisition of a city that offered little real political or economic advantage. In the process they squandered men and resources that could have been much better utilized in securing their national aspiration in Macedonia.

Chataldzha

At the same time as the attack on Adrianople, General Savov ordered the Bulgarian 1st Army to attack at Chataldzha to retake the area lost to the Ottomans the previous month. This, in the words of General Fichev, began a new "bloody round" at Chataldzha.[53] The army and the tsar would have welcomed the opportunity to enter Constantinople. The 1st Army, however, succeeded only in returning to the positions it had evacuated the previous month. Fighting continued until 2 April. The final battle of Chataldzha cost the Bulgarians 2,821 casualties, including 456 dead.[54]

After the fall of Adrianople, the Russians feared that the Bulgarians might again attempt to take that prize that Russia had so long coveted, Constantinople. To avert that embarrassment, St Petersburg promised Sofia full support in the peace process. This was welcome reassurance for the Bulgarian government. It meant that Russia would back Bulgaria's claims to all of Macedonia, including the "disputed zone," and the disputes with Greece and Romania. The Bulgarians then definitely decided against attempting to force the Chataldzha positions.[55] Now they could make peace with the Ottomans and turn their energies to the looming disputes with Greece and Serbia over the partition of Macedonia.

The Ottomans again had exhausted their resources in the latest "round" of fighting. On 7 April, they proposed an armistice. The Bulgarians quickly agreed. At Chataldzha on 15 April, the Bulgarians represented by General Stefan Toshev and the Ottomans represented by Ziya Pasha concluded their second armistice of the war. This truce was valid only for the Bulgarians and the Ottomans. The other Balkan allies were not involved. It would remain in place until the signing of the Treaty of London on 30 May. The fighting in Thrace was over. This afforded the Bulgarians only a slight advantage because they still had to maintain the bulk of their army at Chataldzha confronting the Ottomans until the conclusion of a formal peace. While negotiations for that peace continued in London, the Sofia government anxiously regarded the situation in Macedonia as its relations with its allies deteriorated.

Scutari

The position of the Montenegrins outside Scutari had not appreciably improved during the armistice. Their soldiers remained in poor shelters with scant provisions. Only a trickle of Montenegrins returning from the United States and elsewhere, and South Slavic volunteers from the Habsburg Empire supplemented their forces. During the armistice, they continued to shell Scutari and probe its defenses sporadically.

The Ottomans used the armistice to rest and reprovision their forces. They did what they could to strengthen their defensive positions on Bardanjolt and several other places. They had sortied several times in December to gather food from the countryside after the armistice. On 31 January, the defenders of Scutari acquired a new leader because assassins had shot the able commander Hasan Riza Bey the previous evening. The former second in command, Esad Pasha Toptani, had assumed command. The ambitious Esad Pasha Toptani, who aspired to leadership of the new Albanian state, had apparently instigated his commander's murder.

With the renewal of fighting, King Nikola decided to mount a full-scale attack. Preliminary Montenegrin artillery firing on Ottoman positions on

Bardanjolt began on 6 February. At dawn on 7 February, the Zeta Division again assaulted the Ottoman positions on Bardanjolt east of Scutari. The Coastal Division west of Scutari, together with the Serbian coastal units south of the town, were to provide diversionary attacks. King Nikola's desire to provide the Crown Prince with a military victory seems to have been a major reason for the primary role of the Zeta Division in the attack. This was the most massive attack on Scutari of the entire war. A furious onslaught by the Montenegrins finally got them through the wire on Bardanjolt. They proceeded to drive the Ottomans off the fortified hill and toward the town. Then, however, Esad Pasha Toptani, rallied his troops to counterattack and retake the fortified hill. On 9 February, after three days of fighting, the Montenegrins and Serbs abandoned their attempt to break into Scutari.

Losses were heavy on both sides. Some Montenegrins fell victim to Serbian artillery fire. The Ottomans lost 1,338 men, and the Montenegrins sustained 4,000 casualties. Meanwhile, the diversionary Montenegrin attack on Tarabosh also failed and another 1,500 soldiers were lost. There, too, the Ottomans mounted a counterattack that limited the advance of the besieger. A Montenegrin volunteer recently returned from the United States described the Ottoman counterattack on Tarabosh, "A short jump and crawl brought the Turks higher up from us, so close that we sprayed them with a rapid volley. Soon they had come right up to us. We heard how they heckled us in Turkish and Serbian, clearly and loudly, with various insults and threats."[56] Likewise, the diversionary Serbian efforts to take Brdica, the fortified hill south of the town stalled, at the cost of 1,800 Serbian casualties.[57]

Although this attack was much better conceived and organized than previous Montenegrin efforts, the besiegers still lacked the artillery and the number of troops to give them a decisive advantage against the defenders of Scutari. This was a major failure for the Montengrins and Serbs. It cost them more casualties than had the great Serbian victory at Kumanovo.

After the failure of the February assault, the Montenegrins at Scutari found themselves in a position not unlike that of the Bulgarians at Adrianople. They lacked the military strength to overwhelm Ottoman defenders, but they lacked the political resolve to withdraw. As the Bulgarians had done before them, the Montenegrins turned to their Serbian allies for further help. On 12 February 1913, King Nikola made a formal request for additional aid.[58] The Serbs responded loyally, sending around 30,000 troops under the command of General Peter Bojovich and seventy-two artillery pieces of various sizes to Scutari. The Serbs also sent a squadron of four airplanes to support the siege. Such were the difficulties of moving overland that the Serbs sent their men and equipment by rail to Salonika. The Greeks transported all these troops and equipment from Salonika to San Giovanni di Medua (Serbian, Medov). The first ship arrived there on 18 March. When the soldiers began to disembark, the elusive Ottoman light cruiser *Hamidiye* sailed into the harbor and opened fire. Two mountain guns not yet unloaded from one of the Greek transports drove off the Ottoman warship. The Serbs had seventy-seven soldiers killed and many more wounded.[59] The next day the *Hamidiye* attacked the harbor at Durres and sank several merchant ships.

The Serbian reinforcements came with a price. General Bojovich assumed command of the Scutari operations. This was a further humiliation for the Montenegrins. They had no choice but to accept Serbian leadership.

While the Montenegrins and Ottomans were using military force to decide the ownership of Scutari, the ambassadors of the Great Powers in London were wrangling over the same issue. The Austro-Hungarians wanted Scutari for the new Albanian state, but the Russians sought to obtain it for Montenegro. On 14 February, the Russians seemed prepared to acknowledge that Scutari would become Albanian.[60] On 20 March, in response to this Russian renunciation, the Austrians conceded the Kosovo market town of Djakova to Serbia. Berchtold instructed his minister in London,

> I have decided to renounce the city of Djakova for Albania. Obviously our cooperation in this is tied to the promises of the other (Great Power) cabinets that the north and northeastern frontiers of Albania and also the Bojana River and the shore of Lake Scutari area settled according to our well known desires. Also the representatives of the six Great Powers in Belgrade and Cetinje must immediately demand and enforce the quickest possible evacuation by Serbia and Montenegro of regions assigned to Albania.[61]

This assured the inclusion of Scutari in Albania, and set up a confrontation with Montenegro and Serbia.

The Great Powers applied diplomatic pressure to stop the governments in Athens and Belgrade helping the Montenegrins.[62] Because of the determination of the Great Powers and the strong admonitions of Russia, the Serbs indicated that they would abide by the decision of the Ambassadors Conference. The Serbs were in a difficult situation. They could not afford to abandon their Montenegrin allies in this time of crisis. That could have a negative effect on the nationalist-minded populations of both states. On the other hand, the growing enmity between Bulgaria and Serbia over the division of Macedonia forced the Serbs to allocate their limited resources to the coming struggle there. They had a more direct interest in a Serbian Macedonia than a Montenegrin Scutari. Pashich summarized Serbian policy toward Montenegro succinctly, if not candidly, "We desire nothing more eagerly than a rapid conclusion of peace so that we will not be obligated to make further sacrifices for our allies."[63]

On 28 March the Great Powers presented a collective in Cetinje, and the next day in Belgrade, demanding an end to the siege[64]. The Montenegrins answered the Great Powers with one more assault on Scutari. This began with an artillery barrage on 30 March. The next day the Montenegrin–Serbian force, now under Serbian command, attempted another general attack, with the main thrust on the Tarabosh positions. The Serbian command brought no better results. The attack of 31 March also failed to breach the main Ottoman defenses. This was the last major attempt to attack the Scutari defenses.

In response to this provocation, a fleet made up of ships from five of the Great Powers sailed to the Adriatic to impose a blockade of Montenegro. The fleet under the command of the British admiral Sir Cecil Burney arrived off the coast of Montenegro to carry out the mandate of their governments on 2 April. The Russians, because of feelings of Slavic solidarity with Montenegro, refrained from participating in the blockade. The fleet mounted a "naval demonstration" sailing back and forth off the meager coast of Montenegro. The exact purpose of this demonstration was not clear.

Nevertheless, the Serbs used the naval demonstration as a means to extricate themselves from Scutari. On 2 April, the same day the Great Power fleet appeared off the Albanian and Montenegrin coasts, Pashich told the Serbian high command, "The fate of Scutari is decided."[65] Only on 10 April, however, did they begin to withdraw their troops, leaving behind their artillery for the Montenegrins to use. This five-day gap indicates that the Serbian military was not as eager to comply with the demands of the Great Powers as was the Serbian government.

The Great Power fleet expanded its efforts to impose a naval blockade of the Adriatic coast from the mouth of the Drin River to Durazzo. Nevertheless, the Montenegrins, now without the aid of their Serbian allies, continued their siege. Austro-Hungarian foreign minister Berchtold suggested that it was time to land troops to deal with the Montenegrin defiance of the Great Powers.[66]

After three days of negotiations, Esad Pasha Toptani surrendered to the Montenegrins on 22 April. The defenders were exhausted and running out of food and ammunition. Thirty to forty people died every day.[67] The Ottoman troops were permitted to leave the city with their weapons, except for large artillery. This was a real scoundrels' bargain. King Nikola's army marched into Scutari without firing a shot, in defiance of the Great Powers. In return, Esad Pasha obtained Montenegrin recognition and financial support for his efforts to gain the Albanian throne.[68] Both the Montenegrin and Serbian populations greeted the news of the surrender of Scutari with joy and relief. The realization that further fighting might ensue dampened some of their celebrations however.

After Montenegrin troops entered Scutari on 24 April, the Austro-Hungarians prepared to take coercive action against Montenegro and, possibly, also Serbia, either together with the other Great Powers or without them.[69] The Imperial and Royal army began preparations for war. Scutari was vital for the survival of the new Albanian state. Albania was crucial for sustaining Austro-Hungarian interests in the Balkans. For the second time in the past six months, a Balkan event had brought Austria–Hungary to the brink of war against a Serbian state.

Before the Austro-Hungarians could act, King Nikola, recognizing that he could not retain Scutari in the face of military action from the Great Powers, capitulated. He agreed to surrender Scutari on 5 May. The Montenegrins had occupied the city for less than two weeks. Nine days later a detachment from the Great Power fleet marched into Scutari and assumed control.

Conclusion

The renewed effort to win the war demonstrated the energy and even the imagination of the Young Turk government, but it yielded only additional defeat. All three besieged cities capitulated. By the end of April 1913 Ottoman Europe was reduced to the Gallipoli Peninsula and the tiny area behind the Chataldzha lines.

The Greeks took Janina at relatively little cost to themselves. They demonstrated that they did possess a competent military, capable of functioning in difficult conditions. They also acquired a location that guaranteed them control of an Ionian hinterland stretching from the Gulf of Arta to Corfu. The real losers here were not the Ottomans, but the Albanians. Janina, a predominantly Albanian town, could have secured the southern end of the new state in the same way that Scutari would anchor the north.

The other Balkan victors did not benefit greatly from the Ottoman defeat. The Bulgarians had invested a tremendous effort in the reduction of Adrianople. They achieved a great military victory there. For most Bulgarians, however, Adrianople was secondary to Macedonia. The additional effort to take Adrianople had further stressed an already exhausted Bulgarian military and distracted the Bulgarians from the growing conflict to the west. While the Bulgarians were fighting in Thrace, the Greeks and Serbs were preparing defensive positions to maintain their holds on Macedonia. The Bulgarians might well have applied the men, material, and time utilized to gain Adrianople toward securing Macedonia.

The Montenegrins suffered two defeats at Scutari. With their failure to take the town by military means, they forfeited any claims to predominance in their quest for leadership of the Serbian national cause. By their acceptance of Serbian assistance, they demonstrated their military failure. Their evacuation of Scutari, after the expenditure of so many lives and so much material, yielded the Montenegrins nothing. The money King Nikola received as a bribe/loan hardly compensated for his loss of dignity and prestige.

The end of fighting in the First Balkan War after prolonged sieges left all the participants exhausted. It produced only a brief intermission in the cycle of Balkan wars. Less than two months after Montenegro evacuated Scutari, the Balkan League would collapse in another round of bitter combat.

The end of the fighting also found Austria–Hungary and the other Great Powers more engaged than ever in the Balkans. For the second time in less than six months the Dual Monarchy had threatened war against a Balkan state. Only the concerted action of the other Great Powers, specifically their willingness to send or acquiesce in a joint military force to the Balkans, prevented that war. Such willingness was frail armor indeed against the possibility of Austro-Hungarian intervention in the Balkans.

6

THE INTERBELLUM

The armistice at Chataldzha on 15 April and the surrender of Scutari to the Montenegrins on 22 April ended the fighting of the First Balkan War. Diplomatic activity among the Great Powers and among the Balkan allies intensified. At the same time, the implosion of the Balkan League accelerated. By mid-May, the situation of Bulgaria had become desperate. Pressured by their erstwhile allies and Romania, lacking a final peace with the Ottomans, and increasingly insecure about Russian patronage, the Bulgarians sought a resolution of their problems that would secure Macedonia for themselves.

St Petersburg Ambassadors Conference

The St Petersburg Ambassadors Conference met at the end of March 1913 with the intention of resolving the Romanian–Bulgarian dispute. It was an adjunct to the London Ambassadors Conference, intended primarily to preserve Russian interests in Bulgaria while extending those same interests to Romania. The St Petersburg government ardently sought the detachment of Bucharest from the Triple Alliance. This was an ambitious undertaking that proved beyond the capabilities of Russian diplomacy. At the same time, the Triple Alliance powers endeavored to maintain Romanian loyalty at the expense of pro-Russian Bulgaria. This meant that Bulgaria would have to pay the price for the interests of the Great Powers.

On 8 May, the St Petersburg Ambassadors Conference rendered a decision in the Bulgaro-Romanian dispute that assigned the Bulgarian Danubian port of Silistra to Romania. This was a compromise between the Romanian demands for southern Dobrudzha and the Bulgarian refusal to accept any meaningful cession of its territory. Naturally this decision antagonized both sides. The Romanians sought further concessions from Bulgaria in southern Dobrudzha. At the same time, the loss of this ethnically Bulgarian town outraged the Sofia government. The duplicitous Russian policy also made the Bulgarians, who relied on Russia to mediate the growing dispute with Serbia, uncertain about the reliability of the power they depended upon to protect their interests. If Russia would not preserve the territorial integrity of Bulgaria itself, could the Bulgarians depend upon Russian guarantees for the March 1912 treaty and Bulgarian Macedonia?

Greek–Serbian alliance

In the meantime, the situation between Bulgaria and the erstwhile allies continued to deteriorate. The Bulgarian–Greek dispute over southern Macedonia continued to fester. The major obstacle remained Salonika. Back in February 1913, Prime Minster Venizelos had sojourned in Sofia on his way home from the London conference. Then, he had conceded all southeastern Macedonia, including the towns of Drama, Kavala, and Seres, to Bulgaria, but insisted on retaining Salonika for Greece.[1] The Bulgarian government were divided on the issue, but refused to surrender claims to the major port of Macedonia. Here the Bulgarians missed another opportunity to achieve a settlement with Greece and avoid a Greco-Serbian alliance directed against them. Had they abandoned their pretensions to Salonika at this point, they might have been in a much better position to realize their aspirations in Macedonia, which were increasingly threatened by Serbia. A sated Greece would have been much less likely to ally with Serbia against Bulgaria.

Tensions between the Bulgarians and Greeks had continued to grow throughout the winter of 1913. A report on the anti-Bulgarian activities of the Greek army in northern Macedonia caused great outrage in Sofia.[2] By spring the Bulgarians and Greeks had come to blows. Clashes between Bulgarian and Greek forces around the town of Nigrita northeast of Salonika in March resulted in heavy Bulgarian casualties.[3] The confluence of Greek and Serbian interests in Macedonia at the expense of the Bulgarians became obvious. At the beginning of March, Greek and Serbian officers in Salonika had demonstrated provocatively in the streets, crossing their swords and wearing each other's hats shouting, "Long live Serbo-Greek brotherhood. Long live Greece. Long live Serbia. Long live true allies."[4] Tsar Ferdinand, in mid-March 1913, had warned his son Crown Prince Boris that the Greeks and Serbs had concluded an alliance and that war with Greece and Serbia was imminent. "The situation is deplorable," the tsar asserted.[5] Ferdinand's alert about the alliance was premature. His instincts, however, were correct.

On 18 March, a deranged Greek assassinated King George of Greece in Salonika. This added another emotional dimension to the Bulgarian–Greek dispute over control of the city. In April, fighting between Bulgarian and Greek troops erupted again northeast of Salonika. Once more casualties resulted on both sides.[6] The Bulgarians and Greeks agreed to form a joint commission to investigate these incidents. This commission did little to calm the situation. The reciprocal hostility persisted.

Meanwhile, in Macedonia the Greeks and Serbs continued to consolidate their political and military positions. Further reports of anti-Bulgarian activities by Serbian officials and soldiers in Macedonia reached Sofia in mid-April.[7] At the same time, the Bulgarian military reported that the Greek and Serbian forces in Macedonia had taken positions to wage war against Bulgaria.[8] The Greek navy had transported to Salonika some of the Serbian troops returning from Scutari. The result was that some in Sofia, including Tsar Ferdinand himself, escalated into a state of near panic. Ferdinand, fearing that "savage hordes" would pillage the Bulgarian capital, ordered the removal of works of art, his personal archives, and the foreign ministry.[9] The Bulgarians now realized that they would likely have to fight again for their Macedonian desiderata.

Another issue that brought the Greeks and Serbs together was Albania. The London Ambassadors Conference had in principle established an independent Albanian state. This conflicted with the interests of both Athens and Belgrade. They were eager to avoid any connection between an Albania supported by the Great Powers and an enlarged Bulgaria. In April 1913, Nikola Pashich insisted to St Petersburg that, "The Serbian government will not allow Bulgaria to extend between Serbia and Greece and to connect with Albania, even if it loses the sympathy of the whole world."[10] At the same time, he indicated that Serbia was prepared to go to war if the Great Powers did not somehow limit Bulgarian Macedonia to the right (east) bank of the Vardar River.[11] This was an explicit admission that the Serbs did not intend to adhere to the March 1912 agreement. At this point the Russian foreign office might well have intervened to protect its interests in the Balkans. Sazonov should have taken direct steps to resolve the Bulgarian–Serbian dispute. In particular, he should have invoked the arbitration clause of the March 1912 treaty and indicated that the Russian tsar was prepared to assume his obligations under the treaty. This could have kept the dispute within the bounds of Russian control, or at least Russian influence. Instead, the Russian foreign office attempted to ignore the looming collapse of the Balkan League.

With the Serbian problem becoming pronounced, the Sofia government attempted to resolve its dispute with Greece. Prime Minster Geshov abandoned the principle of proportionality in the conflict with Greece and attempted to persuade his government to accept the idea of arbitration. He had some reason to expect success. The Greek prime minister, Venizelos, himself favored a peaceful settlement to the dispute.[12] Other members of the Bulgarian government, however, led by Stoyan Danev, refused to consider arbitration. They were determined to use force to assert Bulgarian claims, especially to Salonika. This left the Sofia government without anything to offer Athens. With the situation increasingly appearing hopeless, fighting again erupted between the Bulgarians and Greeks in the region east of the Struma River at the end of May. This resulted in fifty Bulgarian casualties and the loss of Bulgarian positions around Angista.[13]

At the same time, Geshov sought a peaceful settlement to the dispute with Serbia. This was the critical dispute for Bulgaria. Possession of the greater part of Macedonia, which the Bulgarians had regarded as the amputated third of their country since the Treaty of San Stefano, depended upon the resolution of this issue. If they settled their dispute with Serbia, the Bulgarians could turn their attention to the conflict with the Greeks. In this, they were confident of having their way. Bulgaria was larger than Greece, after all. The Bulgarian military was more powerful than that of Greece. Furthermore, Greece lacked a clear patron among the Great Powers.

On 25 April the Sofia government decided to request formally Russian arbitration under the terms of the 1912 treaty.[14] The Bulgarians regarded Macedonia as theirs. No further concessions were possible after the Bulgarians had agreed to a "disputed zone" in northern Macedonia to obtain the 1912 treaty. In spite of the St Petersburg conference, which awarded Silistra to the Romanians, many Bulgarians still clung to their 'special relationship' with Russia. They could not believe that Russia would liberate the country from the Ottomans only to turn over one-third to Serbia.

The Russians were not eager to assume this role and attempted to evade the Bulgarian request. The Russian foreign minister, Sergei Sazonov, insisted at the beginning of May that the arbitration include the Greeks, a stipulation he knew Danev had already rejected.[15] St Petersburg realized that arbitration of the Serbo-Bulgarian dispute would be a difficult and thankless job that could likely cost Russia the loyalty of at least one Balkan Slavic state.

On 5 May 1913, the Greeks and Serbs finally formalized their relationship. Conversations had begun as early as March.[16] Venizelos argued to the cabinet that because of the ongoing clashes with the Bulgarians a state of war already existed.[17] Clearly, Greece could not fight the much larger and stronger Bulgaria alone. Together with Serbia, however, the Greeks could secure not only the territories in Macedonia that they had already conquered but also insure that their neighbor to the north would not dominate the Balkan Peninsula.

The agreement provided for a common frontier in Macedonia west of the Vardar River and for diplomatic and military support against Bulgaria if the new frontier was unacceptable to Sofia.[18] The Greeks and Serbs essentially divided Macedonia between them. They signed a military convention on 14 May, and a formal alliance agreement ensued on 1 June 1913 with the signing of the Treaty of Salonika, the day after the conclusion of the Treaty of London ending the Balkan War.[19] These agreements also provided for the division of Albania into Greek and Serbian spheres of influence, generally along the Semeni River. The opposition of the Austro-Hungarians the previous autumn to a Serbian presence in northern Albania and on the Adriatic was no deterrent to Serbian aspirations. The Serbs were on a course of conflict with Austria–Hungary.

In April both Athens and Belgrade approached Bucharest separately. The Romanians refused to commit themselves. They wanted to utilize events to their best advantage, without hindrances or obligations.[20] The Romanians thought of themselves as the arbitrators of the Balkans. At this point the position of Russia was not clear. The government in Bucharest could not afford to offend its powerful neighbor. Nevertheless, Romanian continuity of interests with the Greeks and Serbs was clear. At the same time, both the Greeks and the Serbs contacted the Ottomans with the intention of establishing some basis for mutual advantage against Bulgaria.[21] Here again no specific agreements resulted, but intentions and goals were obvious for all parties. Because the Montenegrins were obliged to the Serbs for help at Scutari, and because of their hopes of obtaining a sizeable portion of the Sandjak of Novi Pazar and their isolation they were committed to the Serbian–Greek position.

On 26 May, the Serbs renewed their demands for a formal revision of the March 1912 Treaty.[22] The Bulgarians refused to consider any revision.[23] According to the treaty, they had agreed to allow Russia to adjudicate upon northwestern Macedonia. Now they faced having to relinquish even more territory. Macedonia was, after all, the main reason that Bulgaria had gone to war and sacrificed so many soldiers and so much material. Increasingly the Bulgarians believed that if Russia would not assume responsibilities according to the March 1912 Treaty as arbitrator, then Bulgaria must fight another round for Macedonia.

Treaty of London

Time now became a critical issue for the Bulgarians. They needed a quick conclusion of the formal peace talks in London so that they could transfer their army from Thrace, where it still confronted the Ottomans at Gallipoli and Chataldzha, to Macedonia, where it could enforce Bulgarian claims. Both the Greeks and the Serbs intentionally delayed the signing of the peace treaty.[24] This provided them with the opportunity to further consolidate their defensive positions. Finally, pressure from the Great Powers on the Greeks and the Serbs finally resulted in the signing of the Treaty of London on 30 May 1913.

The Treaty of London brought a formal end to the war between the Balkan allies and the Ottoman Empire. The Ottomans ceded all lands east of a straight line drawn across eastern Thrace from the Aegean port of Enos (Turkish, Enez) to the Black Sea port of Midia (Turkish, Midye). Unimpeded by any topographical characteristics, the Enos–Midia line gave Bulgaria and the Ottoman Empire a virtually indefensible frontier in Thrace. This was to the great disadvantage of the Ottomans. Now shorn of the fortifications at Adrianople and at Lozengrad, the Ottomans had to rely solely on the Chataldzha lines to protect Constantinople.

The Ottomans also renounced claims to Crete and the Aegean Islands. The Treaty of London granted the Great Powers the right to determine the question of the Ottoman Aegean islands and Albanian issues, including borders.[25] The island issue essentially meant that all Ottoman Aegean islands went to Greece, except for Tenedos and Imbros, which the Ottomans retained to facilitate the defense of the straits.

The Albanian problem was more complicated. The Treaty of London was a triumph for the Austrians and the Italians, and a setback for Russia. It clearly recognized the new Albanian state and left to the Great Powers the right to define its borders and organize its government. The establishment of an Albania supported by the Great Powers by no means created a state including all the Albanian population of the western Balkans. Even Albania's staunchest defender at the London Ambassadors Conference, Austria–Hungary, did not propose the inclusion of Kosovo in the new state. Not until August of 1913 did the conference finally determine Albanian frontiers. These excluded many Albanians.

The very existence of an Albanian state, however, did frustrate the interests of Greece and Serbia. This made the securing of compensation in Macedonia even more necessary for them. The treaty left the distribution of Ottoman Europe with the exception of Albania to the Balkan allies. This insured Russian involvement in the growing dispute between Bulgaria and Serbia. The Russians could only lose by exercising their arbitration powers. In attempting to settle the dispute they inevitably would alienate either Bulgaria or Serbia, and in doing so weaken the Russian position in the Balkans.

The signing of the Treaty of London did bestow one important advantage on the Bulgarians. It ended the war with the Ottomans. This enabled them to complete the transfer of their army from the Gallipoli and Chataldzha fronts in Thrace to Macedonia. They could now confront their allies with their total strength and enforce their claims to Macedonia. The sanction of the Great Powers for the treaty appeared to guarantee the new border with the Ottoman Empire.

By the time of the signing of the Treaty of London, Geshov had resigned. The Balkan League he had helped create was in ruins. His attempts at accommodation had failed. Before leaving office, he met with Pashich at Tsaribrod on the Bulgaro-Serbian frontier on 1 June 1913 in a final attempt to resolve the Macedonian problem. This meeting accomplished nothing. After returning to Belgrade, Pashich was certain that war would ensue.[26]

Explosion

After a brief period of political disorder, a new government headed by the pro-Russian hard-liner Stoyan Danev assumed office in Sofia on 15 June. Danev later explained his intentions,

> I hoped I could compel the Serbs to accept the arbitration agreement. I would suffer the consequences for what might happen if they snipped

off part of Macedonia. I did not intent to yield, because we had signed the agreement of 1912.²⁷

Conflict appeared very close. Danev's strong pro-Russian views meant that the Sofia government still depended upon Russia to resolve the conflict with the Serbs.

The attitude of the Russians now became critical. They had been slow to accept their responsibility of arbitration under the conditions of the treaty of March 1912. Whatever the Russian tsar decided, he would antagonize one of the Balkan states. Increasingly, the attitude of the Serbs exasperated them. The Serbian military was pressing the government for war against Bulgaria.²⁸ Foreign Minister Sazonov warned the Serbs that the Bulgarians would "conquer!!!" them.²⁹ The weakening of Serbia would only benefit Russia's Austro-Hungarian adversary.

Sazonov also became frustrated with the attitude of Danev and the Bulgarians. The Bulgarian pretensions to Constantinople had disconcerted St Petersburg since the previous November. The concept of Bulgarian troops in the city so long coveted by Russia was unthinkable.

Another issue had developed to complicate relations between St Petersburg and Sofia. A major problem for the Bulgarians had arisen in their army. Great discontent had emerged in the ranks.³⁰ The soldiers, who were mostly peasants, had been at arms since September 1912. Now they were exhausted and wanted to go home. The American military attaché in Sofia, Lieutenant Miles, reported,

> The discontent in the Bulgarian Army is much fanned by political discussions. All Bulgarians are politicians, and the soldiers are keen students of the negotiations that have taken place with Servia, Greece and Russia. They also hold strong opinions as to whether the interests of the country have been well served by its government or the reverse. This spirit tends no doubt to make discipline difficult to maintain amongst the many who blame the government for the present situation. Discontent will, however, cease to exist when the men are called upon to fight against Servia and Greece, as it does not diminish their strong patriotic feelings.³¹

Lieutenant Miles's assessment was probably a little optimistic. The discontent in the Bulgarian army undoubtedly had consequences. One Bulgarian officer later wrote that on the eve of the interallied war, "The spirit of the soldiers was, in general, considerably reduced and not answerable to the theoretical operative calculations of the high command."³² The army had to either see action soon or demobilize. On 16 June, the army commander, General Mihail Savov, urged the government to either fight or disperse the army.³³ By this time, the Bulgarian military clearly foresaw a military solution to the problem of Macedonia.[34] In spite of the heavy loses in men and material it had sustained in the war against the Ottoman Empire, the leadership of the Bulgarian army was confident it could defeat the Greeks and Serbs.

Danev seemed to agree. On 21 June, he told the Bulgarian Ministerial Council,

> the Serbs do not accept joint occupation and a condominium (in Macedonia), or if they do not state that they accept arbitration on the basis of the convention, we must declare war.[35]

Danev agreed to travel to St Petersburg if the Russians would announce their decision in seven days. Sazonov greatly resented Danev's attempt to impose a time limit. On 24 June he responded in a fit of pique, stating, "you are free. Do not expect anything from us and forget the existence of any of our agreements from 1902 until the present."[36] To Sofia this meant that Sazonov had definitely forsworn the Russo-Bulgarian treaty of 1902, which the Bulgarian government regarded as the legal basis for Russian support for Bulgaria, not only in the case of the March 1912 Treaty but also against Romanian aggression.[37] Several days later Sazonov relented, and Danev and Pashich prepared to travel to St Petersburg to participate in the arbitration process. The fortuitously named Bulgarian gunboat *Nadezhda* (Hope) waited in the harbor at Varna to carry Danev across the Black Sea.

The attitude of Russia was critical. In June 1913 the situation they had sought to avoid had become inescapable. They would have to arbitrate the March 1912 treaty. Obviously, in doing so, they would alienate one side or the other. The trick was not to alienate both sides at once. The Russians further muddled the issue by their attempt to woo Romania away from the Triple Alliance. If the Russians did not arbitrate the Bulgaro-Serbian dispute, they defaulted to the Serbs, who were already in possession of the disputed territory. This had enormous implications. It meant that, given the likelihood of Romanian intervention, Serbia would triumph in the pending armed conflict. It also meant that Russia, having failed to support Bulgaria, would lose that relatively secure position in the Balkans. This would leave Russia, after the Second Balkan War, with a Balkan ally only in Serbia, remote from Russia's traditional goals in the Straits and Constantinople. Serbia had little value in furthering those goals. The only advantage Serbia imparted to Russia was a means of antagonizing Austria–Hungary. The conditions for the outbreak of general fighting in July 1914 were set in June 1913.

The Danev government could not imagine that Russia would fail to support Bulgaria. Russia had fought to free Bulgaria from Ottoman rule in the Russo-Turkish War of 1877–8. Many Bulgarians had been educated in Russia. Bulgaria and Russia had signed a military convention in 1902 and had discussed its renewal in 1909 and 1911. Russia had guaranteed the March

1912 treaty with Serbia. Finally, Russia had provided Bulgaria with substantial material aid during the fighting against the Ottomans, including ammunition, military clothing, food, and airplanes.[38]

Before Danev could depart, however, the situation exploded. For the previous few days Bulgarian and Serbian troops facing each other in Macedonia had provoked each other by carrying out raids and sniper attacks.[39] On the night of 29–30 June, General Savov, on the authority of Tsar Ferdinand, ordered the Bulgarian 4th Army to attack Serbian positions in Macedonia.[40] The order read in part,

> So that we do not ignore the Serbian attacks, which would reflect badly on our army's morale, and to press the enemy further, I am ordering you to attack the enemy by the most energetic means along the entire line, without completely disclosing your strength and without becoming involved in a prolonged battle.[41]

The 2nd Army received similar orders to act against the Greeks.[42] Savov's orders for the attacks indicated limited objectives and a concern for troop morale. Fear of assassination by Macedonian organizations also motivated Ferdinand to approve the order.[43] Undoubtedly, Savov persuaded Ferdinand about the necessity of the order, rather than the other way around.

The government in Sofia was not directly involved in this order. Danev denied knowing of it[44]. It cannot, however, have come as a complete surprise to Danev and the government in Sofia. His own statements were bellicose and contributed to the tensions. Although the military did not act under Danev's orders, they certainly acted in concordance with his statements. The best judgement on this puzzling issue came from the noted historian of the Balkan Wars, E. C. Helmreich, who wrote,

> The Bulgarian attack of June 29/30 is explicable only as part of a policy of arbitration and not as one directly opposed to it. Military action was thus intended as a means of strengthening Bulgarian's position in the settlement which was to come through the mediation of Russia.[45]

Only those Bulgarian armies in Macedonia, the 2nd and 4th, received orders to act. The others remained quiet. Even so, given the extreme tension and bellicosity that existed on both sides, the Bulgarian idea of fighting to improve a negotiating position was, at best, ill-advised.

When he learned of the fighting in Macedonia, Danev made frantic efforts to stop it. He sent messages to Athens and Belgrade indicating Bulgaria's peaceful intentions.[46] The Greeks and Serbs did not respond. They had no confidence in the good faith of the Bulgarian government.[47] The attacks of 29–30 June gave them an excellent opportunity to present themselves to the Great Powers as the victims of Bulgarian aggression. This would prove a great advantage in the resolution of the ownership of Macedonia. The Greeks and Serbs certainly bear no blame for using this considerable boon bestowed upon them by Bulgarian bungling.

Conclusion

By the spring of 1913 antagonisms among the Balkan allies had reached a flash point. Any incident could set off an explosion. As one commentator observed, the general Greek view was,

> war is bound to come: better now while we are in a state of warlike preparedness and before normal lives and occupations are resumed than in a year or two's time when we shall have to begin, as it were, all over again.[48]

The same was true for Bulgaria and Serbia. Bulgaria, Greece, or Serbia could have provided the spark. Their militaries were intent on action. Their politicians were not entirely in control of the diplomatic or military situation. Emotion prevailed over reason. In addition, Romania and the Ottoman Empire waited expectantly for the opportunity to gain advantage from the situation.

Although convinced of the righteousness of their cause and the strength of their armies, the Bulgarians were increasingly isolated militarily and diplomatically. Their Russian liberator and protector seemed to abandon them. Their soldiers, exhausted from their strenuous efforts in the war against the Ottomans, were becoming restive. These circumstances led them to take desperate action and to catastrophe.

Had the Bulgarians been willing to abandon their claims to most of Macedonia at this point, they still would have emerged from the Balkan War with a major territorial increase. Bulgaria would have gained a strong hold on the Aegean Sea, extending from the mouth of the Struma River to the Gallipoli Peninsula. In addition, they would have gained most of eastern Thrace and would retain a strategic threat to Constantinople. Even with these acquisitions, Bulgaria would have been the dominant power in southeastern Europe and a valuable asset to either of the alliance systems of the Great Powers.

Russia the one power that might have directed these circumstances toward a peaceful resolution had neither the strength, the resolve, nor the inclination to do so. Because of the Russian failure to regulate relations in this area so vital to its own interests, the strong Russian position in the Balkans based on a Bulgarian-led Balkan League collapsed. A little over a year later, Balkan events would again escape the weak bonds of Russian control. This time the consequences would expand far beyond the Balkan Peninsula and involve much of the globe.

7

INTERALLIED WAR

The Bulgarian attack on Serbian positions on the night of 29–30 June unleashed the hostilities which had been escalating since the previous autumn. The Bulgarians, Greeks, and Serbs all perceived war as the means to resolve their disputes. Essentially, all three were fighting for Macedonia. The war presented the Bulgarians with an opportunity to reverse the Serbian alliance of 1912 and acquire all Macedonia. A greater Bulgaria could dominate the Balkans. The Greeks and Serbs not only faced the prospect of dividing the rich region between themselves, but also of preventing Bulgarian hegemony. Their alliance agreements in the spring of 1913 provided for northern Macedonia, including Skoplje, to remain with Serbia and southern Macedonia, including Salonika, to stay with Greece. After the fighting began, the Romanians seized the opportunity to resolve their dispute with Bulgaria over Dobrudzha, and the Ottomans used the occasion to take back Adrianople.

Military preparations

The Serbs and Greeks held the advantage militarily. In the war with the Ottomans, they had faced comparatively weak forces and had taken relatively light casualties. Also the fighting in Macedonia and Albania, except around the two besieged Albanian cities of Janina and Scutari, had been of short duration. For the Serbs, the fighting was over after the Battle of Bitola, although they did lend troops to their Bulgarian and Montenegrin allies. For the Greeks, the fighting had ended with the fall of Janina in March 1913. This time had enabled the Greeks and Serbs to construct strong defensive positions in Macedonia. The Bulgarian forces, depleted from the heavy fighting in Thrace and exhausted from standing at arms over nine months since the previous autumn, would have to attack to gain their goal of Macedonia.

The Bulgarians did possess some advantages of their own. They controlled internal lines of communication and supply. A single language and a unified command also aided the Bulgarians. Although the Greek and Serbian commands remained in contact with each other, they generally operated independently of each other and made little effort to coordinate their actions. In addition, a sense of real outrage over what the Bulgarians perceived as their allies' betrayal over the Macedonian issue provided strong motivation for some. Not all Bulgarian soldiers shared this view however. One junior officer serving in the 1st Army recorded in his diary that both officers and men lacked enthusiasm for further fighting over Macedonia. He overheard some arguing regarding Macedonia, "Let's divide the damn thing, since they do not want to give it all to us."[1]

On the eve of the outbreak of the war, Bulgaria had five armies along a front extending from the Danube River to the Aegean Sea, a front 300 miles long. They had added to their depleted forces by drafting young men aged 20–26 years living in the newly occupied territories in Thrace and Macedonia. This enabled the Bulgarians to field a total of 360,000 troops.[2] The Bulgarian forces were arrayed with the 1st Army, under General Kutinchev, from Vidin to Berkovitsa; the 3rd Army, commanded by General Dimitriev, northwest of Sofia; the newly organized 5th Army under General Stefan Toshev, around Kyustendil and Radomir; the 4th Army, commanded by General Kovachev, generally along the east bank of the Zletovska River along a line Strumitsa–Shtip–Kochana; and the 2nd Army, commanded by General Ivanov, facing the Greeks, stretching from near Kavala on the Aegean Sea to near Lake Doiran north of Salonika. In addition, there was a small Bulgarian detachment isolated in Salonika. The 4th and 2nd Armies faced the Greeks and Serbs in Macedonia. The 2nd Army had been in position since May. The 4th Army had been formed only the previous winter but had combat experience in its successful defense of Gallipoli and Sharkoi the previous February. The 1st and 3rd Armies did not move from Thrace until the signing of the London treaty at the end of May. The cavalry division, which had not performed well during the war with the Ottomans, protected the right flank of the Bulgarian Army north of the 1st Army toward the Danube River. The weak positions were on the two flanks of the Bulgarian forces, especially in the south where the 2nd Army was overextended against the Greeks. Finally, the Bulgarians made little effort to protect the northern frontier against Romania and their southeastern frontier against the Ottoman Empire. They assumed that Russia would insure they would not come under attack from either of these directions.

The Greek army, commanded by King Constantine, who had succeeded to the throne after his father's assassination, had about nine divisions plus a cavalry division totaling around 121,000 men facing the Bulgarian 2nd Army north of Salonika[3]. This gave the Greeks a big advantage in numbers over their Bulgarian opponents. Two other divisions remained in Epirus to enforce Greek claims to this region.

The Serbs fielded around 300,000 men under the command of Vojvoda Radomir Putnik against the Bulgarians. The remainder of their 348,000-

man army stood in and around the still unsettled border with Albania.[4] Vojvoda Putnik, the Serb commander, deployed his forces into four operation groups. In Macedonia, the Serbian 1st and 3rd Armies formed the southern group. The 1st Army, commanded by Crown Prince Alexander, stood northeast of Skoplje. The 3rd Army, commanded by General Bozhidar Jankovich, formed around Veles. The Serbian 2nd Army, the Central group, commanded by General Stepa Stepanovich, who had fought alongside the Bulgarians at Adrianople, now confronted them around Pirot. The northern group consisted only of the Timok army. It was commanded by Reserve General Staff Colonel Vukoman Arachich and extended to the Danube River. The western group, consisting of about twenty battalions, stood on and about the still uncertain Albanian frontier. Most of the Serbian strength was situated in the south for the defense of Macedonia. The weak point of the Serbian deployment was in the north.

A Montenegrin division of 12,802 men, the Dechani brigade, joined the Serbs. One brigade was attached to the Serbian 3rd Army, the other two to the Serbian 1st Army.[5] Initially, these soldiers were part of the strategic reserve. After the Bregalnitsa battle, all the Montenegrin brigades joined the Serbian 3rd Army. Montenegro had no particular quarrel with Bulgaria. Because King Nikola had to remain in the good graces of the Serbs in order to receive a portion of the Sandjak of Novi Pazar, he sent troops to fight Bulgaria.

The Greeks and Serbs were determined to keep those portions of Macedonia they had occupied. The military convention signed between Greece and Serbia on 1 June in Salonika had envisioned three possible scenarios for a war with Bulgaria: Greece assisting Serbia in an offensive in the case of a Bulgarian concentration against Serbia; Serbia assisting Greece in an offensive in the case of a Bulgarian concentration against Greece; or a general offensive against Bulgaria in the case of a Bulgarian concentration against both Greece and Serbia.[6] By the summer of 1913, the Serbs realized that the major Bulgarian concentration confronted them in Macedonia. Because they already held the territory that the Bulgarians wanted, they could be fairly certain that the Bulgarians would act first. A directive from the Serbian high command on 8 June stated, "Our troops must be on constant guard, especially at night, and prepared to not only deflect any Bulgarian attack, but also to go over into an attack themselves to punish the Bulgarians for their aggression, and to mercilessly pursue them."[7] The Serbs awaited a Bulgarian move. Adding to Greek and Serb confidence was the expectation of Romanian intervention in Dobrudzha or across the Danube.

The Bulgarians had planned to begin a war against their allies with a general offensive by all five of their armies. An important issue contributing to the Bulgarian plan for an offensive was the proximity of the Bulgarian capital to the frontier. In 1878, the Bulgarians had selected Sofia as their capital because it would be centrally located in a San Stefano Bulgaria, that is in a Bulgaria including Macedonia. In the post Congress of Berlin Bulgaria, Sofia was near the western frontier. Now hostile forces were close. The Greeks were 75 miles from Sofia and the Serbs were only about 35 miles from the Bulgarian capital. The Bulgarians had to undertake an offensive or face a defensive fight near or at their capital.

The mountainous nature of the terrain in eastern Macedonia, eastern Serbia, and western Bulgaria prevented the Bulgarians from attempting the rapid movement and combined attacks that they had used in the open rolling areas of Thrace. All of their armies had to disperse their forces to conform to the mountains and river valleys where they operated. Roads were few, and linear movement was very difficult. The 1st Army was to attack in the direction of Knjazhevats and on toward Pirot; the 3rd Army was to attack toward Pirot, where it would link up with the 1st Army; the new 5th Army would serve as the axis or anchor of the battlefield and cover its two flanks; the 4th Army would attack in the area of Shtip; and the 2nd Army would attack southern Macedonia in the direction of Gevgeli and Salonika.[8] Although the Bulgarian high command approved this plan, it never managed to implement it.

Bregalnitsa

The Bulgarian 4th Army, newly formed the previous winter, occupied the most important position for the conquest of Serbian-held Macedonia. It was the Bulgarian force designated to achieve the purpose that had led Bulgaria into war against the Ottomans the previous autumn. The 4th Army was arrayed in the shape of a bow, with the city of Shtip at the top of the arc. This made its flanks vulnerable to enemy counterattacks, which could cut off and destroy its center positions.

The initial fighting began on the night of 29–30 June. It mainly involved the Bulgarian 4th Army and the Serbian 1st and 3rd Armies, the Serbian southern group, generally along the Zletovska River, and later, after the retreat of the Bulgarian 4th Army, along the Bregalnitsa River. Initially, the Bulgarians were able to advance against the Serbs on both flanks, crossing the Zletovska. The left flank of the 4th Army advanced to Udovo on the Vardar River after heavy fighting. The Bulgarian center made no progress. The confusion in Sofia, however, undermined this initial success on the flanks.

The spontaneous explosion that started the fighting disrupted the Bulgarian lines of command. Danev ordered Savov to stop the fighting on 1 July. The same day, Ferdinand ordered him to continue the attack. On 3 July Ferdinand fired Savov for failing to continue the attack and replaced him with General Dimitriev, the commander of the 3rd Army. The appointment of the Russophile General Dimitriev was a signal to St Petersburg of Buglaria's continued hopes for Russian intervention. Lieutenant General Racho Petrov assumed command of the 3rd Army. In these actions, Tsar Ferdinand was probably acting on the urgent advice of his senior military officers.

The same day, 3 July, the government fired Savov, because of the initial attacks of the night of 16–17 July. Savov was thus fired twice on the same day. A strong advocate of military action, Savov found himself caught between the tsar and the government. The failure of his armies to gain quick successes was the real reason for his loss of command.

These halts and changes of command had a confusing and even paralyzing effect on the Bulgarian forces. The order to break off fighting and return to their initial positions came as a "genuine surprise" to elements of the 13th Infantry Regiment of the 7th Rila Division of the 4th Army, who had the Serbs pinned down in front of their positions.[9] The retreat to the positions of 29 June was dangerous for the 4th Army because of the proximity of the Serbs. Under these circumstances, Bulgarian losses were heavy.

The three-day hiatus in attacks permitted the Greeks and Serbs to recover from the initial Bulgarian blows. They did not stop fighting and continued to fire upon the Bulgarians. Some Bulgarian officers under flags of truce attempted to persuade them that the fighting was a mistake. Other Bulgarian units were caught off guard by the fighting. The Serbs even took one bewildered company from the 7th Infantry Division of the 4th Army prisoner without any fighting at all. The Bulgarians never recovered their rhythm of action. These halts and changes in command also emphasized the Bulgarians' limited, though naive, intentions and expectations for their attacks of 29–30 June. By 1 July the Serbs had gone on the offensive all along their lines.

The initial Bulgarian attacks had squeezed the Serbian 3rd Army. Its commander, General Jankovich, requested authority to retreat. Vojvoda Putnik, however, refused to grant the request. He ordered his 3rd Army to hold on and counterattack.[10] After the Bulgarian attacks had abated, the Serbs counterattacked on 1 July between Shtip and Kochana and succeeded in driving the right flank of the Bulgarian 4th Army back across the Zletovska River, reaching the Bregalnitsa River. By 4 July, they had the opportunity to break through the Bulgarian lines toward Gornya Dzhumaya (now Blagoevgrad). Had the Serbs succeeded, they might have destroyed the Bulgarian 4th Army, and possibly also the 2nd Army. This could have ended the war.

A major factor in the Serbian success was the inertia of the Bulgarian 5th Army, which lacked orders to act. On 30 June, General Toshev, the 5th Army commander, did request authority from the Bulgarian high command to move into Macedonia.[11] In the confusion that beset the Bulgarian headquarters at the beginning of the fighting, the request was denied. The next day, the 5th Army did receive orders to attack, then, after initiating fighting, to break off the attack. Under such muddled circumstances, the 5th Army's efforts lost direction. Had the 5th Army adopted a more aggressive posture, especially on its left flank, it might have taken some of the pressure off of the Bulgarian 4th Army.

By 8 July, with the Bulgarians in retreat toward the Bregalnitsa River, the fighting died down. The Bulgarian 4th Army had sustained a severe defeat.

It had casualties of about 20,000 men, and the Serbs had casualties of around 16,620 men, including 3,000 dead.[12] At the same time, an even greater Bulgarian debacle had occurred in southern Macedonia in the fighting against the Greeks.

The defeat of the Bulgarian 2nd Army

From the beginning of the fighting on 30 June, the Bulgarian 2nd Army found itself in difficulties. With only 36,000 men, of whom 20,000 were "still untrained," according to General Ivanov, it confronted almost the entire Greek army.[13] Although General Ivanov probably underestimated the number of his soldiers, he still faced a much larger Greek enemy. Even before the 2nd Army transferred from Adrianople, fighting between Bulgarian and Greek forces in eastern Macedonia had become frequent. Skirmishes, sometimes exploding into pitched battles, continued after the 2nd Army took up its new positions. On 26 June the 2nd Army had received orders to destroy the opposing Greek forces and to advance toward Salonika.[14] This proved to be far beyond the offensive capabilities of the 2nd Army. Even if it had more troops than General Ivanov admitted, the 2nd Army still lacked the necessary numbers to carry out a successful attack against the Greeks. When formulating the Bulgarian strategy, General Savov grossly underestimated his opponents here.

Under the command of King Constantine, the Greek army immediately counterattacked. The Greek General Staff considerably overestimated the numbers of Bulgarians, reckoning them to be between 80,000 and 105,000.[15] The Greeks divided their forces into left, center, and right groups. They planned to push strongly on their own center and left positions in order to cut the Bulgarian line of retreat toward Strumitsa.[16] They hoped to link their left flank to the Serbian right flank. This plan would, if successful, eliminate the Bulgarians from Macedonia.

When fighting began on 30 June, strong pressure developed on both flanks of the Bulgarian 2nd Army. Greek warships pounded Bulgarian positions on the Gulf of Orfanos, a finger of the Aegean Sea. At the same time, the right flank of the Bulgarian 2nd Army came under attack by strong Greek units. Stretched along a front 120 miles long and heavily outnumbered by the Greek forces, the overextended 2nd Army began to withdraw from its position northeast of Salonika on 1 July in a northerly direction toward the left flank of the Bulgarian 4th Army near Strumitsa. The 4th Army, itself in difficulties from Serbian counterattacks, could offer no support to the 2nd Army. The Bulgarians had constructed strong defensive positions, including trenches and masked batteries with multiple guns, including some taken from the Ottomans at Kilkis (Bulgarian, Kukush) north of Salonkia. There they attempted to make a stand. After a battle lasting from 30 June to 4 July, they were forced to abandon these positions. The attempts of the 2nd Army to restore its positions through counterattacks had clearly failed. In his memoirs General Ivanov explained,

> That day, 21 June (4 July), was the day of the crisis of the 2nd Army. This crisis was not so much material as moral, which was important in the situation. The soldiers lost faith in themselves, mainly because of seeing the numerical superiority of the enemy, and seeing no help anywhere. The situation became so depressing, that the soldiers in the several day long battles estimated the size of the enemy and realized, that they were so outnumbered that they could only lose.[17]

In the fighting around Kilkis the Bulgarians admitted to casualties of 4,227 dead, 1,977 wounded, and 767 missing.[18]

The Bulgarians would return to some of the same positions in the hills northeast of Salonika two and a half years later after chasing British and French troops down the valley of the Vardar River all the way to Salonika. If not for German insistence on a halt near the Greco-Serbian frontier, they might well have taken Salonika and forced the British and French to return to their boats. This time the Bulgarians would be much more difficult to dislodge from their positions northeast of Salonkia. Ensconced in these hills, they succeeded in containing the "Gardeners of Salonika" until almost the end of the First World War.

Bulgarian headquarters in Sofia ordered limited reserves to bolster the 2nd Army, but these forces arrived only to join in the retreat to the north. With the Bulgarian center unable to hold, the right and left also had to retreat. The retreat threatened to become a rout. The retreat of the 2nd Army uncovered the left flank of the 4th Army around Strumitsa. This forced the 4th Army also to retreat further to the east.

The defeat of the 2nd Army by the Greeks was the most serious military disaster suffered by the Bulgarians in the Second Balkan War, and the greatest Greek success of both Balkan Wars. The Greeks took more than 6,000 prisoners and more than 130 artillery pieces.[19] The cost of victory, however, was heavy. The Greeks suffered 8,700 casualties.[20] Although the 2nd Army remained intact as a fighting force, its retreat from the towns of Seres and Drama represented the end of Bulgarian hopes to retain much of Aegean Macedonia. Because of the Serbian pressure on the Bulgarian 4th Army, a return to this region during the Second Balkan War proved impossible. The unrealistic goal of Salonika not only ruptured the Bulgarian–Greek alliance but also helped to bring about the defeat of the Bulgarian 2nd Army.

Salonika

An important aspect of the defeat of the Bulgarian 2nd Army was the annihilation of the Bulgarian unit in Salonika. The Bulgarian attacks of the night of 29–30 June brought about the loss of Salonika and the Bulgarian soldiers stationed there. Fighting began in Salonika on 30 June 1913 between the Bulgarian and Greek garrisons. The Greek 2nd Division and around 2,000 Cretan police were in Salonika. The Bulgarian 3rd Battalion of the 14th Macedonian regiment stationed in Salonika was isolated and outnumbered. Back in April, Savov had ordered this battalion to withdraw because of its exposed position, but the Sofia government had overridden this order.[21] The Bulgarian soldiers had to remain so that they could embody Bulgarian claims to Salonika. This small Bulgarian force was in no position to offer serious resistance to the Greeks. There was little hope of relief from the Bulgarian 2nd Army, located northeast of Salonika. The Bulgarian command should have withdrawn the Salonika force before initiating any attacks, however limited their aims, on the Greeks.

The Bulgarian representative to the Greek General Staff, Major General Kristofor Hesapchiev, was based in Salonika. He evidently learned in advance of the Bulgarian attack orders. He hurriedly left Salonika on 30 June. Soon after his departure, the Greeks initiated hostilities. Attempts at negotiation became bogged down because of the Bulgarian insistence at communicating with 2nd Army headquarters.[22] The urban fighting in Salonika was of brief duration, ending the next day on 1 July. In the city fighting, the Bulgarians, who had only 200 rounds per rifle, sometimes used their bayonets to repulse the Greeks. The Greeks used artillery against the Bulgarians and inflicted casualties on the civilian population of Salonika. After sustaining heavy losses, the surviving Bulgarians surrendered. The Bulgarians asserted that 237 of there men were killed and around 100 were wounded.[23] They had been sacrificed by the Bulgarian government in a hopeless endeavor. In addition, the Bulgarians insisted that a number of Bulgarian civilians residing in Salonika had also been killed during the fighting or deliberately killed afterwards by the Greeks. The Greeks gave lower figures for the Bulgarian losses. Greek losses amounted to eighteen dead and thirteen wounded.[24] Thus ended Bulgarian hopes of acquiring the largest city in Macedonia. The Bulgarians experienced a major defeat at the beginning of the Second Balkan War, losing the entire battalion and their claims to Salonika. The initial Greek effort in the Second Balkan War was an outstanding success. Held in disrespect by many observers since the disaster of the war of 1897, the Greek army had overcome a numerically inferior but still formidable Bulgarian army. In the first week of the war, the Greek army succeeded in occupying most of the disputed territories. Furthermore, it had defeated the Bulgarian 2nd Army and had begun to pursue it toward the old Bulgarian frontier.

Bulgarian retreats

On 4 July, after the situation in Sofia had somewhat clarified, the Bulgarians attempted to resume their attacks. This time all their armies participated.

Nevertheless, on the Macedonian front, the situation continued to deteriorate. Vigorous Serbian attacks compelled the Bulgarian 4th Army to retreat all along its line. The initial successes of the left flank had to be abandoned. By 7 July the 4th Army's situation was, according to General Dimitriev, "near to catastrophe."[25] He ordered both armies to retreat further toward the old Bulgarian frontier. The same day, however, the 2nd Army received orders to cover the 4th Army's retreat. The exhausted Bulgarian 4th Army retreated behind the Bregalnitsa, assuming defensive positions there on 11 July.

The right wing of the Bulgarian 2nd Army suffered another defeat at the hands of the Greeks south of Lake Doiran on 7 July. Here, in September 1918, the Bulgarian defenders of Doiran would have greater success against a larger combined British and Greek force, holding it off until the armistice of 29 September 1918. The Bulgarian defeat in 1913 forced a retreat to the northeast. The center of the 2nd Army, supported by strong artillery, held out around the Rupel Gorge, which controlled the Struma River route to the north. Three years later, on 26 May 1916, the Greek commander of the defensive positions around Rupel would surrender his soldiers to the Bulgarians without a fight. This secured Bulgarian control of much of Greek Macedonia.

On 9 July 1913, the 2nd Army resumed its general retreat up the valley of the Struma River toward Gornya Dzhumaya. That same day, the Greek army entered Strumitsa. On 11 July, the Greeks met up with the Serbs in Macedonia. The Greek advance up the valley of the Struma continued until 24 July, when it reached the Kresna Gorge of the Struma River. Here the Greeks spread out to the east and west. At this point, their attack stalled. King Constantine had reached the limits of his logistical and communication systems. His troops were exhausted after their victories and their rapid march north.

On the other side of the southern theater of war, the Greek navy occupied the Aegean port of Kavala on 11 July. Nevrokop fell to the Greeks on 19 July. By 23 July, the 2nd Army was up against the old Bulgarian–Ottoman frontier. The Greek fleet took Dedeagach on 25 July. This cut off the Bulgarians completely from the Aegean Sea.

In the center, the Bulgarian 5th Army, finally taking action, made some progress against the Serbs attacking southwest of Kyustendil on 4 July. The defeat and retreat of the 2nd Army and the difficulties of the 4th Army, however, made the advance of the 5th Army untenable. On 6 July, it retreated back toward the old Bulgarian frontier, where it remained on the defense for the duration of the conflict. Its role was to protect the important town of Kyustendil and the southwestern approach to Sofia. The Serbian 1st Army, weakened from the Bregalnitsa Battle, attempted on 14–15 July and 20–22 July to break through, but without success. This front then remained static until the end of the war. Some of the 5th Army soldiers might have been better used elsewhere, especially for reinforcing the two hard-pressed armies to the south.

In the north, on 7 July, the Bulgarian 3rd Army moved forward in two groups toward the town of Pirot and ultimately to Nish in order to cut the railroad line between that city and Skoplje. Initial 3rd Army advances toward Pirot succeeded in threatening the city. This caused great disconcertion in the Serbian command.

In response to this threat, Vojvoda Putnik shifted some of his forces away from the Southern group to defend the approaches to Pirot. This alleviated some of the pressure from the Bulgarian 4th Army. Had the Serbian attacks continued against the Bulgarian 4th Army, the Serbs might have achieved a decisive breakthrough all the way to the rear of the retreating Bulgarian 2nd Army. Putnik's decision to send troops to the north cost Serbia an opportunity to achieve an overwhelming victory in the war.[26] The reinforced Serbs succeeded in removing the Bulgarian threat to Pirot.

The Bulgarian 3rd Army continued to attack toward Pirot until 23 July. Then it assumed defensive positions in order to protect the capital, which was only about 30 miles to the southeast. These positions were strong enough to block any Serbian advance toward Sofia for the remainder of the war.

Further north, the Bulgarian 1st Army began its offensive on 4 July. After heavy fighting, it took the Serbian town of Knjazhevats on 7 July and prepared to move on toward Pirot. The Bulgarians admitted to losses of 280 dead and 820 wounded in the Battle for Knjazhevats.[27] The next day, however, the Bulgarian high command ordered a retreat to the Bulgarian frontier. It determined that the 1st Army would be better employed on the southern front. The 1st Army accordingly evacuated the town. The Serbs continued to fight however. As the 9th Division of the Bulgarian 1st Army retreated, it entered a ravine where a Serbian artillery barrage trapped it. The Serbs later found 5,000 men, which they described as, "chopped to pieces, like cabbages."[28] This was a grim foreshadowing of the effective role of artillery during the First World War. After it regained its original positions, most of the 1st Army prepared for movement to the south. On 17 July the staff of the 1st Army moved to the south. The movement of the 1st Army, however, left northwestern Bulgaria open to attack from the Romanians and the Serbs.

By this time, the soldiers on both sides had become exhausted. The initial enthusiasm of the previous autumn had long since evaporated during the summer. After the Battle of the Bregalnitsa, some Bulgarian and Serbian troops appear to have arranged informal truces between themselves, without the sanction of their officers.[29] Even general officers were becoming weary of the fighting. In a dispatch written on July 1913, General Stepanovich of the Serbian 2nd Army advised a subordinate,

> I received your report of the losses of the night of 10/11 of this month with a heavy heart, because these sacrifices were unnecessary since there

was no urgent and pressing need which required such risky action. I recommend in the future the prudent conservation of fighting power, which has to be totally committed only those situations where there would be a pressing demand in the interest of the campaign.[30]

Soldiers would again die in "Japanese" numbers in Europe a little over one year later, when the lessons of the Balkan Wars would be ignored or forgotten.

By the second week of the war, the Bulgarian position had improved somewhat. Although their armies in Macedonia had given up considerable territory, they continued to fight as intact forces. In addition, their lines of supply and communication, as well as retreat, remained open. In the northern theater, the Serbs had stopped the Bulgarian offensive but had made little headway themselves against the Bulgarians. Just as they were stabilizing their situation, the Bulgarians had to confront two insurmountable problems.

Romanian intervention

Perceiving an opportunity to realize their still unfulfilled aspirations in Dobrudzha, the Romanians mobilized against Bulgaria on 5 July 1913. The Romanians maintained a well-equipped army with a peacetime strength of 6,149 officers and 94,170 enlisted men, which mobilization could raise to 417,720 men in the operating army.[31] They had 126 field batteries, fifteen howitzer batteries, and three mountain batteries. Most of these guns were manufactured by Krupp, as befitting an ally of the Triple Alliance. The Romanian army had not seen foreign action since 1878, although it had suppressed a large domestic peasant revolt in 1907. Nevertheless, possessing the largest army in the Balkans, the Romanians were well situated to play a decisive role in the conflict on their southern borders. The Bulgarians were already outnumbered by and heavily engaged with their Greek and Serbian opponents. The entrance of Romania into the conflict made the Bulgarian situation untenable.

The Romanian government declared war on 10 July. The Bucharest government gave assurances in a diplomatic circular that, "Romania does not intend either to subjugate the policy nor defeat the army of Bulgaria."[32] This was a rather innocuous way to begin a war. It was hardly reassuring for the Bulgarians however. That same day, 80,000 soldiers of the Romanian 5th Corps under General Ioan Culcer crossed the border into Dobrudzha and occupied the line from Tutrakan to Balchik. This was the same territory they had demanded in St Petersburg. The cavalry attached to this corps briefly occupied the Black Sea port of Varna, but withdrew back into Dobrudzha when the absence of Bulgarian resistance became apparent.

On the night of 14–15 July the 250,000-strong Romanian Danube Army under the command of Crown Prince Ferdinand crossed the Danube at Oryahovo, Gigen, and Nikopol. The Sofia government decided not to contest the Romanian invasion.[33] Meeting no resistance, the Romanian forces regrouped into two elements. One element moved in a westerly direction toward the town of Ferdinand (now Mihailovgrad) in northwestern Bulgaria. The other proceeded in a southwesterly direction toward the Iskar River and the Bulgarian capital, Sofia. Cavalry from both elements fanned out in western Bulgaria.

The Romanian thrust across the Danube was the decisive military act of the Second Balkan War. By the time of the Romanian invasion, the Bulgarians had managed to stabilize the Greek and Serbian fronts. They were preparing a counteroffensive. Even the Romanian seizure of southern Dobrudzha was not fatal to the Bulgarian cause. With their entire army fighting in the west and southwest of the country, however, the Bulgarians could not offer the slightest resistance to the Romanian invasion that thrust into the heart of Bulgaria and threatened the capital.

On 18 July Romanian troops entered Ferdinand in northwestern Bulgaria. On 20 July they took Vratsa north of Sofia. By 23 July, a Romanian cavalry division reached the village of Vrzhdebna, only about 7 miles from Sofia. This meant that not only could the Romanians take Sofia, but they were in position to move against the rear of the Bulgarian 3rd Army, which was then fighting the Serbs. On 25 July the Romanians and Serbs met at Belogradchik. This isolated Vidin, the largest and most important city in northwestern Bulgaria.

In support of their invasion of Bulgaria the Romanians utilized airplanes mainly for reconnaissance purposes. Romanian aviators also took pictures from their airplanes and dropped leaflets over Sofia.[34] Even though the Romanian aviators caused no physical damage, their appearance in the skies over Sofia must have been a cause for wonder and fear. Sofia thus enjoyed the dubious distinction of being the first European capitol to come under the shadows of enemy aircraft.

Although the Romanians did not suffer any combat casualties in the invasion of Bulgaria, they did sustain losses. Cholera swept through the Romanian ranks. Around 6,000 soldiers died[35]. Undoubtedly, Romanian civilians contracted the disease from returning soldiers and added to the numbers of dead. These casualties represented the human cost of southern Dobrudzha for Romania.

In September 1916, when Romania joined the Entente, Bulgaria replayed this Romanian invasion in reverse. Bulgarian troops seized southern Dobrudzha and in conjunction with German and Austro-Hungarian troops crossed the Danube at Svishtov to invade, defeat, and occupy Romania.

Ottoman invasion of Bulgaria

If the Romanian invasion was not disastrous enough, the Bulgarians also found themselves attacked by their enemy from the First Balkan War, the

Ottoman Empire. The collapse of the Balkan Alliance alerted Enver Bey and the Young Turk government to the opportunity to regain some of the territories lost in the First Balkan War.[36] Eager to take advantage of the Bulgarian catastrophe and especially to recover Adrianople, the Ottoman forces vacated their old positions at Chataldzha and Gallipoli and crossed the Enos–Midia line on 12 July. Ahmed Izzet Pasha commanded this army, which consisted of 200,000–250,000 men divided into four armies, numbered 1 to 4, with the Ottoman 1st Army the furthest east and the 4th Army in Gallipoli. Most Bulgarian troops had left Thrace the previous spring to confront the Greeks and Serbs on Bulgaria's western frontiers. Adrianople itself had only a small garrison of 4,000 men under the command of Major General Vulko Velchev.[37] This garrison in Adrianople, together with the other small forces in eastern Thrace, withdrew to the old frontier in the face of these superior Ottoman numbers. The Bulgarians abandoned Adrianople on 19 July, returned briefly the next day when Ottoman forces failed to arrive and then left for good on 21 July.[38] The Ottomans reoccupied Adrianople on 23 July without firing a shot. Enver Bey claimed credit as the "Second Conqueror of Edirne."[39] The Bulgarian occupation of Adrianople had lasted about as long as the Bulgarian siege. The tremendous effort and sacrifice of the Bulgarian army to take the city vanished on one summer's day. Moreover, the battlefields of eastern Thrace, where so many Bulgarian soldiers had died to win the First Balkan War, were again under Ottoman control.

The Ottomans advanced beyond Adrianople and crossed the old frontier into Bulgaria. Ottoman cavalry rode in the direction of Yambol. This caused a great deal of panic in Bulgaria. Some of the Bulgarian civilian population fled toward the mountains of central Bulgaria. The catastrophe of the war now came home to Bulgaria. Nine months before, Bulgarian soldiers had knocked on the gates of Constantinople, now the Ottomans had invaded Bulgaria.

The Ottomans suffered no combat casualties in their invasion of Bulgaria. They, like the Romanians, did endure a renewed outbreak of cholera and lost 4,000 men to the disease.[40] They either contracted it from the Bulgarian civilian population, or it was latent in their own ranks. In any event, this inadvertent Ottoman biological weapon of the First Balkan War retained its potency during the Second Balkan War.

New Bulgarian government

Amidst the catastrophic reports from the battlefield, the pro-Russian government of Stoyan Danev in Sofia resigned on 13 July. His position became untenable when the Russians failed to do anything to alleviate the disaster encompassing Bulgaria. The government that replaced him four days later consisted of Russophobe politicians who looked to Germany and

Austria–Hungary to save Bulgaria from invasion and to guide Bulgarian policy after the war. This new government, headed by Vasil Radoslavov, immediately began to seek a diplomatic way out of the growing catastrophe.[41] An appeal from Tsar Ferdinand through the Italian ambassador in Bucharest to King Carol on 22 July halted the Romanian advance, and probably preserved Sofia as the only Balkan capital not occupied by foreign troops during the fighting from 1912 to 1918.[42] At the same time, the Russians and the other Great Powers began to take steps to conclude the war. They urged Serbia and Romania to bring the war to and end.[43] On 20 July the new Bulgarian government, at the invitation of Pashich acting through St Petersburg, had sent a delegation to Nish to seek a way out of the war through direct talks with the allies. These talks proved inconclusive. Both the Serbs and the Greeks, whose armies in Macedonia were advancing against the Bulgarians and who wanted to occupy as much territory as possible before any peace talks, were reluctant to agree to any cessation of hostilities.[44] All sides, however, agreed to a Romanian proposal that Bucharest serve as the site of peace talks. The delegations then left Nish on 24 July and traveled to Bucharest.

Kalimantsi

Amidst this difficult situation, a defensive success against the Serbs heartened the Bulgarians. Former Deputy Commander in Chief General Savov had assumed command of the 4th and 5th Armies on 13 July. The Bulgarians dug into strong positions along a wide front southwest of the old Bulgarian–Ottoman frontier on a relatively level region around the village of Kalimantsi, on the Bregalnitsa River in northeastern Macedonia. On 18 July, the Serbian 3rd Army, including the Montenegrin division, attacked. In the pouring rain that seems to have accompanied many Balkan War battles, they advanced close to the Bulgarian positions. The Serbs threw hand grenades in an attempt to dislodge the Bulgarians, who were in sheltered positions about 40 feet away.[45] The Bulgarians held firm. On several occasions, the Bulgarians allowed the Serbs and Montenegrins to advance on their positions, enticing them on with deliberately weak fire. When the attackers got to within 200 yards of the Bulgarian trenches, the Bulgarians charged with fixed bayonets and threw them back. The Bulgarian artillery was also very effective at breaking up the enemy attacks. The Bulgarian lines held. Now that they were fighting to repel a foreign invasion of their homeland, morale among the Bulgarian soldiers had risen considerably.

If the Montenegrins and Serbs had broken through the Bulgarian defenses, they could have overrun the rear of the already hard-pressed Bulgarian 2nd Army. A Serbian success could have doomed the Bulgarian 2nd Army and pushed the Bulgarians entirely out of Macedonia. The Serbs sustained losses of 2,500 dead and 4,850 wounded, and the Montenegrins suffered 107 dead and 570 other casualties.⁴⁶ Bulgarian casualties were probably similar. Although fighting continued around Kalimantsi until the end of the war, the Serbs were unable to overcome the Bulgarian defenses. The Bulgarians remained in the same positions as at the conclusion of the armistice.

At Kalimantsi the Bulgarians won an important defensive battle. The Macedonian front held. This, together with the general defensive successes of the Bulgarian 1st and 3rd Armies to the north, protected western Bulgaria and Sofia from a Serbian invasion. Although this was heartening for the Bulgarians, the situation was still critical as the Greeks were advancing from the south.

Kresna Gorge

The defensive victories against the Serbs enabled the Bulgarian command to carry out a counterattack against the advancing Greeks. They had begun to plan this action even before the success at Kalimantsi. On 29 July the Bulgarian armies, compacted by their retreats, seized the initiative. Further consolidation had resulted in the 2nd, 4th, and 5th Armies under General Savov's command. General Ivanov, who had led the 2nd Army to victory at Adrianople and to defeat in southern Macedonia, lost his position on the eve of the Bulgarian counteroffensive because of a dispute with General Savov.⁴⁷ Although still retreating north, the Bulgarians planned a counterattack against the Greeks in the area of the Kresna Gorge at the Struma River south of Gornya Dzhumaya (now Blagoevgrad). This is a narrow defile where the Struma River intersects the Rhodope Mountains, an excellent defensive position. By the last week of July, the Greek advance had stalled at the Kresna Gorge. They were exhausted and had reached the limits of their logistical capabilities.

At this point, the Greek government was prepared to accept an armistice. Venizelos visited the headquarters of the army in an attempt to gain the agreement of the King.⁴⁸ Constantine, however, still sought a decisive result on the battlefield. He was reluctant to accede to the appeals of his prime minister.

Meanwhile, the Bulgarian high command began to shift the 1st Army from northwestern Bulgaria to Macedonia to reinforce the 2nd Army on 25 July. This concentrated force had been prepared to prevent the Greeks from invading pre-war Bulgaria. With the left of the consolidated army blocking the Serbs, the center and right flank were able to counterattack against the overextended Greeks. On 29 July, striking out from their positions against the Rila Mountain at the left and right flanks of the Greeks while holding them in the center, the Bulgarians thrust them back down the valleys of the Struma and Mesta Rivers. The Bulgarian left flank, advancing down the Struma valley, and the right flank, advancing down the Mesta valley, were in position to turn toward each other and completely encircle the Greeks. A lack of artillery support because of the difficulties of moving guns over the rugged terrain compounded the difficulties of the Greeks.

The inability of the Greek and Serbian commands to effectively coordinate their actions now became evident. Pleas for assistance directed to their Serbian allies brought the Greeks no relief. The Serbs were nervous about the early Greek successes and feared that the Greeks had designs on Bitola. Moreover, they had troubles of their own after their rebuff at Kalimantsi. The Serbs could offer little help. By 30 July, the Greek army faced annihilation in a large Cannae-type battle. King Constantine sent a telegram to Venizelos in Bucharest, "My army is physically and morally exhausted. In the light of these conditions I can no longer refuse the armistice or suspension of hostilities. Endeavor to find some way of securing a suspension of hostilities."[49] The Kresna Gorge counterattack had succeeded brilliantly for the Bulgarians.

Constantine's presence with his troops, first as crown prince and after the assassination of his father as king, was an admirable example of royal military leadership. King Albert of the Belgians demonstrated the same type of authority a little over one year later. Constantine, however, overreached himself at Kresna Gorge. He had already occupied the territory Greece wanted. He had no need to take his overextended army further into Bulgaria. In attempting to do so, King Constantine very nearly emulated the unfortunate precedent of Napoleon III in being capured by the opposing army.

Even before the imminent annihilation of the Greeks, the Bulgarian government had demanded that its army cease military activity.[50] With the Romanians camped outside Sofia and the Ottomans advancing into southeastern Bulgaria, Radoslavov realized that negotiations were the only solution to Bulgaria's difficulties. A last-minute victory over the Greeks, however emotionally satisfying, could only exacerbate Bulgaria's predicament. The Bulgarian high command complied. Bulgaria's agreement to a general armistice on 31 July in Bucharest saved the Greek army from destruction.

This Bulgarian success against the Greeks around Kresna Gorge could not have reversed the outcome of the war. For Bulgaria the war, and with it most of Macedonia and eastern Thrace, was lost. The defensive victory, however, did help insure that the newly acquired regions of southeastern Macedonia (Pirin Macedonia) would not become Greek. It also restored Bulgarian confidence to some degree in their military.

Vidin

The transfer of the Bulgarian 1st Army to Macedonia for the operation against the Greeks allowed the Serbian 2nd Army to advance into northwestern Bulgaria. The northwestern fortified city of Vidin had limited defensive forces. Only seven infantry companies and some militia units, in all 5,730 men and sixteen antiquated pieces of artillery, remained to protect the city.[51] After taking Rakovitsa and Belogradchik, the Serbs moved toward Vidin. Directly across the Danube, a Romanian detachment concentrated around the town of Calafat. Together the Serbs and Romanians effectively surrounded and isolated Vidin. The Serbs bombarded Vidin on 29 July, but were unable to take it with an infantry attack. Vidin remained in Bulgarian hands when the fighting ended on 31 July. Because of its isolation and the small number of its defenders, however, Vidin probably would have fallen to the Serbs had the war continued for any length of time.

Treaty of Bucharest

The peace delegations, having arrived from Nish, met in Bucharest on 30 July. Venizelos headed the Greek delegation and Pashich led the Serbian delegation. Prime Minister Vukotich represented Montenegro. Titu Majorescu led the host deputation. Working through their ambassadors in Bucharest, the Great Powers maintained a presence at the peace talks. They did not dominate the proceedings, but they did remain very influential. The Romanians rejected an Ottoman request to participate, asserting that the talks were to deal with matters exclusively among the Balkan allies.[52] This meant that, unfortunately for the Bulgarians, they would have to deal with the Ottomans on their own. The delegates agreed to a five-day armistice starting the next day. The fighting had lasted thirty-three days.

Dimitur Tonchev, the new Bulgarian finance minister, led the Bulgarian delegation at Bucharest. The head of the new Bulgarian government, Vasil Radoslavov, was not noted for his diplomatic skills. Nor did he wish to personally negotiate the confirmation of Bulgaria's defeat. He remained in Sofia. Tonchev hoped to divide the victorious coalition. This expectation, however, immediately dissolved into disappointment when the Greeks, Romanians, and Serbs presented a united front.

The Bulgarians settled first with the Romanians, conceding the loss of the southern Dobrudzha. The Bulgarians had already agreed to the cessation on 19 July, well before the Bucharest talks began.[53] Romania, having obtained both southern Dobrudzha and a weakening of Bulgaria, then acted as a force for moderation. The Romanians did not want the Greek–Serbian coalition to become overly strong, any more than they wanted a powerful Bulgaria. That way Romania remained the single strongest power in the Balkans. In addition, the outbreak of cholera in the Romanian army in Bulgaria acted as an incentive to resolve the conflict.

The settlement between Bulgaria and the former allies was more difficult to achieve. It centered around the old issue of Macedonia. Both sides wanted to obtain as much of Macedonia as possible. The Bulgarians had hoped to acquire the east bank of the Vardar River as their frontier.[54] They were unable to realize this object. Serbia initially wanted to acquire Macedonia as far as the Struma valley. This would have deprived Bulgaria of all Macedonia. Pressure on Serbia from both Russia, who hoped to retain influence in Sofia, and Austria–Hungary, who wanted to increase influence there, forced the Serbs to moderate their demands. Nevertheless, they insisted on retaining most of Macedonia in the Vardar watershed. Pashich conceded only the town of Shtip, "in honor of General Fichev," a member of the Bulgarian delegation.[55]

The major difficulty between Bulgaria and Greece was the Aegean port of Kavala. Having lost Salonika, the Bulgarians wanted to retain one good maritime commercial facility to serve their newly acquired territories that lay across the Rhodopes. Kavala was also at the center of a rich tobacco-producing region in eastern Macedonia. The Greeks would not concede Kavala. Venizelos explained the situation to General Fichev, "General, we are not responsible. Before 16 June (29 June) we were afraid of you and offered you Seres and Drama and Kavala, but now when we see you, we assume the role of victors and will take care of our interests only."[56] In an unusual pairing of the Great Powers, Austria and Russia wanted Bulgaria to obtain Kavala, whereas Germany and France supported the Greeks. Kaiser Wilhelm's desire to support his brother-in-law King Constantine was important in securing the port for Greece. This controversy demonstrated that on some Balkan issues, the alliance of the Great Powers retained some flexibility. As a result, Bulgaria kept only the relatively undeveloped facility at Dedeagach as an Aegean outlet.

A Montenegrin delegation attended the Bucharest conference. Even though they had no territorial disputes with Bulgaria, the Montenegrins participated in the determination of the new frontiers. The Montenegrin delegation merely asked the conference to keep them in mind when assigning territory to Serbia.[57] By supporting Serbian aspirations in Macedonia, the Montenegrins hoped to obtain a favorable division of the Sandjak of Novi Pazar with the Serbs. Montenegrin armies had failed to occupy much of this region in the war. Their participation in the Second Balkan War was largely to insure a favorable division of this territory from the Serbs. In this they were successful, as Serbia would concede a good part of the Sandjak to Montenegro at Bucharest.[58] An agreement between Montenegro and Serbia signed on 7 November in Belgrade confirmed the division of territories.[59]

The delegates concluded their work on 8 August. Two days later they signed the Treaty of Bucharest. The major result of this agreement was the division of Macedonia into three parts. Greece obtained the Aegean regions. Serbia received the largest portion of Macedonia, the area of the Vardar watershed. This included both the "disputed zone" and the area promised outright to Bulgaria in the March 1912 treaty. Bulgaria acquired only the southeastern corner, known as Pirin Macedonia.

For Greece and Serbia, Bucharest was a success beyond their expectations of the previous year. Not only did they acquire more territory than they had anticipated, but the strong position of Bulgaria in the Balkan Peninsula had greatly diminished, at least for the time being. Serbia in particular was now the strongest military power south of the Danube. After the Bucharest conference, Serbia also enjoyed exclusive Russian patronage in the region, save for Tsar Nicholas's familial interest in Montenegro. Romania also benefited from the Bucharest settlement. The Romanians had obtained southern Dobrudzha. By bringing all that region under their rule they had eliminated the opportunity a divided province gave the Bulgarians to call for unity under the Sofia government. In addition, the Romanians had established themselves as the arbitrators of the Balkan peninsula.

For Bulgaria, the Bucharest conference was a catastrophe. Bulgaria did retain considerable territory from the victories of the First Balkan War, especially in western Thrace, and did secure an Aegean outlet. Macedonia, Bulgaria's reason for fighting in the first place, for the most part remained under foreign rule. Although the country was exhausted from two wars, the Bulgarians could not regard the Bucharest settlement as permanent. Dimitur Tonchev, the leader of the Bulgarian delegation at Bucharest, observed, "Either the Powers will change it, or we ourselves will destroy it."[60]

Treaty of Constantinople

Unable to deal with the Ottoman invasion at Bucharest, the Bulgarians had to approach Constantinople directly and sue for peace. They had no other choice because the Ottomans had reoccupied most of eastern Thrace and Ottoman cavalry units were roving in pre-war Bulgaria. During August, the Russians made several half-hearted diplomatic attempts to retain Adrianople for Bulgaria.[61] No other Great Power was interested in the issue, and the Russians were not prepared to act alone. Andrei Toshev, one of the Bulgarian representatives in Constantinople, reflected the new attitude in Sofia toward the Russians when he remarked to an Ottoman diplomat, "The Russians consider Constantinople their natural inheritance. Their main concern is that when Constantinople falls into their hands it shall have the largest possible hinterland. If Adrianople is in the possession of the Turks, they shall get it too."[62] When these Russian initiatives had clearly failed, the Bulgarians recognized that they had to come to terms with the Ottomans.

Talks between the Bulgarians and the Ottomans only began in Constantinople on 6 September. General Savov, along with the diplomats Andrei Toshev and Grigor Nachovich, represented Bulgaria. The Ottoman foreign minister, Mehmed Talat Bey, Mahmud Pasha, and Halil Bey represented the Ottomans. The Bulgarians still hoped to retain at least Lozengrad. General Savov insisted, "Bulgaria, who defeated the Turks on all fronts, cannot end this glorious campaign with the signing of an agreement which retains none of the battlefields on which so much Bulgarian blood has been shed."[63] This hope was soon dashed. The Ottomans bluntly stated their position. "What we have taken is ours." was the way Mahmud Pasha, the Ottoman Naval Minister, explained it.[64] The proclamation of a "Provisional Government" of western Thrace at Gyumyurdzhina by the Ottoman forces there increased the pressure on Bulgaria. Under these circumstances, they had to accept the Ottoman position. The straight line of the Enos–Midia border became a short-lived geographic curiosity. The battlefields of Lozengrad, Lyule Burgas–Buni Hisar, and Adrianople, the scenes of outstanding Bulgarian victories, reverted to the Ottomans. The Bulgarians retained only the northeastern corner of eastern Thrace abutting the Black Sea. After the conclusion of an agreement, the "Provisional Government" disappeared. Only in October did Bulgarian troops reoccupy the new lands south of the Rhodopes.

In an effort to obtain something out of this debacle, the Radoslavov government sought not only a resolution of the conflict but also a strengthening of relations with the Ottomans, with a view to recovering Macedonia at some future date in a war against Greece and Serbia. The Treaty of Constantinople was finally signed on 30 September 1913, but negotiations for an alliance continued throughout the autumn. No definitive agreement ever resulted however.[65]

The Treaty of Constantinople deprived Bulgaria of eastern Thrace, on whose battlefield so many Bulgarian soldiers had died during the First Balkan War, and the important prize of Adrianople. Although this was an emotional and regrettable misfortune, it was not as catastrophic as the loss of Macedonia. Most of the exceedingly mixed population of eastern Thrace were not Bulgarians after all. For the Ottomans, the Treaty of Constantinople represented a positive coda to the disaster of the First Balkan War. They had regained Adrianople, and with it not only the first Ottoman capital in Europe but also a great deal of security for Constantinople. In addition, the alliance talks with Bulgaria promised the elimination of a serious threat. Even though this alliance was not realized until 1915 when Bulgaria joined the Central Powers, with the Treaty of Constantinople Bulgaria and the Ottoman Empire entered an era of détente that would last until 1918.

The signing of the Treaty of Constantinople did not quite end the Balkan Wars. On 14 November 1913 the Treaty of Athens concluded the conflict between the Greeks and the Ottomans. This treaty restored relations but left the question of the Aegean Islands open. The Italian occupation of the Dodecanese Islands and the strategic importance of Tenedos and Imbros to access to the Dardanelles complicated this issue. The Great Powers had not resolved it before July 1914. Relations between the Greeks and the Ottomans continued to be very bad. War between them almost broke out in the spring of 1914 and did erupt in 1922.

The Ottomans and Serbs signed the Treaty of Constantinople on 14 March 1914. This reaffirmed the London agreement and restored relations. The

Montenegrins never signed a final treaty with the Ottomans. With this second Treaty of Constantinople, the Balkan Wars were finally over. The fighting had lasted, off and on, for nine and a half months. In only ten months fighting in the Balkans would begin again and become general in Europe and spread throughout the world.

Conclusion

Having provoked the Second Balkan War, the Bulgarians recovered from initial catastrophes to successfully defend their country against a Greek and Serbian invasion. Indeed, the defeat of the Greeks at the end of the war might have enabled the Bulgarians to then turn on the Serbs and push them out of Macedonia. The presence of the Romanians and the Ottomans on Bulgarian soil, however, negated any advantage this victory brought. The Bulgarians lost the war the day the Romanians crossed the Danube.

To a great degree, the Bulgarians were the authors of their own catastrophe in the Second Balkan War. In diplomacy this began as early as the spring and summer of 1912, when they failed to arrive at a territorial settlement as part of their alliance with Greece. A recognition of Greek claims to Salonika in the initial alliance agreement might have achieved such a settlement. A satisfied Greece would have been unlikely to ally with Serbia in support of Serbian claims for revision. Another major diplomatic error was Bulgaria's inability to resolve the dispute with Romania. Understandably regarding Romanian demands as blackmail, the Bulgarians refused to make any significant concessions in Dobrudzha. This cost them Macedonia. Had the Bulgarians conceded some territory in Dobrudzha to Romania, they probably would not have had to endure a Romanian invasion in July 1913. The Ottomans would have been unlikely to attempt the revision of the London settlement without the Romanian cover.

If the Bulgarian government and military command had decided that force against Serbia and Greece was the preferable means to resolve the Macedonian dispute, then the government certainly failed to establish the diplomatic prerequisites for the use of force. It did not secure the support of Bulgaria's traditional patron Russia. The Danev government did flirt with Austria–Hungary, but received only vague assurances, certainly nothing on which to base a military campaign. Secure patronage from Russia or even from Austria–Hungary could have deterred the Romanian and Ottoman attacks on Bulgaria's undefended northern and southeastern frontiers. Under these conditions Bulgaria might well have defeated the Greeks and Serbs. This was the opinion of the former deputy commander in chief General Dimitriev.[66]

Another factor in the Bulgarian defeat was the social and political unrest manifest in the army during June 1913. This was not symptomatic of any rejection of the national cause by Bulgarian soldiers. Nevertheless, concerns about this unrest were a factor in the decision of the Bulgarian command to adopt an aggressive policy. Similar social and political, not national, unrest would be an important reason for the collapse of Bulgaria and the Macedonian front in September 1918.

The Bulgarians also made several important military mistakes. Their 2nd Army was stretched too thin to cover the strategic corner of southwestern Bulgaria. Given that it was inferior in numbers to the Greek forces it faced, the Bulgarian 2nd Army should have remained on the defensive from the beginning and not attempted a foolhardy attack toward Salonika. Clearly the Bulgarians grossly underestimated the military capabilities of the Greek army. The 1st Army or the 3rd Army should have also acted in the Macedonian theater, rather than attempting to invade Serbia. The Bulgarian goals, after all, were in Macedonia, not in Serbia. In addition, having determined upon an attack, the Bulgarians needed to deliver a decisive blow at the beginning. All five of the Bulgarian armies should have initiated simultaneous offensive activity. This would have given them the opportunity to quickly seize Macedonia and present the Great Powers with a *fait accompli*.

Finally, the breakdown in communication between the government in Sofia and army headquarters had terrible consequences. The army's attacks of 29–30 June were a catastrophic miscalculation. Not only did they bring about counterattacks from a well-rested and numerous enemy, but they also caused Bulgaria to lose whatever moral support she might have had among the Great Powers. The Bulgarians were the apparent aggressors and so deserved failure. Although the Bulgarian defeat was complete, it did not extinguish the idea of a greater Bulgaria including Macedonia and Thrace.

To win the war, the Bulgarians had to either destroy the enemy forces or occupy Macedonia, preferably both. They also had to accomplish this quickly. Although the Bulgarians did advance in some places against the Serbs on the first day of the war, none of the Bulgarian armies succeeded in inflicting decisive defeats on their Serbian opponents. The difficult mountainous terrain of eastern Macedonia together with Greek and Serbian resistance hampered Bulgarian attempts to advance against entrenched enemy positions. The Greeks and Serbs remained in control of most of the region.

The Greeks, Ottomans, Romanians, and Serbs were all big winners in the Second Balkan War. The Greek army established a record of military success not evident in the First Balkan War. The Greek army, however, soon reached the limits of its logistical and communication lines. This, together with a lack of coordination between the commands of the allied Greek and Serbian armies, contributed to a Greek defeat and near disaster at Kresna Gorge at the end of the war. The Treaty of Bucharest not only confirmed to Greece important parts of eastern Macedonia, including Seres, Drama, and Kavala, it also established a substantial border with Serbia. This insured that a strong Bulgaria could not exclude Greece from the Balkans.

The Ottomans recovered crucial territory during the Second Balkan War.

Their eradication of the absurd Enos–Midia line made their capital Constantinople once again defensible. Their recapture of Adrianople made Thrace once again a viable Ottoman province. Had the Bulgarians remained in Adrianople, it is unlikely the Ottomans could have held out for long at Gallipoli in 1915.

Romania's actions in the Second Balkan War were marked by decisiveness and restraint, determined to a great degree by awareness that more important national goals lay in Transylvania and Bessarabia. Bucharest used its army only to occupy the desired southern Dobrudzha and to insure Bulgarian acquiescence to that occupation. The Romanians eschewed other temptations, such as the occupation of Varna or entry into Sofia. After they had obtained their goal, they worked to terminate the conflict. They had no desire to replace a strong Bulgaria with a strong Serbia.

With their victory in the Second Balkan War, the Serbs became the dominate south Slavic power. The war confirmed that most Macedonians would live under direct Serbian control. By the time of the Treaty of Bucharest, Montenegro had become a Serbian satellite. The victory also bestowed upon the Serbs great prestige among the south Slavs in the Dual Monarchy. Afterwards Belgrade competed directly with Vienna and Budapest for the loyalty of the Serbs, Croats, Slovenes, and Bosnians who lived in the empire.

The victory over Bulgaria also left Serbia as the only remaining Russian ally in the Balkans. Bulgaria, was resentful over the Russian reluctance to uphold the March 1912 Treaty, and even more over Russia's failure to save Bulgaria from catastrophe. A pro-Austrian and pro-Triple Alliance government had come to power in Sofia even before the Treaty of Bucharest. The loss of Bulgaria made Russia dependent upon Serbia in order to retain any influence in the Balkans. With Serbia alienated, or under Austrian influence or control, Russia could be completely shut out of the Balkans. This situation reversed the traditional reliance of the Slavic Balkan states on Russia. Russia now had to rely upon Serbia in order to maintain a profile in the lower Balkans. The consequences of Russian dependence on Serbia became manifest at the end of July of the following year.

8

CONSEQUENCES AND CONCLUSIONS

As the first all-European conflict of the twentieth century, the Balkan Wars introduced an age of modern warfare encompassing mass armies, machines, and entire civilian populations. These wars eliminated the Ottoman Empire from Europe, except for the eastern corner of Thrace, scrambled the borders of the Balkan Peninsula, and established a frail but independent Albanian state. The conflict initiated in the Balkan Peninsula in 1912 would continue in Europe, with relatively brief interruptions, until 1945. Even after that, many of the problems associated with the Balkan Wars re-emerged during and after the second collapse of Yugoslavia in 1991. These include the status of Macedonia and Kosovo and the establishment of a maximalist Serbian national state.

Albania

One of the most important consequences of the Balkan Wars was the emergence of an independent Albanian state for the first time since the fifteenth century. All of Albania's neighbors had claims to its territories. The self-destruction of the Balkan Alliance presented the infant Albanian state with a brief opportunity to develop without interference from Greece, Montenegro, and Serbia. At the conclusion of the Second Balkan War, these three Balkan states renewed their attempts to further their own interests at the expense of Albania.

In London, on 29 July, the Ambassadors Conference had agreed on an Organization Statute for Albania that established a neutral princedom under the guarantee of the Great Powers.[1] In August 1913, efforts within Albania began to establish a state infrastructure and firm frontiers. The Great Powers, who had undertaken the responsibility to accomplish these tasks, soon ran into difficulties over the frontier issue. In the south the Greeks claimed considerable territory as "Northern Epirus." In the north, Serbian troops invaded Albania in the autumn and initiated a rule of terror against the local Albanian population. The Serbs hoped for a revision of the border decided at the Ambassadors Conference.

CONSEQUENCES AND CONCLUSIONS

The Austrians, with German support, presented an ultimatum in Belgrade on 18 October that demanded the evacuation of Albanian territory.[2] As E. C. Helmreich pointed out, "The whole procedure followed at this time was later duplicated in July, 1914: the warning to Serbia, the general promise of support from Germany, the independent presentation of the ultimatum, the subsequent notification of ally and rival."[3] After a tense week, the Serbs announced that their soldiers had left Albania. The Austrians had established a precedent for dealing with a Balkan crisis. This time the Balkan powder keg's fuse had fizzled out. In the next crisis it would ignite.

Even after the announcement of the departure of Serbian troops from northern Albania, the new state had many difficulties to overcome. An agreement by the Great Powers in the Protocol of Florence on 19 December 1913 confirmed the frontiers for Albania, including Scutari in the north and Korce in the south. It excluded, however, considerable areas containing Albanian-speaking populations, including all of Kosovo and northwestern Macedonia, and territories in the south. Nevertheless, the Greek army continued to occupy the south of the country, and Serbian troops lingered on in the northeast. Although the Greek government accepted the frontiers set by the Council of Florence in February 1914 and withdrew the Greek army, fighting continued between Greek and Albanian irregulars in southern Albania throughout the spring of 1914.[4] The disorders in the north and south greatly complicated the establishment of a stable Albanian government.

Albania only obtained a government recognized by the Great Powers with the arrival of the German Prince William of Wied on 7 March 1914. The Great Powers had themselves selected Wied, a German army officer and the nephew of Queen Elizabeth of Romania, from a field of candidates that included Swedish, German, and Turkish princes. He replaced the provisional government established by Ismail Kemal in November 1912. Wied was totally unprepared for the difficulties facing him. The machinations of the treacherous Esad Pasha Toptani, who was Minister of the Interior and War in Wied's government, but also in contact with the Italians and Serbs, helped to undermine Wied's effectiveness. His authority never extended much beyond Durrës and ended entirely with the outbreak of the First World War. Wied left Albania never to return without abdicating on 3 September 1914. Esad Pasha Toptani attempted to fill the vacuum created by Wied's departure. Soon after the renewal of war in the Balkan Peninsula, the Greeks, Montenegrins, and Serbs, however, all sent troops back into Albania. Austrian, Italian, and French soldiers would follow. Esad Pasha Toptani never realized his ambition to become king of Albania. He remained a disruptive element in Albanian politics until his assassination in Paris on 13 June 1920. Only after the end of the war did the Albanian state proclaimed in November 1912 become a fully functioning member of the international community.

The next war

The proximity and similarity of the experiences in the Balkan Wars and the First World War emphasizes the connection between these conflicts. The Balkan Wars were the first phase of the First World War. They were the same war. In them, conscripted soldiers, motivated by nationalist ideologies, often fought to the point of material, moral, and physical exhaustion. They used many of the same weapons, tactics, and strategies. The trench warfare impasse at Chataldzha foreshadowed the stalemate of the Western Front. Although cholera developed during the war rather than toward the end of the war, like influenza, it attacked all sides, observed no armistice and ravished military and civilian populations alike. Finally, although the end of the fighting produced clear victories, the vanquished endeavored, as soon as they recovered, to restore their position and regain their national objectives. Elements in Serbia initiated actions directed against Austria–Hungary, Serbia's consistent adversary during the Balkan Wars, soon after the signing of the Treaty of Bucharest. Bulgaria, the most devastated of the Balkan states in terms of losses of men and material, would return to the fighting only in October 1915. Many of the same battlefields during the Balkan Wars again saw fighting in the renewed struggles after July 1914. Gallipoli, the Dardanelles, and Salonika as well as Strumitsa, Bitola, and Doiran were all scenes of combat during the Balkan Wars and the First World War.

For the peoples of the Balkans, the short interlude in the fighting hardly warranted the acknowledgment of a new war. Indeed, the Serbs continued to fight Albanians in northern Albania and Kosovo and Macedonians in Macedonia throughout the year separating the Treaty of Bucharest from the Austro-Hungarian declaration of war. For the Balkans, the Balkan Wars and the First World War were inseparable.

The conduct of the war by the Balkan allies echoed the conduct of the war by the Entente the next time around. There was little cooperation among the allies. As in the First Word War, each of the allied armies undertook its own campaign, without much reference to its confederates. The Balkan League made no attempt to create a singular command structure. This failure was due to the singular and conflicting interests of the Balkan allies.

There were several exceptions to this disunity however. The Bulgarians and Serbs fought in a mixed army briefly in Macedonia and then again around Adrianople. The Montenegrins and Serbs besieged Scutari. The single most unifying factor in the First Balkan War was the Greek fleet, which blockaded Ottoman shores, transported Bulgarian and Serbian troops, and carried supplies for all three other armies. In this it evoked the role of the British fleet in the First World War.

In the Second Balkan War, however, the situation of Bulgaria recalled that of Poland during the years of the "Deluge" (1648–68), or France after the Battle of Nations in 1813, or perhaps Nazi Germany after the summer of 1944, when all or almost all allies had deserted the protagonist. Few other countries in European history have endured the catastrophe of invasion on all possible fronts. In the summer of 1913, only Bulgaria's Black Sea littoral remained safe from the intrusion of foreign armies.

All the participants in the Balkan Wars, except for Montenegro, used military airplanes. The Bulgarians used airplanes at Adrianople and at Chataldzha. The Greeks utilized airplanes at Janina and the Dardanelles, and the Serbs at Scutari. The Romanians brought airplanes with them when they invaded Bulgaria. The Ottomans had airplanes, but do not seem to have used them against the Balkan allies. Airplanes mainly served for reconnaissance purposes during the Balkan Wars. The Bulgarians bombed Adrianople, and the Greeks bombed Janina, and the Serbs Scutari, although these cites did not suffer major damage.

Greek sea power secured the control of the Aegean Sea and its islands for the Greeks. It also played an important logistical role in the Balkan wars by transporting and supplying Bulgarian and Serbian troops. It also blockaded the Ottoman Aegean coastline. In these regards, the role of the Greek navy during the Balkan Wars was similar to that of the British navy during the First World War. The attempted Ottoman landing at Sharkoi on the Sea of Marmara was an ambitious attempt at amphibious warfare. Its failure foreshadowed the British and French defeat some 50 miles to the west at Gallipoli in 1915.

Except for Montenegro, which because of the traditional rule of King Nikola had not developed a real parliamentary government, the participants of the Balkan Wars all experienced conflict between their civilian governments and the military establishments. These conflicts arose over the direction of national policy and war goals. In two cases the consequences of the conflict were serious. In the Ottoman Empire, the conflict resulted in what amounted to a military take over of the government in January 1913. In Bulgaria, the lack of communication between the government and the military contributed to the accidental offensives of 29–30 June 1913 and Bulgaria's ultimate defeat in the Second Balkan War. The discord between the civilian government and the military were not so extreme in Greece and Serbia during the Balkan Wars. Nevertheless, friction continued in Greece until the defeat in the war against Turkey in 1922 established a strong military presence in government lasting until the Greek defeat and occupation by Germany in 1941. In Serbia, the divergence of methods, if not goals, between the government and the military contributed to planning and enactment of the Sarajevo assassination of June 1914.

The experience of the Balkan Wars singularly failed to enlighten the military establishments of the other European states about the nature of modern warfare. These soldiers would undergo many of the same experiences that Balkan soldiers had endured, facing each other moldering in trenches, massing infantry attacks in the face of heavy artillery fire, charging into the maws of machine guns. One reason other states did not learn from the Balkan Wars was the brief time between the cessation of fighting in the Balkans at the end of July 1913 and its renewal precisely one year later. The European military establishments did not have time to assimilate the lessons of the fighting.

Another reason the Balkan Wars did so little to instruct observers on aspects of contemporary warfare was the reluctance of the Balkan armies to open up their operations to foreigners. The Bulgarians, Greeks, and Serbs were hesitant about allowing foreign military attachés and journalists access to front line areas. The Montenegrin and Ottoman forward areas, probably because of their lower standards of organization, were more accessible. Much of the information on the Thracian battles, for instance, came from foreign journalists who had wandered back and forth amidst scenes of Ottoman confusion and defeat.

Yet another issue involved the military interests of the attachés detached to gather information. In the autumn of 1912 the American military attaché assigned to Belgrade, Bucharest, and Sofia, Lieutenant Sherman Miles, traveled with several European military attachés from Sofia toward the Bulgarian front. He noted that many of his colleagues were greatly concerned for their own material comfort as they toured the sights of recent battles. Furthermore, he reported,

> The attachés were extremely keen on the strategy of the campaign, on the strategic possibilities, on map discussions, and on map movements of Divisions and Armies. But the construction and position of trenches, the effect of fire on trenches, the lay of the country, and the handling of men they did not regard as of much interest to General Staff officers.[5]

The military attachés observing the Balkan Wars ignored many of the tactical lessons that would become very important during the First World War. Because of this failure to pay attention to various aspects of field fortifications, for instance, many soldiers would lose their lives during the grinding trench warfare of the First World War. In addition, the post-1914 combatants had to discover all over again the devastating impact of modern rapid-firing artillery upon infantry attacks. Implicit in this attitude was the assumption that events in regions of lesser development such as the Balkans could do little to instruct the Great Powers.

Many observations of the Balkan Wars tended to confirm existing doctrines rather than lead to new conclusions. German reports tended to discern the superiority of Krupp artillery, whereas those of the French emphasized the excellence of Schneider weapons. Although the rash offensives of the Ottomans received little notice, the massed infantry attacks of the Bulgarians and Serbs often warranted intense praise from European observers. Many observers insisted that assaults in the "Japanese" style, although costly, could win the objective.

This is not to say that observers ignored all pertinent aspects of the Balkan Wars. Among the prescient observations emanating from the Balkan Wars was one regarding the value of the machine gun, written by a military journalist accompanying the Greek forces in their advance to and investiture of Janina. He noted, "The machine gun is obviously *the* weapon of the future; in the opinion of the author the next war between first-class military powers will establish the vast superiority of the machine gunner over the rifleman, both as regards accuracy and control of fire."[6] This was a valuable observation. It failed to enlighten many General Staffs about the nature of contemporary warfare.

Casualties

Military casualty figures for the Balkan Wars demonstrate considerable variation. This was due to confusion on the battlefield, the renewed chaos of the fighting in July 1913 and again after August 1914, and poor record management and preservation. Epidemic diseases and the resulting civilian casualties further obscured the issue.

In the First Balkan War the Bulgarian losses were 14,000 killed, 50,000 wounded, and 19,000 dead from disease. This means that in the First Balkan War alone the Bulgarian army suffered an overall casualty rate of 21%. In the Second Balkan, or Interallied War, the Bulgarian losses were 18,000 dead, 60,000 wounded, and 15,000 dead from disease.[7] The high losses in the Second Balkan War occurred during intense fighting of only six weeks' duration. The Greek losses were 5,169 dead and 23,502 wounded or sick in the First Balkan War, and 2,563 dead and 19,307 wounded or sick in the Second Balkan War.[8] The First Balkan War cost Montenegro 2,836 dead and 6,602 wounded.[9] Most of these losses resulted from the operations around Scutari. The Montenegrins lost another 240 dead and 961 wounded in the Second Balkan War.[10] These were high casualty rates for a small country. A recent estimate gives Serbian casualties for both Balkan Wars as 36,550 dead and 55,000 wounded, totaling 82,000, although the real figure may go as high as 91,000.[11] Other figures for Serbian losses indicate that in the war against Bulgaria, the Serbs suffered 9,000 dead, 5,000 dead from cholera, and 36,000 wounded.[12] The Serbs probably suffered higher casualties during the war with Bulgaria than during the war with the Ottoman Empire. The Balkan Wars erased a generation of Bulgarians, Greeks, Montenegrins, and Serbs. This was especially true for Bulgaria, which suffered high casualties in both wars.

Ottoman casualty figures are very difficult to ascertain. They were often the result of estimates on the part of journalists or other observers. Since Ottoman forces frequently retreated or fled from the battlefields, the Ottomans were not always able to produce reliable estimates of the numbers of killed and wounded. During the First Balkan War, total Ottoman casualties probably amounted to around 100,000 men. These high Ottoman military casualties eliminated one of the last buttresses of the Ottoman state and accelerated the process of its final disintegration.

In addition, large numbers of civilians in Ottoman Thrace and Bulgaria succumbed to the cholera and dysentery plagues that swept through the Balkans in the autumn of 1912. During the Second Balkan War, refugees and the Ottoman and Romanian invaders of Bulgaria spread disease throughout the Balkans. Cholera and dysentery still prevailed at the time of the outbreak of World War I and reappeared with devastating results in Serbia during that war.

Atrocities

The Balkan Wars initiated an age of horrible actions committed upon both military and civilian populations in Europe. Atrocities of course have never been entirely absent from Europe. Indeed, as recently as 1876 reports of Ottoman massacres of Bulgarians were instrumental in provoking the Russo-Turkish war. The slaughter of Islamic Slavs and Turks by Bulgarians received much less attention. Nevertheless, the suffering of prisoners of war and targeting of civilians by military units initiated an age of inhumanity in Europe that spanned the entire century. The soldiers of the Balkan and Ottoman armies often behaved brutally toward their adversaries. Both sides frequently refused to take prisoners and killed any wounded enemy that they encountered. The Carnegie Report reproduced Greek posters showing Greek soldiers biting and stabbing Bulgarian soldiers. "In talk and in print one phrase summed up the general feelings of the Greeks toward the Bulgarians, '*Dhen einai anthropoi!*' (They are not human beings.)[13] The Serbs might also have uttered this phrase in regard to Albanians, or Bulgarians in regard to Turks. Many of those soldiers taken prisoner by all sides were subject to disease, starvation, and exposure. Montenegrins were notorious for slicing off the lips and noses of Ottoman soldiers as trophies of war. One Montenegrin soldier explained to M. E. Durham, "It is our old national custom, how can a soldier prove his heroism to his commander if he does not bring in noses? Of course we shall cut noses: we always have."[14] Another British observer, however, insisted that scavenging birds and the effects of exposure to the sun were responsible for facial deformities on Ottoman corpses.[15] Ottoman soldiers, as they retreated from the fields of their defeat, sometimes vented their frustrations on Christian villages they passed through with the usual actions of murder, arson, pillage, and rape.

A tendency to regard civilian populations as targets of war marked the Balkan Wars. This was not the first nor last time atrocities directed against civilians occurred during a European conflict. It was, however, the first time in the twentieth century that opposing military forces targeted civilians.

Accusations of atrocities were made against all sides in the Balkan Wars.

This was one aspect of the Balkan Wars that did not generally prevail in the European fighting after 1914.

Ascribing the Balkan War atrocities to vague pretexts such as "centuries-old hatred" is simplistic. The Albanians, Bulgarians, Greeks, Serbs, and Turks had lived in relative proximity to each other for centuries. If not intimate, they were certainly not isolated from each other. A major reason for the atrocities was abandonment of the Ottoman millet system and the adoption by the Bulgarians, Greeks, and Serbs of an exclusivist national ideology as the moral core of their new states. Toleration in the Balkans became a commodity in short supply.

Some of the terror directed against civilian populations was the reaction to the frustrating and costly guerrilla warfare that troops of the Balkan League encountered as they entered Ottoman territories. This was especially the case for Greek, Montenegrin, and Serbian soldiers intruding into Albanian-inhabited regions. Many of the Albanians fiercely resisted what they correctly perceived as an invasion of their lands. The Greeks, Montenegrins, and Serbs reacted by killing large numbers of Albanians, including civilians. This does not explain, let alone excuse, much of the barbarous behavior of the Balkan armies.

The purpose of many of the atrocities inflicted upon the civilian populations in the Balkans was to achieve a homogenous national state. Deliberate terror created by arson, looting, murder, and rape was intended as a spur to move populations out of a particular piece of territory. One journalist reported that when the Serbian Ibar Army, under General Zivkovich, marched into the Sandjak of Novi Pazar, it pacified the Albanian population living there under old principle, "soletudinem facient, pacem appelant."[16] This sensibility justified atrocities in Albania, Macedonia, and Thrace perpetrated by the armies of the Balkan League.

Undoubtedly the Albanian civilian populations in Kosovo and northern Albania suffered grievously at the hands of the Montenegrin and Serbian armies. Examples of these horrors abound. Fritz Magnussen, a correspondent for the Danish paper *Riget*, wrote,

> Serbian military activities in Macedonia have taken on the character of an extermination of the Arnaut (Albanian) population. The army is conducting an unspeakable war of atrocities. According to officers and soldiers, 3,000 Arnauts were slaughtered in the region between Kumanova/Kumanovo and Skoplje and 5,000 near Prishtina. The Arnaut villages were surrounded and set on fire. The inhabitants were then chased from their homes and shot like rats. The Serb soldiers delighted in telling me of the manhunts they conducted.[17]

The Montenegrins and Serbs intended their presence in these regions to be permanent, and were not disposed to share their conquests with the previous inhabitants. Acts of resistance by these Albanians only increased the sufferings of the civilian populations. The numbers of Albanians murdered or who died as a result of the Montenegrin and Serbian actions is impossible to calculate.

The outbreak of the Second Balkan War was a signal for atrocities to be carried out by former allies on former allied populations. As they retreated, Bulgarians took out their frustrations on Greek civilians. Greeks and Serbians increased their efforts to eradicate the Bulgarian influence in Macedonia. Ottomans returning to eastern Thrace sought revenge on the Bulgarian population remaining there. Even the Romanian invaders of Bulgaria, who met no armed opposition, burned, looted, and raped. Charges and countercharges emanating from all sides considerably obscured these outrages.

Probably the most objective assessment of the question of atrocities in the Balkan Wars is found in the Carnegie Report.[18] A committee of seven men, one from each of Austria–Hungary, Germany, Great Britain, Russia, and the United States and two from France, investigated the Balkan war arenas at the conclusion of the Second Balkan War. They traveled to the battlefields and other scenes of destruction of the wars during August and September 1913 and then returned to Paris to write their report.

The report was pervasive and persuasive in ascribing brutalities and atrocities to all sides in both wars. Its conclusions were based on verbal and written evidence of eyewitnesses and survivors as well as the observations of the committee members themselves. The committee judiciously concluded, "The main fact is that war suspended the restraints of civil life, inflamed the passions that slumber in time of peace, destroyed the national kindliness between neighbors, and set in its place the will to injure. That is everywhere the essence of war."[19] Nevertheless, the Greeks thought that the report was unfavorable to them. They responded with several volumes of Bulgarian atrocities in the Second Balkan War.[20] The Bulgarians eventually answered with charges of their own directed against the Greeks.[21]

Although uncounted numbers of civilians perished in or fled from the horrors of the Balkan Wars, no purely national states resulted. Each postwar state continued to included large national minority communities. Large numbers of refugees inundated Constantinople during the First Balkan War and Bulgaria during the Second Balkan War. The Albanian victims of atrocities had nowhere to flee during the wars.

Costs

According to a recent estimate, the First Balkan War cost Serbia 590,000,000 francs, Montenegro 100,000,000 francs, Greece 467,000,000 francs, and Bulgaria 1,300,000,000 francs.[22] Of course, these figures were contemporary, and probably only gesture toward a more precise economic evaluation of the general Balkan disaster of 1912–13. Ottoman costs remain unclear. All of these countries might well have spent this enormous sum on economic development, rather than on destruction. Certainly, the economic costs of these wars was an important factor in the retardation of development in the Balkans. The Balkan countries did not bear the cost alone. They had obtained much of the money used to wage the war in loans from the Great Powers. They had repaid little of it by August 1914, and none of it thereafter.

Conclusion

One of the greatest of the many tragedies of the Balkan Wars was the missed opportunity of especially Bulgaria and Serbia to establish a lasting Balkan union. The March 1912 agreement between Bulgaria and Serbia provided a strong basis for such a union. A united Balkans could have facilitated economic development in the peninsula, and it could have avoided years of wasting of lives and material in Bulgarian–Serbian (Yugoslav) rivalries. A solid Balkan front also might have dissuaded Austria–Hungary from taking the first fatal steps against Serbian terrorism in July 1914.

The alliance failed for three reasons. It failed primarily because Bulgaria did not seek a geographic division of Macedonia with Greece. Bulgaria and Greece could have reached a settlement as late as the spring of 1913. The unrealistic expectations of the Bulgarians, especially in regards to Salonika, prevented this. A territorially satisfied Greece would have been unlikely to come to an agreement with Serbia.

A second reason for the failure of the Balkan alliance was the Austro-Hungarian and Italian interest in the Adriatic Sea. This interest led to the creation of an independent Albanian state in order to thwart Greek, Montenegrin, and Serbian ambitions in this region. Their failure to establish a presence on the Adriatic led the Serbians to seek compensation in Macedonia on territory claimed by the Bulgarians. Even so, the Serbs might well have attempted to retain much of Macedonia even if they had stayed in Durres.

A third reason for the failure of the Balkan alliance was the inconsistent attitude of the guarantor of the March 1912 Treaty, Russia. The Russians failed miserably to promote a sense of fairness and moderation between Bulgaria and Serbia. Their representatives in Belgrade and Sofia gave conflicting advice. As a result, St Petersburg lost its firm position in Sofia and with it a realistic opportunity to finally establish physical control of the Straits. In its place, the Russians found themselves tied to a less advantageous position in Serbia. In the end, Russia had to follow Serbia's lead into the catastrophe of 1914.

The Ottomans notably failed to take advantage of the inherent fissures in the Balkan League. Their major enemy was Bulgaria, because of its proximity to their capital. The Ottomans might well have attempted to make an arrangement with Serbia by ceding the Sandjak outright and by making overt concessions to the Serbs in Macedonia and Kosovo. An Ottoman arrangement with Greece would have been more problematical, but not impossible in terms of concessions in Crete and the Aegean Islands. At the very least, an Ottoman attempt to exploit the divisions in the Balkan League could have bought them the time to shift their forces from Asia Minor to Thrace and to achieve a successful offensive there. The Ottomans, to paraphrase Frederick II, attempted to defend everything and as a result lost everything.

All of the participants in the Balkan Wars suffered disappointment and defeat in the pursuit of the issues that had led to the wars. In the space of two months Bulgaria went from exhilarating victory to catastrophic defeat. The chimeras of Salonika and Adrianople diverted Bulgaria from its main objective, Macedonia. Had the Bulgarians abandoned their desire for Adrianople, they could have achieved a final peace agreement in London on December 1912 or January 1913. Had the Bulgarians reached an accommodation with Greece over Salonika at any time from the autumn of 1912 to the spring of 1913, they might not have had to fight the Second Balkan War. Had Bulgaria satisfied Romanian territorial demands in Dobrudzha during the spring of 1913, they might well have managed to win the Second Balkan war.

In the Second Balkan War, Bulgaria became the only country in modern Europe to suffer invasion on every frontier from every neighbor. Its inability to realize its Macedonian ambitions in the Balkan Wars would lead Bulgaria to enter the fighting on the side of the Central Powers in 1915 and the Germans in 1941. On both occasions Bulgarian troops occupied Macedonia. The Bulgarian presence there, however, would prove ephemeral. The legacy of defeat in the Second Balkan War would lead Bulgaria to defeats in the First and Second World Wars. Macedonia remained beyond Bulgaria's reach.

Greece enjoyed stunning victories in both Balkan Wars, but material exhaustion and political discord led to national inertia and foreign occupation during the First World War. The renewed Greek effort to achieve national goals in Anatolia in 1921 and 1922, however, resulted in military rout. The ensuing catastrophe brought about the eradication of a several millennia old Hellenic presence in Anatolia and eastern Thrace, and a flood of refugees into an exhausted and defeated Greece.

Montenegro gained considerable territory from victory in the First Balkan War. The failure of the Montenegrin army before Scutari, however, exposed the fundamental weakness of the Petrovich dynasty and the Montenegrin state. After the Balkan Wars, King Nikola could have no pretensions to the throne of a unified Serbian state. Indeed, the continued existence of an independent Montenegro became problematic as the power of Serbia drew many Montenegrins toward Belgrade.

The big winner in the Balkan Wars was Serbia. Not only had Serbian armies triumphed over Ottoman troops in Albania, in Macedonia, and in

Thrace and then over Bulgarian soldiers in Macedonia, but Serbia had greatly expanded its territory and population. These gains brought Serbia enhanced power and prestige, but also many difficulties. The new territories contained large non-Serbian populations. Armed rebellions by Albanians in Kosovo and by supporters of IMRO and Bulgaria in Macedonia opposed Serbian rule from 1913. Nevertheless, Serbia's national appetite remained ravenous, especially in regards to Albania and Bosnia. Within a year of the Treaty of Bucharest, Serbia would defeat two Austro-Hungarian invasions. A third invasion, in the autumn of 1915, would bring catastrophic defeat and harsh foreign occupation. Even though Serbia emerged from the First World War on the winning side, the rewards of victory ultimately proved impossible to be fully realized. The Serbian-dominated Yugoslav state only lasted twenty-three years before it collapsed in the face of a Nazi invasion.

Ironically, of all the participants in the Balkan Wars, only the Young Turks succeeded in forging a maximalist national state. Although their vision of Ottoman nationality failed, they did manage, perhaps inadvertently, to create and sustain viable Turkish nationalism. This development only came at the price of devastating defeat, not only in the First Balkan War but also in the First World War, and after still more fighting in Anatolia against the Greeks after 1918. Nevertheless, the beginnings of a Turkish military identity, leading eventually to victories at the Dardanelles in 1915 and at Sakarya River in 1921, began in the Chataldzha lines in November 1912 with the successful defense of Constantinople. Even this resulting Turkish national state had frayed by the end of the twentieth century because of incessant warfare between the Kurds, who sought greater opportunity to realize their identity, and the government in Ankara.

The number of Albanians who were killed or wounded during the Balkan Wars defies easy determination. Many Albanians fought as members of or alongside Ottoman forces, others resisted the Greek, Montenegrin, and Serbian invasions of their lands separately. These invasions caused untold numbers of civilian casualties and much destruction in many areas of the country. Undoubtedly, the north and the south, the areas of the most intensive fighting and the regions coveted by the invaders, suffered the greatest demographic loses.

The Treaty of London of May 1912 proved to be ephemeral. The dissolution of the Balkan League rendered the conditions of the Treaty of London obsolete scarcely one month after its signing. The stipulations of the Treaty of Bucharest survived considerable effort at their revision. In 1915–16 and again in 1941 the Bulgarians annexed all of Serbian-held (Yugoslav) Macedonia and also occupied parts of Greek Macedonia, including the towns of Seres, Drama, and Kavala. Defeat in both World Wars ended these occupations, but only the World War I settlement at Neuilly in 1919 altered the borders laid down under the Treaty of Bucharest. Under the conditions of the Treaty of Neuilly in 1919, Bulgaria lost western Thrace, with its Aegean coastline, and four small pieces of land along the western frontier to the new Yugoslav state, including General Fichev's Strumitsa. In 1940 in the Treaty of Craiova, Romania re-ceded southern Dobrudzha to Bulgaria. The frontiers decided by the Treaty of Constantinople have remained largely unchanged since 1913. Bulgaria did obtain the Maritsa valley as a precondition for entering the First World War on the side of the Central Powers but lost this territory to Greece after 1919.

The Treaty of Bucharest assigned most of Macedonia and all of Kosovo to Serbia. These areas proved to be difficult for the Serbs to control. Rebellions against Serbian rule broke out almost immediately in both locations. The Serbs did not re-establish complete control of these regions until after 1918. During the inter-war period, IMRO contested Serbian rule in Macedonia. During World War II the Bulgarians once again occupied Macedonia, and the Italians annexed Kosovo to their Albanian "kingdom." Those Serbs remaining in Macedonia and Kosovo suffered greatly during the war. After World War II Tito's federal Yugoslavia separated both regions from Serbia.

The Balkan Wars commanded the attentions and energies of the Great Powers of Europe. Although the powers failed to prevent the outbreak of war in October 1912 and again in June 1913, they managed to cooperate diplomatically at the Ambassadors Conferences of London and St Petersburg and militarily at Constantinople in November 1912 and again at Scutari in April 1913. In their efforts to limit the outcome of the Balkan Wars, the Great Powers enacted the final efforts of a Concert of Europe, which had functioned more or less to maintain the balance on the continent since 1648.

Nevertheless, the Balkan Wars greatly increased Austro-Hungarian antipathy toward Montenegro and Serbia. The assaults by these Serbian states on Albania caused the Dual Monarchy, with German support, to threaten war in the autumn of 1912, in the spring of 1913, and again immediately after the Balkan Wars in the autumn of 1913. Although the events in the summer of 1914 that led to war occurred in Bosnia, not Albania, the heightened hostility as a result of the Balkan Wars made the decision in Vienna to go to war much more facile.

As noted above, Russian policy regarding the Balkan Wars was inconsistent and ineffective. The Russians had viewed the treaty of March 1912 as a weapon directed against the Habsburg Empire, not the Ottoman Empire. Yet St Petersburg did little to prevent the outbreak of war. The foreign office of Sergei Sazonov had little clear idea of Russia's real interests in the Balkans. He merely reacted to various issues as they came along, usually without much effectiveness. His major error was his failure to maintain the fundamental Bulgarian–Serbian alliance. If that was not possible, he should have clearly supported Bulgaria, which represented a much more strategically important position for Russia in the Balkans.

The Balkan Wars initiated an era of conflict in Europe lasting, with some gaps, until the end of the century. At the beginning of the century the Balkan

Wars opened a six-year period of conflict in Europe and in a wider sense, a Great European War lasting from 1912 to 1945. These conflicts were to a considerable degree based in the Balkans and elsewhere in Europe on attempts by those involved to realize greater nationalist states. At the end of the twentieth century, the Balkan Peninsula again became an arena for nationalist conflict. This suggests that national states are not the best means to structure the Balkan Peninsula politically. Only by finding a political framework that accommodates ethnic and cultural diversification can the Balkan Peninsula develop economically and politically enough to join the European community.

NOTES

1 BALKAN WAR ORIGINS

1 Konstantin Pandev, *Borbite v Makedoniya i Odrinsko, 1878–1912, Spomeni* (Sofia, 1982) 5.
2 W. N. Medlicott, *The Congress of Berlin and After* (London, 1938) 22.
3 Ivan E. Geshov, *Spomeni iz godini na borbi i pobedi* (Sofia, 1916) 94.
4 Ivan E. Geshov, *Lichna korespondentsiya* (Sofia, 1994) no. 7 letter of 30 June 1878 o.s. to Hristo N. Puliev, 29.
5 Medlicott, 208.
6 B. D. Kesiyakov, *Prinos kûm diplomaticheskata istoriya na Bûlgariya 1878–1925* (Sofia, 1925) I 20–21. See also E. C. Helmreich and C. E. Black, "The Russo-Bulgarian Military Convention of 1902." *Journal of Modern History* IX (December 1937) 471–82.
7 St Danev, "Kabinetût D-r. St Danev 1901–1903 godina," *Rodina* III 4 (1941) 70.
8 Ministerstvo na Voinata, *Shtab na Armiyata voenno istoricheska komisiya. Voinata mezhdu Bûlgariya i Turtsiya 1912–13 god.* (hereafter referred to as *Voinata*) (Sofia, 1933–7) I 83–4.
9 A. Toshev, *Balkanskite voini*, (Sofia, 1929–31) I 153–8. See also E. C. Helmreich, *The Diplomacy of the Balkan Wars 1912–13* (New York, 1969) 4–11.
10 Foreign Office, *British Documents on the Origins of the War 1898–1914*, eds G. P. Gooch and Harold Temperley (London, 1926–38) (hereafter referred to as BD) IX ii 454.
11 Auswärtiges Amt, *Die Grosse Politik der Europäischen Kabinette 1871–1914*, eds Johannes Lepsius, Albrecht Mendelssohn-Bartholdy and Friedrich Thimme (Berlin, 1927) (hereafter referred to as GP) XXVI i 9119. In 1909 Crown Prince George, in a fit of pique, killed his manservant. His younger brother Alexander then replaced him as heir to the throne.
12 BD V 140.
13 *Voinata* I 155.
14 Ministerium des k. und k. Hauses und des Äussern, *Österreich-Ungarns Aussenpolitik von der Bosnischen Krise 1908 bis zum Kriegsausbruch 1914. Diplomatische Aktenstucke des Österreichisch-Ungarischen Ministerium des Äussern*, eds Ludwig Bittner, Alfred F. Pribram, Heinrich Srbik and Hans Uebersberger (Vienna, 1930) (hereafter referred to as OUA) I 187, 198.
15 Ibid., 450, 454, 599.
16 Jovan M. Jovanovich, *Borba za narodno ujedinjenje 1903–1908* (Belgrade, no date) 81–4.
17 B. Kondis, "The Role of the Albanian Factor upon the Greek-Bulgarian Understanding of 1912," *Balkan Studies* 25 2 (1984) 378.

18 See Radoslav Popov, "Balkanskite dûrzhavi i krayat na krizata ot 1908–1909 g." in *V chest na Akademik Dimitûr Kosev* (Sofia, 1974) 262–63.
19 See Helmreich, 40–41.
20 *Voinata* I 37.
21 Ibid., 36.
22 See Edward Thaden, *Russia and the Balkan Alliance of 1912* (University Park, Pennsylvania, 1965) 38–57.
23 *Dnevnitsi (stenografski) na petato veliko narodno sûbranie v gr. Veliko Tûrnovo* (Sofia, 1911) speech by Ivan E. Geshov, 17 July 1911 o.s. 230.
24 George Young (Diplomatist) *Nationalism and War in the Near East*, (Oxford, 1915) 160.
25 For text of the treaty see Kesiyakov, I 36–48; Young, 387–9; BD IX ii appendix II.
26 Alex N. Dragnich, *Serbia, Nikola Pasic and Yugoslavia* (New Brunswick, NJ, 1974) 101.
27 Elena Statelova, "Bûlgaro-Grûtskite politicheski otnosheniya v navecherieto na Balkanskata voina," *Izvestia na Instituta za voenna istoriya* XXXVI (1984) 49.
28 For text of the treaty see Kesiyakov, I 148–151; Young, 396–400.
29 Katrin Boeckh, *Von den Balkankriegen zum Ersten Weltkrieg* (Munich, 1996) 29.
30 Otto Hoetzsch, ed., *Die internationalen Beziehungen im Zeitalter des Imperialismus: Dokumente aus den Archiven der zarischen und der provisorischen Regierungen* (Berlin, 1942) (hereafter referred to as RD) 3rd series I i 6.
31 Mary Edith Durham, *Twenty Years of Balkan Tangle* (New York, 1920) 222–3; John D. Treadway, *The Falcon and the Eagle* (West Lafayette, IN, 1983) 106.
32 *Voinata* I 62; Kesiyakov I 45 (footnote).
33 Ernst C. Helmreich, "The Serbo-Montenegrin Alliance of September 23/October 6, 1912," *Journal of Central European Affairs* XIX (January 1960) 412–13; Henryk Batowski, "The Failure of the Balkan Alliance of 1912," *Balkan Studies* 7 1 (1966) 113.
34 Draga Vuksanovich-Antich, *Stvaranje moderne Srpske vojske. Frantsuske utitsaj na njeno formiranje* (Belgrade, 1993) 135–6.
35 Yucel Aktar, "The Impact of the 1912 'War Meetings' on the Balkan Wars," *Revue internationale d'histoire militaire* 67 (1988) 169–75.
36 See Istoriski institut Jugoslovenske narodne armije, *Prvi Balkanski rat* (Operatsije Srpske vojske) ed. Branko Perovich (Belgrade, 1959) (hereafter referred to as *Rat*) I 144–5; Ivan Fichev, *Balkanskata voina 1912–13. Preshivelitsi, belezhki i dokumenti* (Sofia, 1941) 68–9.
37 Vojvoda Zhivojin Mishish, *Moje uspomene* 2nd edn (Belgrade, 1980) 268.
38 Fichev, 69; Georgi Markov, "Voennite sporazumeniya v Balkanskiya sûyuz i obyavavaneto na obshta mobilizatsiya v Bûlgariya (Mart-Septembri 1912 g.)" *Voennoistoricheski sbornik* 58 1 (1989) 18–19.
39 National Archives, Washington DC, War College Division, General Correspondence 1902–1920, Records Group (hereafter referred to as RG) 165-5964-3. Report of Major T. Bentley Mott, 28 July 1910.
40 Philip Howell, *The Campaign in Thrace 1912* (London, 1913) 56–7.
41 Yako Molhov, "Bûlgarskata artileriya prez Balkanskata voina 1912 g." *Voennoistoricheski sbornik* 57 1 (1988) 74.
42 D. J. Cassavetti, *Hellas and the Balkan Wars* (London, 1914) 26.
43 Ibid., 31.
44 Novica Rakocevic, "The Organization and Character of the Montenegrin Army in the First Balkan War," eds Bela Kiraly and Dimitrije Djordjevic in *East Central European Society and the Balkan Wars* (Boulder, 1987) 122–3.

45 The figures for the Balkan states are from Carnegie Endowment for International Peace, *Report of the International Commission to Inquire into the Causes and Conduct of the Balkan Wars*, Washington DC, 1913, 418 facing map.
46 The Italians did not fulfill this obligation, claiming that they needed to protect the islands from the effects of the Balkan War. They would retain the Dodecanese Islands until the end of the Second World War.
47 Feroz Ahmad, *The Young Turks. The Committee of Union and Progress in Turkish Politics 1908–1914* (Oxford, 1969) 113. Mehmud Shevket Pasha was Ottoman minister of war from January 1910 until Nizam Pasha succeeded him in July 1912.
48 Cherif Pacha, *Quelques réflexions sur la guerre turco-balkanique* (Paris, 1913) 49.
49 General Staff, War Office (Great Britain) *Armies of the Balkan States, 1914–1918* (London and Nashville, 1996); "Military Notes on the Balkan States," 63.

2 THE FIRST BALKAN WAR: THRACIAN THEATER

1 Kemal Soyupak and Huseyin Kabasakal, "The Turkish Army in the First Balkan War," in Kiraly and Djordjevic, 159. Estimates of the actual strength of the Turkish forces vary. One Ottoman commander stated that the Eastern (Thracian) army had 150,000 men. Mahmoud Moukhtar Pasha (Mahmut Muhtar Pasha), *Mon commandement au cours de la campagne des Balkans de 1912* (Paris, 1913) 2. The Ottoman forces were observed to be understrength. Lionel James, *With the Conquered Turk* (London, 1913) 53–4.
2 Ronald Tarnstrom, *Balkan Battles* (Lindsborg, KA, 1998) 58.
3 *Voinata* I 363–71.
4 Fichev, 90.
5 S. Toshev, *Pobedeni bez da bûdem biti* (Sofia, 1924) 246–7. The Bulgarian General Staff made a thorough study of this region in 1911.
6 The figures for the 1st and 3rd Armies are from *Voinata* II 657–8. The figure for the 2nd Army is from *Voinata* I 566. The figure for the western troops is from *Voinata* VI 258. The number of volunteers is from Nikola T. Zhekov, *Bûlgarskoto voinstvo 1878–1928 g.* (Sofia, 1928) 204. The total number comes from *Voinata* I 308–9. This includes men serving in such capacities as railroad work, but nonetheless was almost one-third of the total male population.
7 Henry Dugard (Louis Thomas), *Histoire de la guerre contre les Turcs 1912–13* (Paris, 1913) 71.
8 Howell, 33.
9 *Voinata* II 41.
10 Dr Borislav Ratkovich, "Prvi Balkanski rat 1912–13," *Vojnoistorijski glasnik* 39 2–3 (1988) 118.
11 See Captain Willard Vickers, "The Ottoman Army in the Balkan Wars," unpublished thesis, Princeton University, 1958, 83.
12 Izzet Pasha, *Denkwürdigkeiten des Marschalls Izzet Pascha*, trans. Karl Klinghardt (Leipzig, 1927) 172–80. The author of the plan, Izzet Pasha, was at the outbreak of the Balkan War in remote Yemen.
13 Field Marshall von der Goltz, "Causes of the Late Turkish Defeat," *Infantry Journal* IX (March-April 1913) 731.
14 Ellis Ashmead-Bartlett, *With the Turks in Thrace* (London, 1913) 78.
15 *Voinata* II 130.
16 Cherif Pacha, 21.
17 Dugard, 76.
18 Moukhtar Pasha, 43.
19 RG 165-7277-213 2. Lieutenant Sherman Miles, "Captured Turkish despatch," 11 January 1913.

20 *Voinata* II 285, 313, 404, 414, 457, 483.
21 Aram Andonyan, *Balkan harbi tarihi* (Istanbul, 1975) 490; Bernard P. L. Boucabeille, *La guerre Turco-Balkanique 1912–1913* (Paris, 1913) 155.
22 *Voinata* II 574. According to the chief of the bureau of operations of the Bulgarian 3rd Army, Lieutenant Colonel Asmanov, the Bulgarians were prepared to beseige Lozengrad if their attack failed. Alain de Penennum, *La guerre des Balkans en 1912. Campagne de Thrace* (Paris, 1913) 55.
23 Radko Dimitriev, *Treta armiya v Balkanskata voina 1912 godina* (Sofia, 1922) 155.
24 Cherif Pacha, 26.
25 RG 7277-213 1–2. Miles, "Captured Turkish despatch." 11 January 1913.
26 Moukhtar Pasha, 49.
27 Cherif Pasha, 33; Momchil Yonov, "Bulgarian Military Operations in the Balkan Wars," in Kiraly and Djordjevic, 70.
28 *Voinata* III 149. This was Lieutenant Stefan Ionov.
29 Boris, Nikolov, "Balkanskata voina v spomenite na General-Maior Iordan Venedikov," *Voennoistoricheski sbornik* 57 5 (1988) 177.
30 Ashmead-Bartlett, 155. Along these same lines see also Friedrich Immanuel, *Der Balkankrieg 1912* (Berlin 1913–14) II 41.
31 Moukhtar Pacha, 134.
32 Ashmead-Bartlett, 145.
33 *Voinata* III 525, 618–20.
34 Stefka Slavova and Tsvetana Doinova, eds, *Balkanskata voina prez pogleda na edin Frantsuzin* (Sofia, 1977) (hereafter referred to as Martharel) no. 26, 7 January 1913, 133. These are the reports of the French military attaché in Sofia, Major Camille Louis de Martharel.
35 Moukhtar Pacha, 138. Dimitriev, 296. The usually reliable Immanuel speaks of "extraordinarily high" Turkish battlefield losses and gives the figure of 25,000. *Immanuel* II 37.
36 Colin Ross, *Im Balkankrieg* (Munich, 1913) 83–4. Unlikely name for a German journalist.
37 The American military attaché in Constantinople, Major Taylor, reported that at the height of the epidemic 2,000–3,000 Ottoman soldiers died of cholera every day. He wrote, "No exaggeration of the condition is possible." RG 165-7277-127. Major J. R. M. Taylor, "Cholera," 20 November 1912.
38 Howell, 157–8. In their capacity for self-sacrifice the Bulgarian troops were often compared to the Japanese. Howell also noted, "Like the Japanese the Bulgarians have made a fetish of the bayonnette."
39 A. Toshev, II 47, BD IX ii 192.
40 Ministère des Affaires étrangères, *Documents diplomatiques français* (Paris 1929–59) (hereafter referred to as DDF) 3rd series IV 429.
41 RG 165-7277-175 1. Major J. R. M. Taylor, "Conditions in Constantinople," 17 December 1912.
42 *Voinata* IV 173.
43 Hans Graf von Podewils, "Taktisches vom thrazichen Kriegsschauplatz," *Vierteljahrshefte für Truppenführung und Heerskunde* X (1913) 185.
44 RG 7277-174, 1–2. Major J. R. M. Taylor, "Report" 16 December 1912.
45 Narodno sûbranie, *Doklad na parlamentarnata izpitatelna komisiya* (Sofia, 1918–19) (hereafter referred to as DPIK) 261–2 no. 3; RD 3rd series IV i 231.
46 Ivan Geshov, *Prestupnoto bezumie i anketata po nego. Fakti i dokumenti* (Sofia, 1914) 32–3. The five men referred to were Savov, the three army commanders, and Fichev.
47 See Hans Roger Madol, *Ferdinand von Bulgarien. Der Traum von Byzanz* (Berlin, 1931) 141–8. The portrait is the frontispiece.

48 Fichev, 200.
49 *Voinata* IV 625.
50 Ibid., 608; Kiril Kosev, *Podvigût* (Sofia, 1983) 109.
51 Dimitriev, 318. Krum (*c*. 803–814) and Simeon (893–927) were medieval Bulgarian rulers who led their armies up to Constantinople but failed to take it.
52 *Voinata* IV 427; A. Toshev, II 69; Fichev, 204–5.
53 Narodno sûbranie, *Prilozhenie kûm tom vtori ot doklada na parlamentarnata izpitatelna komisiya* (Sofia, 1918) (Savov) 290.
54 Ashmead Bartlet, 288.
55 Penenerum, 97.
56 James, 343. Another English observer, to the contrary, stated that, "certainly it seemed beyond argument that the Bulgarian artillery was very much better than that of the defense." Philip Gibbs and Bernard Grant, *The Balkan War. Adventures of War with Cross and Crescent* (Boston, 1912) 233.
57 *Voinata* IV 138; Kosev, 119.
58 Andonyan, 516.
59 Fichev, 221; *Narodno sûbranie, Prilozhenie kûm tom pûrvi ot doklada na parlamentarnata izpitatelna komisiya* (Sofia, 1918) hereafter referred to as *Prilozhenie* I (Savov) 274.
60 G. von Hochwächter, *Mit den Türken in der Front. Im Stab Mahmud Muchtar Paschas* (Berlin, 1913) 121.
61 RG 7277-223-1. "Present conditions on the Tchataldja lines to Jan. 17 1913." Major J. R. M. Taylor, 23 January 1913.
62 *Voinata* IV 466. This figure did not include specialists such as engineers, etc.
63 The Bulgarians did not take seriously a Greek proposal in December 1912 to cooperate against Constantinople with a combined operation using the Bulgarian army against Chataldzha and the Greek fleet against the Dardanelles was not taken seriously by the Bulgarians. Archive of Bûlgarska akademiya naukite, Sofia, Fond 58, diary of former Minister of Justice Petûr Abrashev (hereafter referred to as BAN) 51-I-17-127; DPIK I, 576–7 no. 32.
64 *Voinata* V i 9, 27.
65 Nazmi Çagan, "Balkan harbinde Edirne (1912–1913)" in *Edirne* (Ankara, 1965) 200. There were in addition 106,000 civilians in the city, of whom around 20,000 were refugees from the surrounding countryside.
66 *Voinata* I 503.
67 Major General Pantelei Tsenov "Za atakata na Odrinskata krepost" ed. Momchil P. Ionov in *Odrin 1912–1913 Spomeni* (Sofia, 1983) (hereafter referred to as *Odrin*) 40.
68 *Voinata* V i 38–41.
69 Nikola Ivanov, "Spomeni 1861–1918" in *Odrin* 21.
70 Fichev, 86.
71 BAN 51-I-17-95. See also RD series 3 vols IV i 96.
72 RD 3rd series IV i 204 no. 1 p. 214.
73 *Voinata* V i 275–76; Aleksandûr Ganchev, *Voinite prez tretoto Bûlgarsko tsarstvo* (Sofia, no date) 115.
74 BAN 51-17-I-68. Fichev proposed the use of Serbian troops at Adrianople to the Serbian General Radomir Putnik in August 1912. Fichev, 64–5. See also Georgi Markov, "Bûlgariya i neinite sûyuznitsi prez Balkanskata voina (1912–1913 g.)" *Istoricheski pregled* XXXIX (1983) 42.
75 Petar Opachich, "Political Ramifications of Serbo-Bulgarian Military Cooperation in the First Balkan War," in Kiraly and Djordjevic, 93.
76 Gibbs and Grant, 102. Gibbs and Grant place this raid in the first week of November.
77 Howell, 121.
78 *Voinata* V i 612.

79 Fichev, 224.
80 C. Zoli, *Der Balkankrieg. Mit den Bulgaren gegen die Türken* trans. Adolf Sommerfeld (Berlin 1913) 44. These figures are probably a little high.
81 *Voinata* V i 603.

3 FIRST BALKAN WAR: WESTERN THEATER

1 Dr Borislav Ratkovich, "Mobilization of the Serbian Army for the First Balkan War, October, 1912," in Kiraly and Djordjevic, 155. This is the source of numbers for all four Serbian army.
2 *Rat* I 279; Ratkovich, "Mobilization," 156.
3 Stojan Stojanovich, "Kumanovo-mladno nagorichino, (1912)" *Nova Evropa* 6 12 (1922) 366.
4 Borislav Ratkovich, "Prvi Balkanski rat," *Vojnoistorisjski glasnik* 39 2–3 (1988) 118.
5 Soyupak and Kabasakal, 159. This seems a little high in terms of what the Ottomans actually put into the field.
6 Dordje Mikich, "The Albanians and Serbia during the Balkan Wars," in Kiraly and Djordjevic, 171.
7 Dr Borislav Ratkovich, "Mobilizacija Srpske i Turski vojske za prvi balkanski rat Oktobra 1912 godine," *Vojnoistoriski glasnik*, 36 1 (1985) 201.
8 Izzet Pasha, 196.
9 Ratkovich, "Prvi Balkanski rat," 127.
10 Savo Skoko, "An Analysis of the Strategy of Vojvoda Putnik during the Balkan Wars," in Kiraly and Djordjevic, 18.
11 The German advisor von der Golz had thought that in the west the Ottomans should fight a defensive battle around Shtip, in southeastern Macedonia. Von der Goltz, 732.
12 Stevan S. Shapinac, "Kako smo ushli u Kumanovsku bitku," *Nova Evropa*, 6 12 (1922) 373.
13 Vatslav Kolfach, "Bitka kod Kumanova," ed. Silvija Djurich in *Dnevnik pobeda* (Belgrade, 1988) 71. These were the same terms used to describe a Bulgarian attack. See above.
14 Dr Petar Opachich, "Kumanovska bitka," *Vojnoistoriski glasnik* 39 1 (1988) 220.
15 Cherif Pacha, 58.
16 *Rat* I 718.
17 Aleksandar M. Stojichevich, *Istorija nashih ratova za oslobodjenje i ujedinjenje od 1912–1918 god* (Belgrade, 1932) 164.
18 Ivan. S. Pavlovich, *Od Skoplja ka Bitolju u ratu s Turtsima 1912 godine* (Belgrade, 1925) 40 no. 1. The source of the quotation is not identified.
19 A. Kutschbach, *Die Serben im Balkankrieg 1912–13 und im Kriege gegen die Bulgaren* (Stuttgart, 1913) 50.
20 A. Toshev, II 47; *Prilozhenie* (Danev) 41.
21 Ratkovich, "Prvi Balkanski rat," 130.
22 Dr Borislav Ratkovich, "Bitoljska bitka," *Vojnoistoriski glasnik* 39 2 (1988) 207.
23 Skoko, "Putnik," 23.
24 Savo Skoko and Petar Opachich, *Vojvoda Stepa Stepanovich u ratovima Srbije 1876–1918* (Belgrade, 1984) 235–7.
25 Petar Opachich, "Political Ramifications of Serbo-Bulgarian Military Cooperation in the First Balkan War," in Kiraly and Djordjevic, 91.
26 Jasha Tomich, *Rat na Kosovu i Staroj Srbiji. 1912 godine* (Nish, 1988) 119, 125. The Nemanjas were the most important medieval Serbian dynasty. Tsar Lazar was the Serbian ruler who led the Serbs at the battle of Kosovo Polje in 1389.

27 Mishich, 282.
28 Mitar Durishich, "Operations of the Montenegrin Army during the First Balkan War," in Kiraly and Djordjevic, 127.
29 Dragich Vujoshevich, "Operatcije Crnogorski Primorskog odreda u ratu 1912 g.," *Istoriski zapisi* 10 2 (1954) 465.
30 Durishich, "Operations," 127.
31 M. E. Durham, *The Struggle for Scutari* (London, 1914) 183.
32 Mitar Djurishich, "Uloga Kralja Nikole u Prvom Balkanskom ratu." *Istoriski zapisi* 17 1 (1960) 91.
33 F. S. Stevenson, *A History of Montenegro* (New York, 1971) 210.
34 Eleutherios Prevelakis, "Eleutherios Venizelos and the Balkan Wars." *Balkan Studies*, VII 2 (1966) 372.
35 Dr Kleanthes Nikolaides, *Griechenlands anteil an den Balkankriege 1912/1913* (Vienna, 1914) 41–2. This is the source of both Ottoman figures.
36 Ibid., 55,
37 Captain A. H. Trapmann, *The Greeks Triumphant* (London, 1915) 89 (original in italics).
38 Gregor Manousakis, *Hellas-Wohin? Das Verhaltnis von Militar und Politik in Griechenland seit 1900* (Godesberg, 1967) 94.
39 Nikolaides, 63.
40 Georgi Markov, *Bûlgariya v Balkanskiya sûyuz sreshtu Osmanskata imperiya 1912–1913* (Sofia, 1989) 91–2. The Bulgarians claimed that the Greeks spent large sums of money to induce the Turkish commanders to surrender to them.
41 Hellenic Army History Directorate, Army General Headquarters, "Hellenic Army Operations during the Balkan Wars," in Kiraly and Djordjevic, 102. A Turkish source gave the number as 40,000. Soyupak and Kabasakal, 161.
42 Douglas Dakin, *The Greek Struggle in Macedonia 1897–1913* (Thessaloniki, 1966) 449, no. 10.
43 Fichev, 231, *Voinata* VI 194.
44 Hoover Institute, Stanford, CA, Archive of Tsar Ferdinand of Bulgaria (hereafter referred to as Ferdinand) telegram from Ferdinand to the Prince of Turnovo (Boris) no date (probably late autumn 1912).
45 Opachich, "Political Ramifications," 92.
46 Trapmann, 71.
47 Tarnstrom, 195.
48 Nikolaides, 200.

4 THE ARMISTICE

1 DPIK I 268 no. 20.
2 BD IX ii no. 332.
3 St Danev, "Primirieto v Chataldzha na 20 Noemvri 1912." *Rodina* I 3 (1939) 94.
4 *Nashata duma. Vûzrazheniya na bivshite ministri I. E. Geshov, Dr S. Danev, T. Teodorov, M. I. Madzharov, I. Peev i P. Abrashev sreshtu obvineniyata na dûrzhavniya sûd ot 1923 godina* (Sofia, 1925) (Teodorov) 108.
5 RG 165 7277-184, 2. Lieutenant Sherman Miles, "Present condition of the Bulgarian and Serbian Armies in view of a possible continuation of the war against Turkey," 22 December 1912.
6 BAN 51-I-18-310. This was Hak Pasha, a member of the Ottoman delegation sent to London to sign the preliminary peace treaty between the Ottoman Empire and the Balkan allies in May 1913.
7 Ahmad, 115.

NOTES

8 Narodno sûbranie, *Dnevnitsi (stenografski) na sedemnadesetoto obiknoveno narodno sûbranie. Pûrva redovna sesiya.* (Sofia, 1914) 5 May 1914, Speech by Stoyan Danev, 645.
9 Helmreich, 461–62.
10 Alfred Rappaport, "Albaniens Werdegang," *Die Kriegsschuldfrage*, V (September 1927) 824.
11 See Stefanaq Pollo, "La proclamation de l'independance de l'Albanie," *Studica Albanica*, 24 2 (1987) 3–18.
12 OUA IV 4170.
13 J. Swire, *Albania: The Rise of a Kingdom* (New York, 1930) 147.
14 Andrew Rossos, *Russia and the Balkans. Inter-Balkan rivialries and Russian foreign policy 1908–1914* (Toronto, 1981) 102.
15 M. Boghitschewitsch (Bogiechivich) (ed), *Die Auswärtige Politik Serbiens, 1903–1914* (Berlin, 1928–31) (hereafter referred to as SD) II 694.
16 DPIK I 396 no. 10.
17 Dimitrije Djordjevich, *Izlazak Srbije na Jadransko more i konferentsija ambasadora u Londonu 1912* (Belgrade, 1956) 57.
18 OUA V 4928.
19 DPIK I 560 no. 3, 560–1 no. 4, 561 no. 5.
20 Ibid., 562 no. 7.
21 Ibid., 572 no. 23.
22 BAN 51-17-I-132.
23 Edouard Driault, *Historie diplomatique de la Grèce de 1821 a nos jours* (Paris, 1926) V 85.
24 DPIK I 583 nos 49, 50; *Prilozhenie* I (Danev) 50–1.
25 Popovich, Ched. A., "Srpsko-Bulgarski rat, 1913 godine, (Rad organizacije "Ujedinjenje ili Smrt") *Nova Evropa* 18 10–11 (1928) 319–21.
26 Dimitûr G. Gotsev, *Natsional-osvoboditelnata borba v Makedoniya 1912–1915* (Sofia, 1981) 54–69, 78–9, 96–104; Toshev, II 82–3.
27 Tomich, 139.
28 Helmreich, 353–4.
29 Tsentralen dûrzhaven istoricheski arkiv, Sofia, fond 176 opus 2 a.e. 1254, 14–16.
30 BAN 51-I-17-92; I. E. Geshov, *Prestupnoto bezumie* 62.
31 BAN 51-I-17-168.
32 Ahmad, 116–19.
33 Helmreich, 268.

5 THREE SIEGES

1 Georges Redmond, *Avec les vaincus. La campagne en Thrace (Octobre 1912–Mai 1913)* (Paris, 1913) 181.
2 *Voinata* VII 518.
3 Ibid., 235.
4 Cherif Pacha, 67; Teno Tonchev, *Hrabrostta na Bûlgariya* (Sofia, 1981) 136.
5 *Voinata* VII 167.
6 *Istoriyata na Riltsi. 13. Pehoten Rilski polk v voinite za obedinenie na Bûlgarskiya narod. 1912–13. g. i 1915–1918. g.* (Kyustendil, 1931) 87.
7 "Dnevnik na Todor Dichev Slavchev," in *Balkanskata voina v spomenite na sûvremnitsi i uchastnitsi*, (Sofia, 1973) 171.
8 Cherif Pacha, 67.
9 Markov, *Bûlgariya*, 275.
10 Ganchev, 191–2.

11 Stiliyan Noikov, "Iz spomenite na General Stiliyan Kovachev za Balkanskata voina 1912–1913 godina," *Voennoistoricheski sbornik* 57 1 (1988) 99. According to General Kovachev, Enver Bey was in little danger of capture by the Bulgarians.
12 Izzet Pascha, 208–9.
13 Guy Chantepleure, *La Ville assiégée. Janina octobre 1912–mars 1913* (Paris, 1913) 115.
14 Nikolaides, 118.
15 T. S. Hutchison, *An American Soldier under the Greek Flag at Bezanie* (Nashville, 1913) 151.
16 Cassavetti, 146.
17 Chantepleure, 149.
18 Trapmann, 115.
19 Hellenic Army, 104.
20 Nikolaides, 139.
21 *Rat* II 234.
22 Hasan Dzhemal, "Novata voina" in *Odrin 1912–13* 145, 147. Hasan Dzhemal was a young Ottoman subaltern serving with the Adrianople garrison.
23 Immanuel, IV 28.
24 Fichev, 290–2.
25 Vojvodich, Mihailo, ed. *Dokumenti o spoljnoj politisi Kraljevina Srbije 1903–1914* (Belgrade, 1985) (hereafter referred to as DSPKS) VI 1 nos 133, 136.
26 A. Toshev, II 189.
27 DSPKS V, 1 nos 187, 271; DPIK I no. 24, 409–13 no. 25. For a summation of Pashich's four-point demand see Helmreich, 353–4; Rossos, 165; Gunnar Hering, "Die Serbisch-Bulgarischen Beziehungen am vorabend und während der Balkankriege." *Balkan Studies* IV (1963) 361–2. These three objective scholars agree that the Serbian case for revision of the agreement was weak.
28 Gustave Cirilli, *Journal du siège d'Andrinople. (Impressions d'un assiégé)* (Paris, 1913) 142.
29 Fichev, 307.
30 Vladimir Pavlov, "The Bulgarian Navy (1879–1914)." *Bulgarian Historical Review* XVIII 3 (1990) 68.
31 Opachich, "Political Ramifications," 93.
32 BAN 51-I-17-195, 218.
33 Fichev, 313.
34 Immanuel, IV 30.
35 Fichev, 311.
36 DPIK, I 147 no. 316; P. Peshev, *Istoricheskite sûbitiya i zhivota mi ot navecherieto na osvobozhdenieto ni do dnes. (Chuto, videno i prezhiveno)* (Sofia, 1925) 178.
37 Ferdinand, Letter from Crown Prince Boris (Rylski) to Ferdinand, 27 February 1913.
38 Ibid., Letter from Crown Pince Boris (Rylski) to Ferdinand, 14 March 1913.
39 Major S. C. Vestal, "The Siege of Adrianople," Unpublished manuscript, United States Army War College, Carlisle, Pennsylvania, 1915.
40 Dimitûr Tangulov, "Koga za prûv pût Bûlgarskata aviatsiya izpolzva samoleta za bombardirane na protivnika." *Voennoistoricheski sbornik* 59 1 (1994) 145. The bombing seems to have occurred on 30 November 1912. See also Michael Paris, "The First Air Wars – North Africa and the Balkans, 1911–1913," *Journal of Contemporary History* 26 1 (1991) 97–109. The Bulgarians were also the first to use their national colors on their aircraft for identification.
41 Hasan Dzhemal, 159; GP XXXIV ii 13056; Carnegie, 110–11.
42 *Voinata* V ii 923–4.
43 Stiliyan Noikov, "Dokladût na komisiyata na Avstro-Ungarskiya generalen shtab za atakata na Odrin prez 1913 g." *Izvestiya na Institut za voenna istoriya* 48 (1989) 185.

44 Nikola Ivanov, "Spomeni 1861–1918," in *Odrin*, 17.
45 Peshadijski pukovnik Borislav Ratkovich, "Operacije Srpskih i Bugarskih snaga pod Jedrenom 1912–13 godine," *Vojnoistorijski glasnik* 22 1 (1971) 73.
46 Klavdiya Zaimova, "Spomeni na General-Maior Vasil Popov ot Balkanskata voina 1912–13 godina," *Voennoistoricheski sbornik* 59 6 (1990) 114.
47 Martharel, no. 44, 22 April 1913, 247.
48 Stefan S. Bobchev, *Stranitsi iz moyata diplomaticheska misiya v Petrograd, 1912–1913* (Sofia, 1940) 107.
49 *Voinata* V ii 1057, 1092–3, 1103. Serbian troops and casualty figures are included with the Bulgarian. The Serbs suatained losses of 292 dead and 1156 wounded at Adrianople. Opachich, "Political Ramifications," 93. Of course many of the troops at Adrianople were non-combatant personnel such as cooks, animal handlers, etc. Ivanov estimated that the Bulgarians would lose 6000–7,000 killed and wounded in an attack on the fortress. Nikola Ivanov, *Balkanskata voina 1912–13 god* (Sofia, 1924) I 227.
50 *Voinata* V ii 1058–64.
51 Vestal, 49; Clyde Sinclair Ford, *The Balkan Wars* (Fort Leavenworth, KS, 1915) 42.
52 Fichev, 337.
53 Ibid., 338. He called this a "kurvavo horo." A horo is a Balkan round dance.
54 Ibid., 344.
55 Geshov, *Prestupnoto bezumie* 96, 106. Not all Bulgarians were content to stop with Adrianople. After taking Adrianople General Savov wanted to concentrate all his forces and march on Constantinople to dictate peace to the Ottomans in their capital. DDF 3rd series VIII 170.
56 Ilija R. Ljubibratich, "Od San Frantsiska do Skadra," in *Dobrovoljtsi u ratovima 1912–1918, Dozhivljaji i setchanja*. (Belgrade, 1971) I 33.
57 Durishich, "Operations," 136–8. This is the source of all the casualty figures for the battle of 7–9 February.
58 Djurishich, "Kralja Nikole," 87; OUA V 5770.
59 Kutschbach, 85.
60 OUA V 5801.
61 Ibid., 6230.
62 Dr Mihailo Vojvodich, *Skadarska kriza 1913 godine* (Belgrade, 1970) 103. The Great Powers pressured the Serbs because of their military assistance to Montenegro, and the Greeks because of their logistical assistance to the Montenegrins and Serbs.
63 OUA V 6095.
64 Helmreich, 298, no. 70.
65 Mitar Djurishich, *Prvi Balkanski rat 1912–1913 (Operatsije Tsrnogorske vojske)* (hereafter referred to as *Rat* III) 343, no. 1.
66 OUA, VI 6664.
67 Durham, *Scutari*, 277.
68 Treadway, 142.
69 Helmreich, 321–2.

6 THE INTERBELLUM

1 A. Nekludoff (Neklyudov) *Diplomatic Reminiscences Before and During the World War, 1911–1917* (New York, 1920) 140.
2 Ferdinand 41–8 1913, untitled report on the situation of the Bulgarian population in Kosura, Voden, and Salonika after the entry of the Greek army, no date. See also ibid., 47–9 1913, untitled report of A. Shopov to Ivan Geshov, 2 April1913 o.s.
3 Ministerstvo na Voinata shtab na voiskata, voenno-istoricheska komisiya, *Voinata mezhdu Bûlgariya i drugite Balkanski dûrzhavi prez 1913 god*. (Sofia, 1941) I 73–81.

4   Fichev, 325.
5   Ferdinand, letter from Ferdinand to Crown Prince Boris, 10 March 1913; 45–1 1913, letter from Ferdinand to Crown Prince Boris, 12 March 1913.
6   *Voinata mezhdu Bûlgariya i drugite Balkanski dûrzhavi* I 92–101.
7   DPIK I 446–8 no. 78.
8   Ibid., 434–5 no. 61. See also Carnegie, 61.
9   Ferdinand, 46–7 1913, note from Ferdinand to S. Dobrovich, 4 May 1913 o.s.
10 Savo Skoko, "Rukovodjenje operacijama Srpske vojske u ratu s Bulgarskom 1913 godine," *Vojnoistorijski glasnik* 33 1–2 (1982) 244.
11 Dr Djordje Dj. Stankovich, *Nikola Pashich i Jugoslovensko pitanje* (Belgrade, 1985) I 134.
12 Herbert A. Gibbons, *Venizelos* (Boston, 1920) 138.
13 Cassavetti, 316–17; *Voinata mezhdu Bûlgariya i drugite Balkanski dûrzhavi*, I 107.
14 BAN 51-I-18-266.
15 Geshov, *Lichna korespondentsiya*, Letter of Ivan E. Geshov to Evstrati I. Geshov, 20 October 1913, 270.
16 DSPKS V, 1 no. 296; Ganchev, 229.
17 Prevelakis, 374.
18 DSPKS V 2 136; Driault, 96.
19 DSPKS V 2 186, 308; Driault, 115–20.
20 Ljudmil Spasov, "La Serbie et le Differend territorial bulgaro-roumain (Janvier-Aout 1913)" *Etudes Balkanques* 23 3 (1987) 63.
21 Helmreich, 350.
22 DPIK I 474–80 no. 121; DSPKS VII, 2 no. 501; Ganchev, 209–10.
23 A. Toshev, II 279.
24 Helmreich, 330; Rossos, 131–2.
25 For the peace agreement see Helmreich, 331; DSPKS V 2 no. 291.
26 Carnegie, 63.
27 *Prilozhenie* (Danev) 104.
28 Dragnich, 104.
29 DSPKS V 2 no. 401 (punctuation and underlining as in original).
30 BAN 51-I-18-336; Mariya Veleva, "Voinishkite buntove prez 1913 g." *Istoricheski pregled* XIV (1958) 3–33.
31 RG 165 5964-287-1, Lt. Sherman Miles, "Discontent and indiscipline in the Bulgarian Army," 4 July 1913.
32 Zhekov, 269.
33 BAN 51-I-18-334.
34 See Georgi Markov, *Bûlgarskoto krushenie 1913* (Sofia, 1991) 48–9.
35 BAN 51-I-18-343.
36 DPIK I 532-3 no. 205. At this time, Sazonov was suffering from several physical complaints.
37 Boeckh, 58.
38 See, for example, Petûr St Goranov, "Ruskite voenni dostavki za Bûlgarskata voinska prez Balkanskata voina" ed. Ivan Todorov in *Balkanskite voini 1912–1913*. (Veliko Tûrnovo, 1995) 43–56,
39 *Prilozhenie* (Savov) 278; Savo Skoko, *Drugi Balkanski rat* (Belgrade, 1968) I 341.
40 Georges Bourdon, "Innocent Bulgaria. M. Georges Bourdon's interview with M. Theodoroff," *Balkan Review* II (1919) 110; DPIK I 1202.
41 *Voinata mezhdu Bûglariya i drugite Balkanski dûrzhavi*, I 301.
42 Ibid., 399.

43 Helmreich, 362. Serbian sources often attribute the attack to Tsar Ferdinand's desire to disrupt the Balkan Alliance because of his Austrian background. See, for example, Savo Skoko, "Bukureshki mir 1913 godine," *Vojnoistorijski glasnik* 23 3 (1972) 7–8. They overestimate Ferdinand's authority. It is unlikely that Bulgaria, having acquired Macedonia under the aegis of Russia, would heed Austrian blandishments.
44 See, for instance, Danev's interview in *Le Temps*, 9 December 1913.
45 Helmreich, 366–7.
46 DPIK I 537–8 no. 225, 622 no. 131; A. Toshev, II 357–9.
47 Skoko, "Rukovodjenje operacijama Srpske vojske," 260.
48 Cassavetti, 308.

7 INTERALLIED WAR

1 Oton Barbar, *Moite spomeni ot voinite* 1912–1918. (Sofia, 1923) 81. Thanks to Dr Tatyana Nestorova for the explanation of this phrase rendered in the Shop dialect.
2 Ganchev, 266. The numbers of Bulgarian soldiers in the Second Balkan War remains unclear. General Ivanov insisted that of the five Bulgarian armies only the 4th Army had more than 50,000 men. Ivanov II, 335.
3 Hellenic Army, 107.
4 Skoko, *Drugi Balkanski rat*, I 255. Of the total of 348,000, 252,000 were combat soldiers.
5 Mitar Djurishich, "Crnogorska divizija u Drugom Balkanskom ratu." *Vojnoistorijski glasnik* 35 3 (1984) 112.
6 Skoko, *Drugi Balkanski rat* I 329.
7 Ibid., 333.
8 *Voinata mezhdu Bûlgariya i drugite Balkanski dûrzhavi* I 182. According to Colonel de Dreyer of the Russian General Staff, Colonel Stefan Nerezov, a man of "complete conceit and huge presumption, but with a remarkable absence of all military talent," assisted Savov in the preparation of the plan. Colonel de Dreyer, *La Debacle Bulgare. Deuxième Guerre Balkanique de 1913* (Paris, 1916) 17.
9 *Istoriyata na Riltsi* 124.
10 Skoko, "Putnik," 28–29.
11 S. Toshev, 265.
12 Stojichivich, 256; Skoko, *Drugi Balkanski rat* II 159; Skoko and Opachich, *Vojvoda Stepanovich* 282.
13 Ivanov, II 92.
14 Ganchev, 286.
15 Cassavetti, 325; Nikolaides, 253.
16 de Dreyer, 101–102.
17 Ivanov, II 113–114.
18 *Voinata mezhdu Bûlgariya i Drugite Balkanski dûrzhavi* I 818.
19 Nikoalides, 256.
20 Hellenic Army, 107.
21 Richard C. Hall, *Bulgaria's Road to the First World War* (Boulder, 1996) 196.
22 Carnegie, 188.
23 *Voinata mezhdu Bûlgariya i Drugite Balkanski dûrzhavi* I 418. Illustrative of the ethnic complexity of the Balkans was the circumstance that one of the Bulgarian company commanders in Salonika was Captain Andreadis, a member of a Greek family from Varna, a Black Sea port founded by the Greeks in the sixth century b.c.e. According to the Bulgarian official history, Captain Andreadis, "behaved gallantly." Ibid., 415.
24 Ibid.
25 Zhekov, 276.

26 Skoko, "Rukovodjenjie operacijama Srpske vojske," 272.
27 A. Hristov, Polkovnik, *Istoricheski pregled na voinata na Bûlgariya sreshtu vsichki Balkanski dûrzhavi 1913 g.* (Sofia, 1924) 184.
28 de Dreyer, 64.
29 Leon Trotsky, *The War Correspondence of Leon Trotsky. The Balkan Wars 1912–13* (New York, 1980) 351. Trotsky places these troops between Sultan Tepe and Gyushevo. This suggests that they were from the Bulgarian 5th Army and the Serbian 3rd Army.
30 Skoko and Opachich, *Vojvoda Stepanovich* 294–295.
31 Constantin Cazanistenanu, "The Military Potential of Romania, 1900–1914," in Kiraly and Djordjevich, 143; *Istoria Militara a Poporului Roman* (Bucharest, 1988) V 276.
32 Radulescu-Zoner, Serban, "Romania si Razboaiele Balcaniece," *Anale de Istorie* 29 1 (1983) 131.
33 Ganchev, 302.
34 Colonel Paul Baltagi, "Beginning of Aviation Integrating into Romania's Military System," ed. Colonel Dr Al. Gh. Savu in *The Army and The Romanian Society* (Bucharest, 1980) 276.
35 Hristov, 232.
36 Izzet Pasha, 210.
37 de Dreyer, 159.
38 See Carnegie, 120–122.
39 William M. Hale, *Turkish Politics and the Military* (London, 1994) 45. Sultan Murad (1359–1389) later to fall at Kosovo Polje was the first conqueror of Edirne in 1361.
40 Hristov, 232.
41 See Hall, 251–253.
42 Fichev, 451. This was actually the third such appeal sent by Ferdinand to Carol.
43 Ministère des Affaires étrangères, *Documents diplomatiques. Les événements de la peninsule balkanique. L'action de la Roumaine septembre 1912–août 1913* (Bucharest, 1913) (hereafter referred to as Rom Doc) 207; DSPKS V 3 nos 20, 57.
44 Helmreich, 385–86.
45 de Dreyer, 70.
46 Skoko, *Drugi Balkanski rat* II 210; Djurishich, 142.
47 Trendofil Mitev, *General Nikola Ivanov* (Sofia, 1986) 247.
48 Manousakis, 99.
49 Prevelakis, 376.
50 Markov, *Bûlgarskoto krushenie* 161–2.
51 Ibid., 161.
52 Rossos, 197.
53 Rom Doc 222.
54 Ferdinand, 43–1, 1913, telegram from Ferdinand to Crown Prince Boris, 4 August 1913 o.s.
55 Fichev, 462.
56 Ibid., 464. Venizelos had made the offer during his stopover in Sofia the previous February. See above. On the Kavala controversy see Boeckh, 64–5.
57 Savo Skoko, "Bukureshki mir," 29.
58 Treadway, 161.
59 DDF, 3rd series VIII 153.
60 Simeon Radev, *Konferentsiyata v Bukuresht i Bukureshtkiyat mir ot 1913g.* (Sofia, 1992) 67.
61 Rossos, 203.

62 Djemal Pasha, Ahmed, *Erinnerungen eines Türkische Staatsmannes* (Munich, 1922) 49.
63 Markow (Markov) Geogri, "Bulgarien auf der Friedenskonferenz in Konstantinopel (August–September 1913)" *Bulgarian Historical Review* XVIII 4 1990, 67–8.
64 A. Toshev, II 453.
65 See Hall, 258.
66 M. I. Madzharov, "Radko Dimitriev za Mezhdusûyuznicheskata voina," *Bûlgarski misûl* XV 9 (November 1940) 488.

8 CONSEQUENCES AND CONCLUSIONS

1 Boeckh, 43.
2 OUA VII 8850.
3 Helmreich, 426.
4 N. Petsalis-Diomidis, *Greece at the Paris Peace Conference* (1919) (Thessaloniki, 1978) 27–8.
5 RG, 165-7277-191, 3, 4. Lieutenant Sherman Miles, "Treatment of foreign military Attaches, military observers, officers without official status and war correspondents by the Bulgarian Government during the Balkan war," 19 December 1912.
6 Trapmann, 294. Trapmann somewhat undercut his prediction by suggesting that machine guns would render infantry riflemen obsolete, and that modern armies would employ machine guns for long-distance shooting. Hand grenades and cutlasses would suffice for close in fighting.
7 Zhekov, 258–9, 287.
8 Diplomatist, 308.
9 Rat III 408.
10 Djurishich, "Csrnogorska divizija," 150.
11 James M. B. Lyon, "'A Peasant Mob': The Serbian Army on the Eve of the Great War." *The Journal of Military History*, 61 (July, 1997) 484.
12 Stojichevich, 283.
13 Carnegie, 95.
14 Durham, *Scutari* 185.
15 Joyce Cary, *Memoir of the Bobotes* (Austin, TX, 1960) 33.
16 Cyril Campbell, *The Balkan War Drama* (New York, 1913) 110. "Where they make a desert, they call it peace." Tacitus, *Agricola* §30.
17 Leo Freundlich, "Albania's Golgotha. Indictment of the Exterminators of the Albanian People," ed. Robert Elsie in *Kosovo, In the Heart of the Powder Keg* (Boulder, 1997) 338. Magnussen was known for his pro-Serbian sympathies.
18 On the work of the Carnegie commission see Ivan Ilchev, "Karnegievata anketa prez 1913 g. Obstanovka, izvûrshvane i mezhdunaroden otzvuk." *Istoricheski pregled* XLV 10 (1989) 15–28.
19 Carnegie, 108.
20 See, for instance, *Les cruautés Bulgares en Macédoine orientale et en Thrace 1912–1913. Faits, Rapports, Documents Témoignages officiels* (Athens, 1914).
21 L. Miletitch, *Documents relatifs aux actions antibulgares des pouvoirs Serbes et Grecs en Macédoine au cours de l'année 1912–1913* (Sofia, 1930).
22 Ratkovich, "Prvi Balkanski rat," 134.

WORKS CITED

Archival material

Archive of Tsar Ferdinand of Bulgaria, Hoover Institute, Stanford, CA, USA.
Bûlgarska akademiya naukite, Sofia. Fond 58, Diary of former Minister of Justice Petûr Abrashev.
National Archives, Washington DC War College Division, General Correspondence 1902–20 Records Group 165.
Tsentralen dûrzhaven istoricheski arhiv, Sofia. Fond 176, Foreign Ministry Papers.

General

Books

(Austria–Hungary) Ministerium des k. und k. Hauses und des Äussern. *Österreich–Ungarns Aussenpolitik von der Bosnischen Krise 1908 bis zum Kriegsausbruch 1914. Diplomatische Aktenstücke des Österreichisch–Ungarischen Ministerium des Äussern*, eds Ludwig Bittner, Alfred F. Pribram, Heinrich Srbik, and Hans Uebersber. Vienna: Österreicher Bundesverlag für Unterricht, Wissenschaft und Kunst, 1930, 9 vols.
Boeckh, Kartin, *Von den Balkankriegen zum Ersten Weltkrieg*. Munich: R. Oldenbourg, 1996.
Boucabeille, Bernard, *La guerre Turco-Balkanique 1912–1913*. Paris: Librairie Chapelot, 1913.
Campbell, Cyril (Special Correspondent of the London Times at the Front) *The Balkan War Drama*. New York: McBride, Nast & Co., 1913.
Carnegie Endowment for International Peace, *Report of the International Commission to Inquire into the Causes and Conduct of the Balkan Wars*. Washington DC: The Endowment, 1914.
Dugard, Henry (Louis Thomas) *Histoire de la guerre contre les Turcs 1912–1913*. Paris: Les Marches de l'Est, 1913.
Durham, M. Edith, *Twenty Years of Balkan Tangle*. London: George Allen & Unwin Ltd, 1920.
Ford, Clyde Sinclair, *The Balkan Wars*. Fort Leavenworth, KS: Press of the Army Service Schools, 1915.
(France) Ministère des Affaires étrangères, Commission de Publication des Documents relatifs aux Origines de la Guerre de 1914. *Documents diplomatiques français 1871–1914*. Paris: Alfred Costes, 1929–1959.

General Staff, War Office (Great Britain) *Armies of the Balkan States, 1914–1918*. London: Imperial War Museum, 1996.

(Germany) Auswärtiges Amt, *Die grosse Politik der europäischen Kabinette 1871–1914. Sammlung der diplomatischen Akten des Auswärtiges Amtes, im Auftrage des Auswärtiges Amtes*, ed. Johannes Lepsius, Albrecht Mendelssohn-Bartholdy, and Friedrich Thimme. Berlin: Deutsche Verlagsgesellschaft für Politik und Geschichte, 1922–27.

(Great Britain) Foreign Office, British *Documents on the Origins of the War 1898–1914*, eds G. P. Gooch and Harold Temperly. London: His Majesty's Stationary Office, 1926–38.

Helmreich, E. C., *The Diplomacy of the Balkan Wars 1912–13*. New York: Russell and Russell, 1969.

Howell, Major P, *The Campaign in Thrace*. London: Hugh Rees Ltd, 1913.

Immanuel, Friedrich, *Der Balkankrieg 1912–1913*. Berlin: Ernst Siegfried Mittler und Sohn, 1913–14.

Medlicott, W. N., *The Congress of Berlin and After*. London: Methuen & Co., 1938.

Penennum, Alain de, *La guerre des Balkans en 1912. Campagne de Thrace*. Paris: Charles-Lavauzelle, 1913.

Rossos, Andrew, *Russia and the Balkans. Inter-Balkan Rivalries and Russian Foreign Policy 1908–1914*. Toronto: University of Toronto Press, 1981.

(Russia) *Die internationalen Beziehungen im Zeitalter des Imperialismus: Dokumente aus den Archiven der zarischen und der provisorischen Regierungen*, ed. Otto Hoetzsch. Berlin: Steiniger-Verlag, 1942. 3rd series, 3 vols.

Tarnstrom, Ronald, *Balkan Battles*. Lindsborg, Kansas: Trogen Books, 1998.

Thaden, Edward, *Russia and the Balkan Alliance of 1912*. University Park, PA: Penn State University, 1965.

Trotsky, Leon, *The War Correspondence of Leon Trotsky. The Balkan Wars 1912–13*. New York: Monad, 1980.

Young, George (Diplomatist), *Nationalism and War in the Near East*. Oxford: Clarendon, 1915.

Articles

Batowski, Henryk, "The Failure of the Balkan Alliance of 1912," *Balkan Studies* 1966, 7(1): 111–22.

Helmreich, E. C., "The Serbian-Montenegrin Alliance of September 23/October 6, 1912." *Journal of Central European Affairs* 1960, 19(4): 411–14.

Hering, Gunnar, "Die Serbisch-Bulgarischen Beziehungen am voarbend und während der Balkankriege," *Balkan Studies* 1963, IV(6): 347–78.

Ilchev, Ivan, "Karnegievata anketa prez 1913 g. Obstanovka, izvûrshvane i mezhdunaroden otzvuk," *Istoricheski pregled* 1989, 65(10): 15–28.

Paris, Michael, "The First Air Wars–North Africa and the Balkans, 1911–1913," *Journal of Contemporary History* [GB] 199,1 26(1): 97–109.

Albania

Books

Joyce Cary, *Memoir of the Bobotes*. Austin, TX: University of Texas Press, 1960.

Swire, J. *Albania: The Rise of a Kingdom*. New York: Arno, 1971.

Articles

Freudlich, Leo, "Albania's Golgotha. Indictment of the Exterminators of the Albanian People (1913)," ed. Robert Elsie, in *Kosovo. In the Heart of the Power Keg*. Boulder: East European Monographs, 1997, 332–60.

Kondis, B., "The Role of the Albanian Factor upon the Greek-Bulgarian Understanding of 1912," *Balkan Studies* 1984 25(2): 377–87.

Mikich, Dordje, "The Albanians and Serbia during the Balkan Wars," eds Bela Kiraly and Dimitrije Djordjevich in *East Central European Society and the Balkan Wars*. Boulder: Social Science Monographs, 1987, 165–96.

Pollo, Stefanaq, "La Proclamation de L'Indépendance Albanie," *Studia Albanica* 1965 2(1): 87–107 and *Studia Albanica* 1987, 24(2): 3–18.

Rappaport, Alfred, "Albaniens Werdegang, *Die Kriegsschuldfrage* 1927, V(September): 815–44.

Bulgaria

Books

Barbar, Oton, *Moite spomeni ot voinite 1912–1918*. Sofia: Armeiskiya voenno-izdatelski fond, 1923.

Bobchev, Stefan. S., *Stranitsi iz moyata diplomaticheska misiya v Petrograd, 1912–1913*. Sofia: Slavyanska, 1940.

Dimitriev, Radko, *Treta armiya v Balkanskata voina 1912 godina*. Sofia: Armeiski voenno-izdatelski fond, 1922.

Documents sur les atrocités grecques. Extraits du livre de M. le professeur L. Miletich: "Atrocités Greques en Macédoine." Sofia, 1913.

De Dreyer, Colonel, *La Débâcle Bulgare. Deuxième Guerre Balkanique de 1913*. Paris: Henri Charle-Lavuzelle, 1916.

Fichev, Ivan, *Balkanskata voina 1912–1913. Preshivelitsi, belezhki i dokumenti*. Sofia: Dûrzhavna pechatnitsa, 1940.

Ganchev, Aleksandûr, *Voinite prez tretoto Bûlgarsko tsarstvo*. Sofia: Rodna misûl (no date).

Geshov, Ivan E., *Lichna korespondentsiya*, eds Radoslav Popov and Vasilika Tankova. Sofia: Marin Drinov, 1994.

—— *Prestupnoto bezumie i anketata po nego. Fakti i dokumenti*. Sofia: Balkan, 1914.

—— *Spomeni iz godini na borbi i pobedi*. Sofia: Gutenberg, 1916.

Gotsev, Dimitûr G., *Natsional-osvoboditelnata borba v Makedoniya 1912–1915*. Sofia: Bûlgarska akademiya na naukite, 1983.

Hall, Richard C., *Bulgaria's Road to the First World War*. Boulder: East European Monographs, 1996.

Hristov, A., Polkovnik, *Istoricheski pregled na voinata na Bûlgariya sreshtu vsichki Balkanski dûrzhavi 1913 g.* Sofia: Armeiskiya voenno-izdatelski fond, 1924.

Istoriyata na Riltsi, *13.pehoten Rilski polk v voinite za obedinenie na Bûlgarskiya narod. 1912–1913. g. i 1915–1918. g*. Kyustendil: Trud, 1931.

Ivanov, N., *Balkanskata voina 1912–13 god*. Sofia: Pechatnita na armeiskiya voenna-izdatelski fond, 1924–1925.

WORKS CITED

Kesiyakov, B. D., *Prinos kûm diplomaticheskata istoriya na Bûlgariya 1878–1925*. Sofia: Rodopi, 1925.

Kosev, Kiril, *Podvigût*. Sofia: Voenno izdatelstvo, 1983.

Madol, Hans Roger, *Ferdinand von Bulgarien. Der Traum von Byzanz*. Berlin: Universitas, 1931.

Markov, Georgi, *Bûlgariya v Balkanskiya sûyuz sreshtu Osmanskata imperiya 1912–1913*. Sofia: Nauka i izkustvo, 1989.

—— *Bûlgarskoto krushenie*. Sofia: Bûlgarskata akademiya na naukite, 1991.

Miletitch, L., *Documents relatifs aux actions antibulgares des pouvoirs Serbs et Grecs en Macedoine au cours de l'année 1912–1913*. Sofia: P. Glouchcoff, 1930.

Ministerstvo na Voinata shtab na voiskata, voenno-istoricheska komisiya, *Voinata mezhdu Bûlgariya i drugite balkanski dûrzhavi prez 1913 god. Tom I, Prichinite i podgotovkata na voinata i voenite diestviya do 21–i Yuni*. Sofia: Dûrzhavna pechatnitsa, 1941.

—— *Voinata mezhdu Bûlgariya i Turtsiya 1912–13 god*. Sofia: Dûrzhavna Pechatnitsa.

—— Tom I. Podgotovka na voinata 1937.

—— Tom II. Lozengradskata operatsiya 1928.

—— Tom III. Srazheniteto pri Lyule Burgas–Bunar Hisar 1931.

—— Tom IV. Srazheniteto pri Chataldzha. 1932.

—— Tom V. Operatsite okolo Odrinskata krepost (two parts) 1930.

—— Tom VI. Deistviyata na zapadniaya operatsionen teatûr 1935.

—— Tom VII. Deistviyata na Trakiiskiya operatsionen teatûr ot purvoto primirie do kraya na voinata 1933.

Mitev, Trendofil, *General Nikola Ivanov*. Sofia: Voenno izdatelstvo, 1986.

Narodno sûbranie. *Doklad na parlamentarnata izpitatelna komisiya*. Sofia: Dûrzhavna pechatnitsa, 1918–19. 4 vols.

—— *Prilozhenie kûm tom pûrvi ot doklada na parlamentarnata izpitatelna komisiya*. Sofia: Dûrzhavna pechatnitsa, 1918.

—— *Prilozhenie kûm tom vtori ot doklada na parlamentarnata izpitatelna komisiya*. Sofia: Dûrzhavna pechatnitsa, 1918.

—— *Dnevnitsi (stenografski) na sedemnadesetoto obiknoveno narodno sûbranie. Pûrva redovna sesiya*. Sofia: Dûrzhavna pechatnitsa, 1914.

—— *Dnevnitsi (stenografski) na petoto veliko narodno sûbranie v gr. Veliko Tûrnovo*. Sofia: Dûrzhavna pechatnitsa, 1911.

Nashata duma. *Vûzrazheniya na bivshite ministri I. E. Geshov, Dr S. Danev, T. Teodorov, M. I. Madzharov, I. Peev i P. Abrashev sreshtu obvineniyata na dûrzhavniya sûd ot 1923 godina*. Sofia: Mir, 1925.

Nekludoff (Neklyudov) A., *Diplomatic Reminiscences Before and During the World War 1911–1917*. New York: E. P. Dutton, 1920.

Pandev, Konstantin, *Borbite v Makedoniya i Odrinsko, 1878–1912. Spomeni*. Sofia: Bûlgarski pisatel, 1982.

Penennum, Alain de, *La Guerre des Balkans en 1912. Campagne de Thrace*. Paris: Henri Charles-Lavauzelle, 1913.

Peshev, P., *Istoricheskite sûbitiya i zhivota mi ot navecherieto na osvobozhdenieto ni do dnes. Chuto, videno i preshiveno*. Sofia: Liberalni klub, 1925.

Radev, Simeon, *Konferentsiyata v Bukuresht i Bukureshtkiyat mir ot 1913 g*. Sofia: Tinapres, 1992.

Slavova, Stefka, and Tsvetana Doinova (eds) *Balkanskata voina prez pogleda na edin Frantsuzin*. Sofia: Voenno izdatelstvo, 1977.

Tonchev, Teno, *Hrabrostta na Bûlgariya*. Sofia: Voenno izdatelstvo, 1981.
Toshev, A., *Balkanskite voini*. Plovdiv and Sofia: H. G. Danov, 1931.
Toshev, S. *Pobedeni bez da bûdem biti*. Sofia: Pechetnitsa na armeinskiya voenno-izdatelski fond, 1924.
Zhekov, Nikola T., *Bûlgarskoto voinstvo 1878–1928 g*. Sofia: Bratya mladinovi, 1928.

Articles

Bourdon, Georges, "Innocent Bulgaria. M. Georges Bourdon's interview with M. Theodoroff." *Balkan Review* 1919, II: 108–15.
Danev, Stoyan, Interview in *Le Temps*, 9 December 1913.
——— "Kabinetût D-r. St. Danev 1901–1903 godina." *Rodina* 1941, III(4): 63–88.
———"Primirieto v Chataldzha na 20 Noemvri 1912." *Rodina* 1939, I(3): 94–106.
"Dnevnik na Todor Dichev Slavchev," in *Balkanskata voina v spomenite na sûvremennitsi i uchastnitsi*. Sofia: Dûrzhavno voenno izdatelstvo, 1973, 159–73.
Goranov, Petûr St, "Ruskite voenni dostavki za Bûlgarskata voinska prez Balkanskata voina," ed. Ivan Todorov, in *Balkanskite voini 1912–13*. Veliko Tûrnovo: Sv.sv Kiril i Metodii, 1995, 43–56.
Helmreich, E. C. and C. E. Black, "The Russo-Bulgarian Military Convention of 1902. *Journal of Modern History* 1937, IX(December): 471–82.
Ivanov, Nikola, "Spomeni 1861–1918 g," ed. Momchil P. Ionov, in *Odrin 1912–13 Spomeni*. Sofia: Voenno izdatelstvo, 1983, 17–38.
Madzharov, M., "Radko Dimitriev za Mezhdusûyuznicheskata voina." *Bûlgaraki misûl* 1940 15(9): 485–91.
Markov, Georgi, "Voennite sporazumeniya v balkanskiya sûyuz i obiaviavaneto na obshta mobilizatsiya." *Voennoistoricheski sbornik* 198,9 58(1): 3–19.
Markow, (Markov) Georgi, "Bulgarien auf der Friedenskonferenz in Konstantinople (August-September 1913)." *Bulgarian Historical Review* 1990, 18(4): 66–76.
Molhov, Yako, "Bûlgarskata artileriya prez Balkanskata voina (1912 g.)." *Voennoistoricheski sbornik* 1988, 57(1): 72–91.
Noikov, Stiliyan, "Dokladût na komisiyata na Avstro-Ungarskiya generalen shtab za atakata na *Odrin* prez 1913 g." *Voennoistoricheski sbornik* 1989, 48(Suppl.): 178–86.
——— "Iz spomenite na General Stiliyan Kovachev za Balkanskata voina 1912–13 godina." *Voennoistoricheski sbornik* 1988, 57(1): 92–104.
Nikolov Boris, "Balkanskata voina v spomenite na Gerneral-Maior Iordan Venedikov." *Voennoistoricheski sbornik* 1988, 57(5): 163–84.
Pavlov, Vladimir, "The Bulgarian Navy (1879–1914)." *Bulgarian Historical Review* 1990, 18(3): 65–9.
Popov, Radoslav, "Balkanskite dûrzhavi i krayat na krizata ot 1908–1909 g." in *V chest na Akademik Dimitûr Kosev*. Sofia: Bûlgarska akademiya na naukite. 1974, 253–63.
Statelova, Elena, "Bûlgaro-Grûtskite politicheski otnosheniya v navecherieto na Balkanskata voina." *Izvestiya na instituta na voenna istoriya* 1984, 36: 48–58.
Tangulov, Dimitûr, "Koga za pûrv pût Bûlgarskata aviatsiya izpolzva samoleta za bombardirane na protivnika." *Voennoistoricheski sbornik* 1990, 59(1): 141–7.
Tsenov, Major General Pantelei, "Zq atakata ma O drinskata krepost," ed. Momchil P. Ionov, in *Odrin 1912–13 Spomeni*. Sofia: Voenna izdatelstvo 1983, 39–54.
Veleva, Mariya, "Voinishkite buntove prez 1913 g." *Istoricheski pregled* 1958, 14: 3–33.
Vestal, Major S. C., "The Siege of Adrianople." Unpublished manuscript, United States Army War College, Carlisle, PA.

Yonov, Momchil, "Bulgarian Military Operations in the Balkan Wars," eds Bela Kiraly and Dimitrije Djordjevich in *East Central European Society and the Balkan Wars*. Boulder: Social Science Monographs, 1987, 63–84.

Zaimova, Klavdiya, "Spomeni na General-Maior Vasil Popov ot Balkanskata voina 1912–13 godina." *Voennoistoricheski sbornik* 1990, 59(6): 100–18.

Greece

Books

Atrocités bulgares en Macedoine. (Faits et Documents). Exposé de la Commission d'enquête de l'Association Macedonienne rendue sur les lieux, Athens, 1913.

Cassevetti, D. J., *Hellas and the Balkan Wars*. London: T. Fisher Unwin, 1914.

Dakin, Douglas, *The Greek Struggle in Macedonia 1897–1913*. Thessaloniki: Institute for Balkan Studies, 1966.

Driault, Edouard, *Historie diplomatique de la Grèce de 1821 a nos jours*. vol 5. Paris: Presses universitaires de France, 1926.

Gibbons, Herbert A., *Venizelos*. Boston: Houghton Mifflin, 1920.

T. S. Hutchison, *An American Soldier under the Greek Flag at Bezanie*. Nashville: Greek-American Publishing Company, 1913.

Les Cruautés bulgares en Macédoine orientale et en Thrace 1912–1913. Athenes: P. D. Sakellarios, 1914.

Manousakis, Gergor, *Hellas-wohin? Das Verhaltnis von Militar und Politik in Griechenland seit 1900*. Verlag Wissenschaftliche Archiv: Godesberg, 1967.

Nikolaides, Kleanthes, *Griechenlands Anteil an den Balkankriegen 1912/1913. I. Der Krieg gegen die Türkei. II. Der Krieg gegen Bulgarien*. Vienna, Leipzig: Alfred Hoelder, 1914.

N. Petsalis-Diomidis, *Greece at the Paris Peace Conference (1919)*. Thessaloniki: Institute for Balkan Studies, 1978.

Trapmann, Captain A. H., *The Greeks Triumphant*, London: Forster Groom & Co., Ltd, 1915.

Articles

Hellenic Army History Directorate, Army General Headquarters, "Hellenic Army Operations during the Balkan Wars," eds Bela Kiraly and Dimitrije Djordjevich, in *East Central European Society and the Balkan Wars*. Boulder: Social Science Monographs, 1987, 99–111.

Prevelakis, Eleutherios, "Eleutherios Venizelos and the Balkan Wars." *Balkan Studies* 1966, 7(2): 363–78.

Montenegro

Books

Durham, M. Edith, *The Struggle for Scutari (Turk, Slav, Albanian)*. London: Edward Arnold, 1914.

Djurishich, Mitar, *Prvi Balkanski rat 1912–1913 (operatsije Tsrnogorske vojske) Book III*. Belgrade: Istoriski institut jugoslovenske narodne armije, 1960.

F. S. Stevenson, *A History of Montenegro*. New York: Arno Press, 1971.
Treadway, John, *The Falcon and the Eagle*. West Lafayette, IN: Purdue, 1983.
Vojvodich, Dr Mihailo, *Skadarska kriza 1913. godine*. Belgrade: Zavod za izdavanje udzhbenika sotsijalistichke republike Srbije, 1970.

Articles

Djurishich, Mitar, "Crnogorska divizija u Drugom Balkanskom ratu." *Vojnoistorijski glasnik* 1984, 35(3): 105–52.
—— "Operations of the Montenegrin Army during the First Balkan War," eds Bela Kiraly and Dimitrije Djordjevich, in *East Central European Society and the Balkan Wars*. Boulder: Social Science Monographs, 1987, 126–40.
—— "Uloga Kralja Nikole u prvom Balkanskom ratu." *Istoriski zapisi* 1960, 17(1): 69–92.
Ljubibratich, Ilija R. "Od San Frantsiska do Skadra," in *Dobrovoljtsi u ratovima 1912–1918, Dozhivljaji i setchanja*. Belgrade: Udruzhenje dobrorvoljatsa 1912–1918, 1971 19–43.
Rakocevich, Novica, "The Organization and Character of the Montenegrin Army in the First Balkan War," eds Bela Kiraly and Dimitrije Djordjevich, in *East Central European Society and the Balkan Wars*. Boulder: Social Science Monographs, 1987, 112–25.
Vujoshevich, Dragich, "Operacije Crnogorskog Primorskog odreda u ratu 1912 godine." *Istoriski zapisi* 1954, 10(2): 458–73.

Ottoman Empire

Books

Ahmad, Feroz, *The Young Turks*. Oxford: Clarendon Press, 1969.
Andonyan, Aram, *Balkan harbi tarihi*. Istanbul: Sander Yayinlari, 1975.
Ashmead-Bartlet, Ellis, *With the Turks in Thrace*. New York: George H. Doran, 1913.
Chantepleure, Guy, *Ville Assiégée. Janina octobre 1912–mars 1913*. Paris: Calmann-Levy, 1913.
Cherif Pacha, General, *Quelques réflexions sur la guerre turco-balkanique par Le Général Cherif-pacha*. Paris: A.-G. L'Hoir, 1913.
Cirilli, Gustave, *Journal du siège d'Andrinople. (Impressions d'un assiégé)*. Paris: Chapelot, 1913.
Djemal Pascha, Ahmed, *Erinnerungen eines Türkischen Staatsmannes*. Munich: Drei Masken Verlag, 2nd edn, 1922.
Gibbs, Phillip and Grant, Bernard, *Adventures of War with Cross and Crescent*. London: Methuen & Co, 1912.
Hale, William T., *Turkish Politics and the Military*. London: Routledge, 1994.
Hochwächter, Gustav von, *Mit den Türken in der Front im Stabe Mahmud Muchtar Paschas*. Berlin: Ernst Siegfried Mittler und Sohn, 1913.
Izzet Pascha, *Denkwürdigkeiten des Marschalls Izzet Pascha*, trans. Karl Klinghardt. Leipzig: K. F. Koeler, 1927.

Mahmoud Moukhtar Pasha (Mahmut Muhtar Pasha), *Mon commandement au cours de la Campagne des Balkans de 1912*. Paris and Nancy: Berger-Levrault, 1913.
Munir Bey, Djemil, *La cavalerie turque pendant la guerre turco-bulgare*. Paris: Chapelot, 1913.
Ross, Colin, *Im Balkankrieg*. Munich: Martin Mörikes Verlag, 1913.
Remond, Georges, *Avec les vaincus. La campagne de Thrace (octobre 1912–mai 1913)*. Paris, Nancy: Berger-Levrault, 1913.

Articles

Aktar, Yucel, "The Impact of the 1912 "War Meetings" upon the Balkan Wars." *Revue Internationale d'Histoire Militaire* 1988, 67: 167–80.
Çagan, Nazmi, "Balkan harbinde Edirne (1912–13)" in *Edirne. Edirne'nin 600 fetih yildonumu armagan kitabi*. Ankara: Turk tarih kurumu basimevi, 1965, 197–213.
Dzhemal, Hasan, "Novata voina," ed. Momchil P. Ionov, in *Odrin 1912–13 Spomeni*. Sofia:Voenno izdatelstvo, 1983, 140–86.
Goltz, Field Marshall von der, "Causes of the Late Turkish Defeat." *Infantry Journal* 1913 9(March–April): 729–35.
Podewils, Hans Graf von, "Taktisches vom thrazichen Kriegsschauplatz." *Vierteljahrshefte für Truppenführung und Heereskunde* 1913 10: 176–89.
Soyupak, Kemal, and Huseyinn Kabaskal, "The Turkish Army in the First Balkan War," eds Bela Kiraly and Dimitrije Djordjevich, in *East Central European Society and the Balkan Wars*. Boulder: Social Science Monographs, 1987, 158–62.
Vickers, Willard, Captain, "The Ottoman Army in the Balkans Wars." unpublished thesis, Princeton University, 1958.

Romania

Books

Ceausescu, Ilie (coordinating ed.) *Istoria Militara a Poporului Roman*. Bucharest: Editura Militara, 1984–8. vol. V.
Ministère des Affaires étrangères, *Documents diplomatiques. Les événements de la peninsule balkanique. L'action de la Roumaine septembre 1912–aout 1913*. Bucharest: Imprimeria statului, 1913.

Articles

Colonel Paul Baltagi, "Beginning of Aviation Integrating into Romania's Military System," ed. Colonel Dr Al. Gh. Savu, in *The Army and The Romanian Society*. Bucharest: Military Publishing House, 1980, 264–77.
Cazanistenanu, Constantin, "The Military Potential of Romania, 1900–1914," eds Bela Kiraly and Dimitrije Djordjevich, in *East Central European Society and the Balkan Wars*. Boulder: Social Science Monographs, 1987, 141–5.
Radulescu-Zoner, Serban, "Romania si Razboaiele Balcaniece." *Anale de Istorie* 1983, 29(1): 126–32.

…

Serbia

Books

Boghitschewitsch, Milosch (ed.) *Die auswärtige Politik Serbiens, 1903–1914*. Berlin: Brükenverlag, 1928–31. 3 vols.
Djordjevich, Dimitrije, *Izlazak Srbije na Jadransko More i konferentsija ambasadora u Londonu 1912*. Belgrade: Slobodan Jovich, 1956.
Dragnich, Alex N. *Serbia, Nikola Pasic and Yugoslavia*. New Brusnwick: Rutgers, 1974.
Istoriski institut jugoslovenske narodne armije, Prvi balkanski rat 1912–13 (Operatsije Srpske vojske) Book I, ed. Branko Perovich. Belgrade: Istoriski institut Jugoslovenske narodne armije, 1959; Book II Dr Borislav Ratkovich, Belgrade: Vojnoistorijski institut, 1975.
Jovanovich, Jovan, *Borba za narodno ujedinjenje 1903–1908*. Belgrade: Getsa Kon A. D. no date.
Kutschbach, A., *Die Serben im Balkankrieg 1912–13 und im Kriege gegen die Bulgaren*. Stuttgart: Franck'sche Verlagshandlung, 1913.
Mishish, Vojvoda Zhivojin, *Moje uspomene*, 2nd edn. Belgrade: Beogradski izdavachko-grafichki zavod, 1980.
Pavlovich, Ivan S. *Od Skoplja ka Bitolju u ratu s Turtsima 1912 godine*. Belgrade: Shtamparija save radenkovicha i brata, 1925.
Skoko, Savo, *Drugi Balkanski rat 1913*. Knjiga prva. Uzroci i pripreme rata. Belgrade: Vojnoistorijski institut 1968.
—— Knjiga druga. Tok i zavrshetak rata. Belgrade: Vojnoistorijski institut, 1975.
—— *Vojovoda Radomir Putnik*. Belgrade: Beogradski izdavachko-grafichki zavod, 1984.
Skoko, Savo and Opachich, Petar, *Vojvoda Stepa Stepanovich u ratovima Srbije 1876–1918*. Belgrade: Beogradski izdavacho-grafichki zavod, 1984.
Stankovich, Dr Djordje Dj., *Nikola Pashich i Jugoslovensko pitanje*. Belgrade, Beogradski izdavachko-grafichki zavod, 1985.
Stojichevich, Aleksandar M. *Istorija nashih ratova za oslobodjenje i ujedinjenje od 1912–1918 god*. Belgrade: Savza srpskih zemljorad. zadruga, 1932.
Tomich, Jasha, *Rat na Kosovu i Staroj Srbiji 1912 godine*. Nish: Prosveta, 1988.
Vojvodich, Mihailo (ed.) *Dokumenti o spoljnoj politisi Kaljevina Srbije 1903–1914*. Belgrade: Srbska Akademija Nauka i Umetnosti, 1985. 7 vols.
Vuksanovich-Antich, *Draga, Stvaranje moderne Srpske vojske. Frantsuske utitsaj na njeno formiranje*. Belgrade: Mala Biblioteka, 1993.

Articles

Helmreich, Ernst C., The Serbo-Montenegrin Alliance of September 23/October 6, 1912." *Journal of Central European Affairs* 1960, 29(January): 411–15.
Kolfach, Vatslav, "Bitka kod Kumanova," ed. Silvija Djurich, in *Dnevnik pobeda*. Belgrade: Biblioteka posbno izdanja, 1988, 70–3.
Limik, "Kumanovo." *Nova Evropa* 1922, 6(12): 361–5.
Lyon, James, "A Peasant Mob: The Serbian Army on the Eve of the Great War." *Journal of Military History* 1997, 61: 481–502.
Opachich, Petar, "Kumanovska bitka." *Vojnoistorijski glasnik* 1988, 39(1): 205–28.

—— "Political Ramifications of Serbo-Bulgarian Military Cooperation in the First Balkan War," eds Bela Kiraly and Dimitrije Djordjevich, in *East Central European Society and the Balkan Wars*. Boulder: Social Science Monographs, 1987, 85–98.

Popovich, Ched. A., "Srpsko-Bulgarski rat, 1913 godine (Rad organizacije 'Ujedinjenei ili Smrt')" *Nova Evropa* 1928, 18(10/11): 309–23.

Ratkovich, Borislav, "Bitoljska bitka." *Vojnoistorijski glasnik* 1988, 39(2): 179–211.

—— "Mobilizacija Srpske i Turske vojske za Prvi Balkanski rat Oktobra 1912 godine." *Vojnoistorijski glasnik* 1985, 36(1): 183–204.

—— "Mobilization of the Serbian Army for the First Balkan War, October 1912," eds Bela Kiraly and Dimitrije Djordjevich, in *East Central European Society and the Balkan Wars*. Boulder: Social Science Monographs, 1987, 146–57.

—— "Operacije Srpskih i Bugarskih snaga pod Jedrenom 1912–13 godine." *Vojnoistorijski glasnik* 1971, 22(1): 45–77.

—— "Prvi Balkanski rat 1912–13." *Vojnoistorijski glasnik* 1988, 39(2–3): 113–40.

Shapinac, Stefan, "Kako smo ushil u Kumanovsku bitku." *Nova Evropa* 1922, 6(12): 371–6.

Skoko, Savo, "An Analysis of the Strategy of Vojvoda Putnik during the Balkan Wars," eds Bela Kiraly and Dimitrije Djordjevich, in *East Central European Society and the Balkan Wars*. Boulder: Social Science Monographs, 1987, 17–34.

——"Bukureshki mir 1913 godine." *Vojnoistorijski glasnik* 1972, 23(3): 7–39.

——"Rukovodjenie operacijama Srpske vojske u ratu s Bugaskom 1913 godine." *Vojnoistorijski glasnik* 1982, 33(1–2): 243–86.

Spasov, Ljudmil, "La Serbie et le différend territorial bulgaro-roumain (Janvier–Août 1913)." *Etudes Balkaniques* [Bul] 1987, 23(3): 58–69.

INDEX

Abdullah Pasha 22, 24, 25, 28, 29
Abuk Pasha, Ahmed 22
Adrianople: bombardment of 38–42, 87–9; Bulgarian objective 24; Bulgaro-Serbian co-operation at 76–7; importance of fortress at 22, 23; negotiations stalled by issue of 71; Ottoman re-occupation of 119; siege of 86–90; sophisticated fortifications of 39; winter conditions difficult at 87–8
Adriatic Sea 54
Aegean Islands 64, 71
Aegean Sea 42, 46, 64, 65
Aehrenthal, Alois 7
airborne power, use of 88, 133
Albania: borders redrawn by Great Powers 102; Bulgaro-Serbian dispute over 99; continued fighting in 85–6; emergence of independent 130–31; new frontiers of 74; stirrings of 8–9
Alessio 54, 57, 74
Alexander, Crown Prince of Serbia 45, 50, 59, 109
Ambassadors Conference, London 72–4
Ambassadors Conference, St Petersburg 97–8
Andjelkovich, Colonel Milovoje 45
Andrassy, Count 3
Antivari 20
Arachich, Colonel Vukoman 109
armies: Bulgarian 1st 23, 24, 26, 29, 34, 38, 40, 41, 82, 108, 116, 121, 122; Bulgarian 2nd 23, 24, 26, 40, 105, 108, 112–13, 114, 115, 120, 121; Bulgarian 3rd 23, 24, 26, 28, 29, 30, 34, 38, 40, 108, 116; Bulgarian 4th 80–81, 105, 108, 110, 111, 115, 116, 121; Bulgarian 5th 108, 111, 121; Bulgarian consolidation at Chataldzha 35, 36; Bulgarian overall strength 108; Bulgarian strength in peacetime 16; Danube (Romanian) 117–18; Epirus (Greek) 52, 59; Greek strength in peacetime 17; Ibar (Serbian) 45, 46, 54; Macedonian 2nd (Ottoman) 22; Montenegrin militia 18; Ottoman 1st 119; Ottoman, in Europe 18–19; Serbian 1st 45, 46, 47, 49, 51, 85, 109, 110; Serbian 2nd 41, 45, 46, 49, 53, 109, 116–17, 122; Serbian 3rd 45, 46, 49, 53, 54, 57, 109, 110, 111, 120; Serbian mobilized strength 18; similarity of Balkan 15; Thessaly (Greece) 59–61, 64, 83; Thracian 1st (Ottoman) 22, 25; Timok (Serbian) 109; Vardar (Ottoman) 47, 48, 49, 51, 52, 60; *see also* brigades; divisions; corps
armistice, negotiations at Chataldzha 69–70
artillery: Bulgarian advantage at Bulair 81; Bulgarian lack of at Adrianople 41, 86; effect of barrage on trapped men 116; effective Ottoman use of at Chataldzha 36; effectiveness of Bulgarian at Kalimantsi 120; effectiveness of Serbian at Bitola 51–2; Greek use at Salonika 114; importance at Lyule Burgas–Buni Hisar 29, 30; ineffective Bulgarian at Chataldzha 37; lack of Ottoman at

168

INDEX

Lozengrad 26; Montenegrin at Scutari 91, 92; Ottoman failure at Janina 84; Ottoman reinforcement at Adrianople 39; Serbian heavy guns at Adrianople 87; Serbian power at Kumanovo 48
aspirations, national 3–7
assasination of George, King of Greece 98
Ataturk, Mustapha Kemal 61, 81
Athens, Treaty of 126
atrocities 136–137

Balagat, skirmish at 85
Balchik 77, 117
Balkan alliance, old idea of 4
Balkan League 9–13, 15, 56, 75, 102
Bansko 43
Bar *see* Antivari
Barbaros Hayrettin (armoured ship) 36, 64, 82
Basil II, Emperor (the Bulgar Slayer) 16
Batak, Bulgaria 43
bayonet charges, Bulgarian at Buni Hisar 30
Belogradchik 123
Berane 58
Berat 52
Berchtold, Leopold 72, 93
Berdan rifles 18
Berlin: Congress of 1–3; Treaty of 3, 4, 5, 15
Bijelo Polje 58
Bilolj *see* Bitola 51
Bismark, Otto von 2–3
Bitola, battle of 49, 50–2, 60
Black Sea 66, 77
blockades: Great Powers on Montenegro 94–5; Greek on Albania 74; *see also* naval power
Bobchev, Stefan S. (Bulgarian Minister in St Petersburg) 89
Bojovich, General Peter 92, 93
Boljetini, Isa 46–47
Boris, Crown Prince of Bulgaria 61, 62, 98
Bosnia-Hercegovina, Austrian annexation of 8
Bosnian crisis 7–8
Brankovich, Vuk 53

Brdica 92
Bregalnitsa, battle of the 109, 110–112, 116
brigades: Dechani (Montenegrin) 109; Javor (Serbian) 45, 46; Javorska (Serbian) 54; Macedonian-Thracian (Bulgarian) 82; *see also* armies; divisions; corps
Bucharest, Treaty of 123–125
Bulair, attacks upon 80–83
Bulgaria: advantage from Treaty of London 102; alliance with Serbia (1904) 6; annihilation in Salonika 113–14; avoidance of siege at Adrianople 39–40; claims to Macedonia 61–2; claims to Salonika 62; decisive ascendancy at Lozengrad 27; defeat of 2nd Army 112–13; defense of Kalimantsi 120–21; defensive success at Bulair 83; deteriorating relations with Serbia 89; discontent of armies of 103; dispute with Greeks 74–5; dispute with Romania 77–8; dispute with Serbia 76–7; exaggerated importance of Ardianople 90; Exarchate of 4; expectation and insistence regarding Adrianople 70; lack of intelligence on Chataldzha 33; logistical faulure of 32; losses resulting from Treaty of San Stefano 3; military advantages of 107–8; military dispositions against Serbs and Greeks 108; mobilization of forces 24; morale, decline of, at Adrianople 88; naval success of 66; new government of 119–20; offensive posture of 23; Ottoman invasion of 118–19; planning deficiencies of 32; plans for general offensive against Serbs and Greeks 109–10; plans for siege of Adrianople 40–1; problem of Romanian intervention 117–18; pursuit of Ottomans to Lyule Burgas–Buni Hisar ridge 28–9; reservations on attacking Chataldzha 34–6; resistance to Romanian demands 78; retreating on all fronts 114–17; Russian support for 91, 104–5; satisfaction from Bosnian crisis 8;

success at Kresna Gorge 121–2; victims of success 38; well-trained army of 16
Bulgarian Agrarian Party 14
Bulgarian Grand National Parliament (*subranie*) 11
Bulgarian Supreme Committee 5
Bulgaro-Greek alliance 12
Buni Hisar–Lyule Burgas, battle of 25, 28–32

Calafat 123
Carol, King of Romania 120
casualties: assault on Adrianople 90; Balagat 85; Bardanjolt, Scutari 92; battle of the Bregalnitsa 111–12; Bitola 52; Bulair, central sector 81; Chataldzha fortifications 37; final assault on Janina 84; final battle for Chataldzha 91; Greeks at Janina (Fort Bezane) 84; Kalimantsi 120; Kilkis 113; Kumanovo 48; landing at Sharkoi 82; Lozengrad 27; Lyule Burgas-Buni Hisar 31; Ottoman sorties from Adrianople 41; overall view of 135–6; Prilep 50; Salonika in Second Balkan War 114; Serbs at Brdica 92; Tarabosh 92; Thessaly campaign 60
Çatalca *see* Chataldzha
Chataldhza: armistice 69–70; armistice, second 91; final battle of 90–1; fortifications and battle of 32–8; supplementary attack on 82
cholera: effect on Bulgarians at Chataldzha 35; Ottoman casualties from 119; Romanian casualties from 118
Chukor 58
conflict, civil governments with military 133
Congress of Berlin 1–3
Congress of Vienna 72
Constantine, Crown Prince of Greece 59, 60, 84
Constantine, King of Greece 108, 112, 115, 121, 122
Constantinople: Bulgarian threat to 32–3; Treaty of 125–7
convention, military, in Belgrade (29 April 1912) 14

convention, military, in Sofia (5 October 1912) 14
corps: Ottoman 10th 82; Ottoman 6th 83, 85; Scutari (Ottoman) 55; *see also* armies; brigades; divisions
costs, financial 138–9
Cretan police 114
Crete: control of 8; Greek annexation attempt 4; union with Greece 15
Crimean War 81
crisis in Bosnia 7–8
Culcer, General Ioan 117

Danev, Stoyan 5–6, 69, 70, 71, 75, 88, 99, 100, 102, 104, 105, 110, 119
Danilo, Crown Prince of Montenegro 6, 55, 59
Danube River 77–8, 108, 109
Dardanelles: Greek blockade of 64; sea battle at 64–5
de Grandmaison, Colonel Louis 16
Dechani 58
Dedeagach 43, 64, 115
Dimitriev, General Radko 24, 27, 28, 29, 30, 31, 35, 36, 38, 108, 110, 115
divisions: Bulgarian 7th Rila 42, 45, 61, 62, 111; Bulgarian 7th Rilski 80–1; Bulgarian cavalry 23, 24, 26; Coastal (Montenegrin) 55, 56, 57, 92; Drina (Serbian) 49–50; Eastern (Montenegrin) 55, 57, 58; Greek 2nd 114; Kochana (Ottoman) 51; Morava (Serbian) 47, 49–50; Myureteb (Ottoman) 81; Ottoman 27th 81; Timok (Serbian) 45; Zeta (Montenegrin) 55, 56, 57, 92, 120; *see also* armies; brigades; corps
Djakova 73, 74, 93
Djavid Pasha 22, 47, 51, 52, 54, 58, 83, 85
Dobrev, Commander Dimitur 66
Dobrudzha (Dobrogea) 77, 78, 117, 118, 123
Dodecanese, Italian-occupied 64
Doiran 115
Dolphin (submarine) 17
Drach *see* Durazzo
Drama 43, 98, 113, 124
du Fournet, Rear Admiral Dartige 33
Durazzo (Durrës) 54, 73, 74, 93, 94
Dushan, Stafan 2, 16

INDEX

Eastern Thrace: Bulgarian reinforcement of 42; Ottoman offensive in 82–3
Edirne *see* Adrianople
Effendi, Noradounghian (Ottoman Foreign Minister) 80
Elassona 59
Elbasan 54, 85
Enos 101
Enver Bey 78, 80, 82, 119
Enver Pasha 7
Epirus, preparation for invasion of 63–4
Ergene River 28
Esad Pasha Toptani 55, 59, 84, 91, 92, 94
Ethniki Etairia 5
Evzones 17
Exarchate, Bulgarian 4
explosion, allies in conflict 102–106

Fahri Pasha 81
Ferdinand (Mihailovgrad) 118
Ferdinand, Crown Prince of Romania 117
Feti pasha 47, 51, 52
Fetik Bouled (warship) 61
Fichev, General Ivan (Bulgarian Chief of Staff) 14, 23, 28, 34, 37, 40, 69, 86, 88, 124
First World War 132–5
Florence, Protocol of 131
Florina 60–61
forces, military (First Balkan War) 15–21
formation of Balkan league 9–13

Gallipoli (Bulair), attacks upon 80–83
Gallipoli Peninsula 43
Garibaldi, General Ricciotti 63
geography: dictates Thrace as major battlefield 22; offensive difficulties resulting from 110; problem of Bulgarian 23
George, King of Greece 60, 98
Georgios Averov (armoured cruiser) 17, 19
Geshov, Ivan E. (Prime Minister of Bulgaria) 3, 11, 14, 17, 51, 69, 75, 88, 99, 102
Gornya Dzhumaya (Blagoevgrad) 115, 111, 121
Gotse Delchev (formerly Nevrokop) 43
Great Powers: Austrians and Russians rivals for Balkan domination 7; and Berlin settlement 2, 3–4; efforts to end siege of Scutari 93; fear of collapse of Ottoman authority 33; intervention sought by Bulgaria 25; London Ambassadors Conference 72–4; and Murzteg reform program 6; pressure on Serbs in Albania 85
Greco-Albanian frontier 73–4
Greco-Serbian alliance 98–101
Greece: defeat at Klidion 60; dispositions, Western theater, First Balkan War 59; dispute with Bulgarians 74–5; military advantage of 107; military dispositions against Bulgarians 108; occupation of Salonika 61–2; officer revolt in 8; reconnaissance deficiencies by 60; Salonika as main objective 60; stalled by fortifications at Janina 63–4; success in defeat of Bulgarian 2nd Army 113; as victim of Bulgarian aggression 105–6; victory at Janina 84–5; victory at Yanitsa 61
Grey, Sir Edward 72
Gulf of Orfanos 112
Gulf of Saros 81
Gushinje 58
Gypsies 15–16

Halil Bey 125
Hamdi Pasha 29
Hamidiye (light cruiser) 19, 65, 66, 92–93
Hartwig, Nicholas 11
Helmreich, E.C. 105
Henri-Martini gun 19
Hesapchiev, Major General Kristofor 114
Hkovo detachment 42–43
Hurshid Pasha 82

Imbros 64
IMRO (Internal Macedonian Revolutionary Organization) 5, 10, 13
infantry tactics; Bulgarian at Buni Hisar 30; Bulgarian at Lozengrad 26–7; Bulgarians taking Adrianople 88–9; Montenegrin simplism 57; Serbian at Kumanovo 47–8; Serbian

171

INDEX

guilelessness at Prilep 49; Serbs at Bitola 51–2
information gathering, difficulties for foreigners 134
intervention by Romania 117–18
invasion, Ottoman of Bulgaria 118–19
Ioannina *see* Janina
Iskar River 118
Ismail Kemal 131
Italo-Turkish war of 1911 11, 19
Ivanov, Lieutenant General Nikola 40, 88, 112–13, 121
Izvolski, Aleksander 7
Izzet Pasha, Ahmed 119

Janina 51, 52, 63, 83–85
Jankovich, General Bozhidar 45, 53, 109, 111
Javer Pasha 22, 42, 43

Kalimantsi, defense of 120–1
Kamil Pasha 78
Karageorgevich, King Peter and Crown Prince George 6
Katinchev, General 108
Katovo 53
Kavala 64, 75, 98, 124
Kemal Bey, Ismail 73
Kilkis 112–13
Kircaali 22
Kirkkillise *see* Lozengrad
Klidion, battle of 60
Knjazhevats 116
Kochana 53, 111
Kolibi Karagach, skirmish at 29
Korce *see* Koritsa
Korchi 52
Koritsa 52, 60, 83
Kosovo: Albanian national self-awareness in 9; Montenegrins in Prizren 58; outside new State of Albania 102; Serbian and Montenegrin claims to 5; Serbian rule harsh in 54; Serbians take Pristina 53
Kostura 52
Kovachev, General Stiliyan 42, 80, 82, 108
Kresna Gorge, Bulgarian success at 115, 121–2

Krupp guns 15, 16, 17, 19, 37, 117
Kukush *see* Kilkis
Kumanovo, battle of 41, 47–9, 77
Kundouriotis, Rear Admiral Paul 17
Kurdzhali *see* Kircaali
Kutinchev, General Hikola 24
Kyril, Prince of Bulgaria 61
Kyustendil 115

Lerin 52
Levski, Vasil 2
Lezhe *see* Alessio
Limnos 64
Ljesh *see* Alessio
London Ambassadors Conference 72–4
London peace conference 70–2
London, Treaty of 91, 100, 101–2
Lozengrad, battle of 23, 25, 26–8, 30
Lushe 85
Lyule Burgas–Buni Hisar 23, 25, 28–32, 41

Macedonia: Bulgarian motivation over 108; determination of Greeks and Serbs to hold 109; focus of aspiration 5; Greek and Serb consolidation in 98–9; problem of 4–5, 10, 11–12, 104; raids and sniper attacks in 105; revolt against Ottomans in 5–6
Makedonia (auxilliary cruiser) 65
Mahmud Pasha 125, 126
Maiorescu, Titu (Prime Minister of Romania) 77
Mannlicher rifle 16
Mannlicher-Schonauer rifle 17
Maritsa River 43, 79
Martinovich, Brigadier Mitar 55
Mathiopulos, Colonel 60
Mauser rifle 18, 19
Maxim guns 16, 18
Medov *see* San Giovanni di Medua 92
Meluna Pass 59
Merhamli, skirmish at 43
Mesta River 121
Mecidiye (armoured cruiser) 19, 64, 81–3
Metaxas, Captain Ioannes 14
Midia 101
Mijushkivich, Lazar 70
Miles, Lieutenant Sherman (US Balkan Military Attaché) 71, 103, 134

military forces (First Balkan War) 15–21
millet system, Ottoman 2
Milovanovich, Foreign Minister Milan 10, 11
Milutin, King 53
Mishich, Colonel Zhivojin 13, 14
Monastir see Bitola 51
Montenegro: commitment to Serbian-Greek position 101; military dispositions, Western theater, First Balkan War 55–6; Greek "gentlemen's agreement" with 12–13; objectives against Ottomans 55–6; occupation of Sandjak 58; prestige of resistance against Ottomans 6; siege (incomplete) of Scutari 56–7; military disposition against Bulgarians 109
Mott, Major T. Bentley (US Military Attaché, Paris) 16
Muhtar Pasha, Mahmut 22, 27, 28, 30, 34
murder at Scutari 91

Nachovich, Grigor 125
Nadezhda (torpedo gunboat) 17
national aspirations 3–7
national rivalries, Serbia and Montenegro 8
national unity 1–2
nationalism, power of 1–3, 35
nationalist goals 13
naval gunfire: at Bulair 81, 82; effective Ottoman use of, at Chataldzha 36
naval power 133; *see also* blockades
navies: Bulgarian 17; Greek 17, 46; Greek blockade on Albania 74; Ottoman 19
Nazim Pasha, Huseyin (Ottoman Minister of War) 20, 24, 25, 26, 34, 48, 78
Nazlumov, Major General Atanas 28, 31
Neklyudov, Anatoli (Russian Minister to Sofia) 11, 34, 40
Nemanjich Dynasty 53
Nevrokop (Gotse Delchev) 115
night attacks Bulgarian at Buni Hisar 30
Nigrita 98
Nikola Petrovich Njegosh, of Montenegro 6, 8, 9, 13, 56, 57, 58, 92, 94, 95, 109

Nish 120
Novakovich, Stojan 70
Novi Pazar, Sandjak of *see* Sandjak

Obrenovich, Alexander 6
Odrin *see* Adrianople
offensive à outrance 24
openness, reluctance of Balkan armies toward 134
Orient Express 20
Ottoman Empire: Albanian irregular support for 46–7, 55–6; armistice request rejected by Bulgaria 34; at Chataldzha, strength of position of 33–4; concentration of troops at Chataldzha 34; defensive strategies of 25; delaying tactics of 70–71; demoralizing defeat at Kumanovo 49; deterioration in control of 13; military dispositions, Western theater, First Balkan War 46–7, 56, 59; impregnability (apparent) of Adrianople 39; invasion of Bulgaria 118–19; logistical failure 29; loss of Lozengrad disaster for 28; naval guns at Chataldzha 65; peace proposal (of 1 January, 1913) 71–2; planning, lack of clarity in 20; plans for defence of West 46, 47; reinforcement at Lyule Burgas–Buni Hisar ridge 28; remarkable recovery at Chataldzha 37–8; retention of fortress cities 69; sell-out at Salonika 62–3; support by Albanian irregulars 85; *see also* Young Turks
Ouchy, Treaty of 56
outbreak of war 24–25
Ovche Polje 46

Panafieu, Hector (French Minister in Sofia) 33
Panas, Demeter (Greek Ambassador to Bulgaria) 14, 17, 69
Paprikov, General Stefan 10
Pashich, Nikola (Serbian Radical Party) 6, 12, 62, 74, 86, 93, 94, 99, 102, 120
peace conference, London 70–72
Pech 58
Petra 59

Petrov, Lieutenant General Racho 110
Pinarhisar *see* Buni Hisar
Pirin Macedonia 124
Pirot 109, 110, 116
Plav 58
Plovdiv 43
Podgoritsa 56
Pomaks (Bulgarian-speaking Muslims) 43
population of Balkan states 18
preparations for war 13–15, 22–4, 107–10
Preveza 63
Prilep, battle of 49–50
Pristina 53
Prizren 58, 73
Prochaska, Oskar 73
Protocol of Florence 131
psychological bombardment 88, 118
Putnik, Vojvoda Radomir 10, 12, 45, 47–9, 52, 53, 62, 108–9, 111, 116

Radoslavov, Vasil 120, 123
Rakitovo, Bulgaria 43
Rakovitsa 123
Rashid Pasha, Mustafa 70, 71
Rauf Bey 65
retreat: Bulgarians on all fronts 114–17; Ottoman rout at Lozengrad 27; stubborn Ottoman resistance at Prilep 50
Rhodopes 24, 42–43, 121
Rila Mountain 121
Risa Pasha, Ali 22, 47, 52
Riza Bey, Hasan 55, 57, 91
Rom *see* Gypsies
Romania: Balkan power of 77; continuity of interest with Greeks and Serbs 101; dispute with Bulgaria 77–8; intervention of 117–18; military disposition of 117–18
Romanovski, Colonel Georgii D. 40, 87
Rumelia, Eastern 3
Rupel Gorge 115
Russia: active policy in Balkans 10–11; critical nature of attitude of 103, 104; dereliction in influence of 99, 100; fears for Constantinople 91; objections to annexation of Adrianople withdrawn 40; Scutari, policy on 93; Serbia as only remaining ally 129; setback of Treaty of London 102; *see also* Great Powers
Russo-Japanese War (of 1904) 7
Russo-Turkish War (of 1877–78) 2, 5, 104

Said Pasha, Kara 47, 51
Salisbury, Lord 3
Salonika: assination of George, King of Greece 98; Bulgarian annihilation in 113–114; major Bulgarian objective 53; central to Bulgaro-Greek dispute 75; major Greek objective 59–60; major obstacle, Greece and Serbia 98; occupation of 61–3; Serbian forces approaching 52; Treaty of 100
Samothrace 64
San Giovanni di Medua 92
San Stefano, Treaty of 2, 7, 38, 54, 100
Sandjak of Novi Pazar: Austrain withdrawal from 7; Montenegrin aspirations for 3, 5, 7, 8, 55; Serbian forces in 46, 54
Santi Quaranta 84
Sarantaporos Pass, battle for 59–60
Sava, Society of Saint 5
Savov, Mihail (Bulgarian Deputy C-in-C) 24, 28, 34, 35, 37, 69, 86–8, 103, 110–12, 120, 121, 125
Sazonov, Sergei (Foreign Minister of Russia) 99, 100, 103, 104
Schneider guns 87
Schneider–Canet guns 17
Schneider–Creusot guns 15, 16, 17, 18
Scutari: surrender of (Ottoman and Montenegrin) 94–5; siege of 54, 55, 56–7, 73, 74, 91–5
Sélanik *see* Salonika
Sea of Marmara 43, 80, 82
sea, war at 64–66
search lights, Bulgarian use of 30
Serbia: Adriatic expansion resisted 73; advance on Bitola 51; alliance with Greece 98–101; assisting Bulgaria at Adrianople 4, 41; Black Hand of 6, 10; and Bulgarian-Greek entente 99; claims on Albania 74; control of

INDEX

Macedonia 53; decisive victory at Kumanovo 48; deteriorating relations with Bulgaria 89; difficulties regarding Scutari 93, 94; military dispositions, Western theater, First Balkan War 45–6; dispute with Bulgaria 76–7; Greece, "gentleman's agreement" with 12–13; and Montenegrins at Scutari 92; military advantages of 107; military dispositions against Bulgarians 108–9; military objectives attained 70; rapport with Bulgaria 10, 11–12; as victim of Bulgarian aggression 105–6; victory at Bitola 52; victory at Kumanovo 77
Serbo-Bulgarian Treaty 87
Serbo-Bulgarian war of 1885 4
Seres 53, 75, 98, 113, 124
Servia (Serfidse) 59
Sharkoi 80, 81, 82
Shevket Pasha, Mahmut 20, 78–9
Shkoder *see* Scutari
Shkumba River 85
Shtip 53, 111
Silistra 100
Skadra *see* Scutari
Skoplje 46, 49, 73, 116
Skouloudis 75
Smyrna 64
Sofia *see* Bulgaria
Solun *see* Salonika
St Petersburg Ambassadors Conference 97–8
stalemate at Scutari 57
Stepanovich, General Stepa 41, 45, 53, 109, 116–17
stirrings in Albania 8–9
Struma River 99, 115, 121
Strumitsa 112, 113, 115
Sukhomlinov, General Vladimir A. 89–90
Sukru Pasha, Ferik Mehmed 22, 41, 39, 87, 89
Sultan Abdul Hamid II 7, 61
Sultan Mohammad V 7, 9

Tahsin Pasha, Hassan 59, 61, 62, 63
Talat Bey, Mehmed 125
Tarabosh, Montenegrin attack on 92, 94

Taylor, Major J.R.M. (US Military Attaché, Constantinople) 33, 34, 37
Temrosh salient 43
Tenedos 64
Teneshdol Pass 53
Thassos 64
Thessaloniki *see* Salonika
Thessaly, campaign in 59–61
Thracian theater, importance of 22–3
The Times –
Todorov, General Georgi 53, 61, 62, 81
Tonchev, Dimitur 123
topography of Balkan Peninsula 20
Toshev, General Stefan 91, 108, 111, 125
transportation difficulties in Balkan Peninsula 20–1
Treaty of Athens 126
Treaty of Berlin 3, 4, 5, 15
Treaty of Bucharest 123–5
Treaty of Constantinople 125–7
Treaty of London 91, 100, 101–2
Treaty of Ouchy 56
Treaty of Salonika 100
Tricoupis, Kharilaos 4
Tsar Ferdinand of Bulgaria 25, 33, 34, 62, 69, 78, 82, 87, 98, 105, 110, 120
Tsar Lazar 53
Tsar Simeon 16
Tsaribrod 102
Tundzha River 24
Turgut Pasha, Shevket 22
Turgut Ries (Ottoman warship) 82
Tutrakan 77, 117

Udovo 110
Union of Death *see* Serbia, Black Hand of
University of Constantinople 14
Uskub *see* Skoplje

Vardar River 60, 99, 100, 110, 113, 123
Varna 77, 117
Velchev, Major General Vulko 119
Veles 49
Venizelos, Eleutherios 8, 15, 59, 70, 75, 84, 98, 99, 100, 123
Victor Emmanuel III, King of Italy 6
Vidin, isolation of 118, 122–3

175

INDEX

Vlore 72, 74
Von Bluhm Pasha 33
Von der Golz, General Field Marshall Colmar 25
Vukotich, Brigadier Janko 55, 123

war: mood in favour of 13–14; outbreak of 24–5; preparations for 13–15, 22–4, 107–10; resumed 79; at sea 64–6
Western Thrace, Ottoman strength in 42
White Drin River 54
William of Wied, Prince 131
World War I 132–5

Yambol 119
Yanitsa, battle for 60
Yenije Vardar *see* Yanitsa
Young Turks 7–8, 9, 13, 18–19, 25, 27, 61, 78–9, 80; *see also* Ottoman Empire
Yugoslavism 10

Zapundzakis, General Constantine 59, 63, 84
Zeki Pasha 47, 48, 49, 51
Zhivkovich, General Mihail 45
Ziya Pasha 91
Zletovska River 110, 111